Life's Greatest Journey

The Partnership

BASED ON A TRUE STORY

Author
Rene` Monroe PhD

A Real Estate career lady goes from city life back to her country roots. With NO children of her own; she becomes a protective mother of eighteen street wise behavioral problem boys, creating many humbling and hilarious experiences. IT'S A MUST READ!

The Chapters of this book
Is written in short story form
Making each chapter a separate story

Youth America Publishing Co.

To order additional copies of this book, contact:
On the web at wwwdrrenemonroe.net
e-mail youthamerica@sbcglobal.net

Available at createspace.com/ 3548052
Amazon.com
And other retailers
Also available on Kindle at Amazon.com

This book was printed in the United States of America.
ISBN: 0983270546
ISBN 13: 9780983270546
Soft cover 978-0-9832705-0-8
Hard cover 978-0-9832705-1-5

DEDICATION

This book is dedicated to the unwanted street children of this country with the hope that readers will recognize the need to participate in making changes for the betterment of our street children and be motivated to act. This statement does not mean there are not wonderful charities for children in the country; however, for the street children, we are lacking in meeting their needs. If you have to ask the question, "What needs?" then you know how very grey this area is in this country. In this book you will see how the children are exposed not only to the elements of reality but also to the sheer political failure of children's programs which use these children as if they were pawns in a chess game, moving them from one placement to another until they are eighteen. The solution is to fund each child privately so that he or she is provided for in a ranch family setting, thus eliminating the large percentage of these children who eventually overload our prison system.

AUTOBIOGRAPHY

Dr. Rene' Monroe has dedicated most of her life to children and the development of better children's programs. Licensing her first facility in 1975, she continued in this field of humanity with children, mainly street children for 25 years licensing six facilities. The author takes you inside a licensed government ranch program for children. You will experience the struggles she experiences with the government written programs. You will see the hilariously funny and happy times a ranch setting for eighteen behavioral problem boys can provide.

The author having lived and experienced most of what is being written leads you through an exciting adventure. She gives an accounting of the horror that our unwanted street children go through when abandoned by their parents and left on the streets.

Monroe goes a step further and explains how private ranch programs work, if properly funded.

The reader is introduced to a complex personality that is full of excitement and adventure. She possesses a unique combination of personal traits that is both fascinating and bold. Rene' is an outdoor sportsman, a marksman who has hunted near the North Pole, an avid fisherman, and an experienced horseman.

Monroe is highly respected by the "inner circle," a family of professional horsemen. She is known for her good stout ranch horses, purchasing from such greats as Walter Merrick. All this and feminine too.

Her character is a determined and devoted career lady, with a split personality, one educated and one country. Both come together taking the reader on an enjoyable and intriguing Journey, awaking all your emotions. From drama, to laughter, sometimes at her expense, heart break, tears and then love.

Monroe dresses with the utmost class in designer suits and hats, but prefers her wranglers and boots. In the two months we worked together I found her positive nature wholesomely addictive. If it was raining, she would declare, God is simply clearing the air of the smog. If it was too hot, God was blessing us with more vitamin D.

Executive editor; Susan Slovene
Manhattan Beach, California

René Monroe, Ph.D.

The author on "I'm Talken Cash," three years old, son of Dash for Cash, purchased from Walter Merrick

PERSONAL DEDICATION

Self-employed people have to remain strong in their beliefs and must to succeed, be fully committed regardless of the verbal abuse they must encounter. There is a saying that all writers must know: "If you want to improve yourself and be successful, be prepared to look stupid and foolish in the eyes of those who have accomplished nothing."

In Memory of Tom Monroe

Tom Monroe died of cancer three months before this book went to publication. He was a good professional PRCA, down to earth cowboy. Tom never met a stranger. A personality and smile, that would melt your heart. It did mine. If there is a cowboy heaven, I imagine, Tom is riding his horse across the green meadows with the other cowboys, telling tales of yester-years gone by. He was my strength during most of the boys' ranches. TOM MONROE I THANK YOU FOR YOUR STRENGTH, LOVE AND SURRORT.

DISCLAIMER

I am notoriously known for my forwardness and it saddens me to be writing a disclaimer in this century. A person should be able to express his or her opinions without this rubbish. We must be able in this society to express our words, thoughts, and opinions under the freedom of speech, which by the way, I believe still exists.

This book is based on my opinions, thoughts, and conclusions; plus twenty-five years of experience with government-run adult and children's programs. Of course, I should make you aware that I never gave birth to a child, and this decision was of my choosing. My spiritual Journey and my career were chosen for me quite some time ago by the Higher Power. There are people who are chosen for a specific Journey, such as Oprah, too many to mention who follow an inner spiritual guidance. They have never given birth to children, but are one of the biggest factors in fighting the injustices in the world for our youth.

Should you decide to follow my insights and opinions and find this a learning experience in the process that may better your situation as a parent or enlighten you as a reader and taxpayer, let it be known for goodness sake. You and only you are responsible for your choice to act on anything that you may read.

This book is based on my life experiences with the boys ranches I owned, mostly in the 80s. The dates and times may differ, and most of the names have been changed to protect the privacy of the children.

The exact conversations may vary according to how I remember the boys. Did I own boys ranches that were licensed by the state and federal government in California? Yes. Is it true our government children's programs are run in this failed structure today; still moving children from place to place? Yes. The stories may vary somewhat, but they were taken from my experiences and my journal. Therefore, because of these "few things not being exact in nature; this will be classified as a novel, based on a true story.

ACKNOWLEDGEMENT

I could make this section a book in itself, to recognize and acknowledge all the friends and family members that encouraged me during this book-writing process. I applaud you and thank you for believing in me.

I cannot name all of you, but you know who you are: the true friends who gave me a place to stay and write, pushing me forward into a greater expansion of my being. You understood that my goal is to give my experience and knowledge freely so others may learn from my Journey. This required many a sacrifice.

The wonderful investor for his marvelous insight believing in me and my potential, to help make the boys ranch become such a success; I could not have survived without you. Bless you, my friend, for allowing me to experience some of the most productive years of my life.

To the two most important business people that continued throughout the years to help my business grow. The first is my attorney who stayed with me through the thin times and raised his fees through the good times. The other person is my accountant and he is the best in the business.

Thank you to the many P.R.C.A. professional cowboys such as Harley May for backing and supporting the boys ranch and being the finance director for my corporation. Thank you to Jack Roddy who took the time to care, inviting my boys to his team roping's and donating many used ropes, which were so needed. Thank you to Ted Nuse, for your time in volunteering to help my little young steer riders.

It is ironic, but I would also like to thank the federal government and their ridiculous children's programs for their constant irritation, directing me towards writing this book, making it public knowledge how these programs are damaging our children and creating an adult population of criminals.

Boys ranches do work provided they are privately funded, not governed by government control programs that are written to fail.

My sincere Thank You to all.

TABLE OF CONTENTS

~ Chapter 1 ~

JAKE'S FATE

Amarillo, Texas

The words "tumor" and "difficult to get to" kept ringing in my head. Surely he could not be talking to me! After all, I did not drink alcohol or smoke cigarettes. The only symptom I had was this darn sore throat and persistent cough. After the initial CAT scan, the doctor asked for a second one. Frankly, I thought they must have made a mess of things and needed a "do over" to correct the situation.

My husband and I were sitting in this new office, listening to a very young doctor tell me what options were available. I was not interested in any of these options! Country gals do not like options that include words such as "surgery," "chemotherapy," "maybe," and "it might be possible."

What this very young doctor did not know is, I came to him for his opinion—not a cure. I had studied herbal cures for years and was already thinking of possible cures. He was thinking, "Hum-m-m, Aetna Insurance—major medical coverage," while I was trying to make sense of his diagnosis and realize the seriousness of the problem.

The more I listened, the more skeptical I became.

As we sat there in our creased Wranglers and Resistol cowboy hats (normal dress for Amarillo, Texas), I could see the doctor and I were miles apart. He kept saying, "For your age," as if sixty was old. I have normal aches and pains, but I do not consider myself old. There is still a little girl in me!

He wanted to schedule more tests. I stared at the cut on his young face where he nicked himself shaving. I looked at the diploma from a very prestigious medical school and wondered at the obvious contradictions.

He asked, "Are you in much pain?" The room was quiet for a long time. He leaned forward to let me know he expected a response.

"How much pain are we discussing?" Wanting to be anywhere but in this room at this time, I responded with a defensive strategy. Answer a question with a question.

Thus, a mind game began between this young doctor and a country-raised, educated metaphysician—he wanted to gain as much information as possible, and I wanted time to process the news that a mass was now living and growing inside me and might eventually take my life. I needed time to absorb the shock.

"Doctor, if I understand what you're saying, I should not go out and buy any broodmares and breed them, in anticipation of seeing how the foals turn out."

This statement went right over his head.

My mind wandered back to happier times with the boys at the ranch. I drifted back to the boys' laughter and their pain, their growth, and successes. Oh yes, we had sad times, and I felt their pain deep within my heart. Every time I could not find a way to heal their pain, it somehow became my own.

Pain of the heart is the hardest of all to handle, especially when it involves a child. Jake's pain was such a pain.

I remember Jake's last visit, in 1989, at the boy's ranch I operated in Oakdale, California.

One day I looked up to see a probation officer's van coming up the driveway toward the ranch house. This was odd because we were not expecting any new residents. The ranch had been full for quite some time, with a waiting list. Since I had not interviewed anyone lately, I was puzzled by his visit.

It was late in the afternoon. As I approached his vehicle, I could see several boys in the van. The probation officer's name was Chuck and he started talking as soon as he stepped out of the van to greet me. "And how are you, René, or should I say mother of the year?" I never really thought of myself as mother of the year. To me, I was doing God's work, and therefore considered myself blessed.

"Oh, I'm fine," I said. "Are you lost? It looks like you are on a delivery trip."

The probation officer had certain days in the month when he delivered boys to different "group homes" for new placement. I really hate the term "group home". I insisted everyone refer to my facility as the boys' ranch.

There was another boy's ranch about fifty miles away and Chuck informed me that he was delivering one of my former residents to that ranch. "The boy had requested I stop so he could see you." Chuck helped a boy out of the back of the van, and there before me stood a very thin-looking Jake. He was handcuffed and wore ankle chains. My heart sank.

Four years earlier when Jake first came to my ranch, he had many, many problems. Yet with time and patience, we worked through them. He stayed at the ranch for two and a half years before state licensing enforced their replacement policy. Jake was moved to a less-expensive foster program.

Jake's father belonged to a motorcycle gang and served time in prison for murder. I guess he was a bad one of sorts. In fact, he threatened anyone and everyone who offered to take the boy.

The first time I met Jake was in 1986. I visited "hardcore" lockups for juveniles to interview boys who might qualify for the ranch. I spotted a boy in quarantine in a cell about twelve by twelve feet. From where I stood, he looked to be eight or nine years old, at least three years younger than his actual age. He had short sandy hair, blue eyes, and a very pale complexion. I had never seen a child so undernourished and frail looking. I was astonished to learn this child was eleven years old. He was too small and frail to be in a place like this. I called one of the guards and asked to speak with the boys' probation officer. This probation officer, whom I knew from previous placements at the ranch, was eager to talk to me. I asked him what the package (the history background) was on the boy.

I asked, "What was it?" Then I answered my own question, "His mother taking drugs while pregnant?"

The probation officer said, "That too," but there was more to the story. Jake's father had shot the boy up with heroin when Jake was a baby. Drugs given a child at a very young age may alter his or her growth pattern and that's why Jake looked stunted in growth. In the business I was in, you ran across all kinds of low life.

The probation officer could not place Jake in foster care anymore because of threats from the father. As young looking as Jake appeared, the state was afraid to put Jake in with the normal juvenile population.

After a brief interview with Jake, I told the probation officer I would take the boy if he would help me with Jake's father. The probation officer went to his supervisor who was delighted to help in any way possible.

Let me explain why the probation officer was so cooperative. The county had no place to go with this boy. Should he end up, at eleven years old, raped by one of the older boys, the county was responsible, triggering a lawsuit of the worst kind.

I suggested we begin by looking for outstanding warrants on the boy's father. We found three in the state of California. I asked the supervisor to hold all information received on the father for at least 60 days. The supervisor asked, "And how do you expect us to do this legally. Withholding information is against the law."

I responded with what I thought to be a logical answer, "Lose it on your desk, in a file, I don't care how you do it. You want the boy placed at my ranch, lose the darn thing." This was my strategy to use against the father, if I needed it. If we had him arrested, he would simply make bail, and we would lose our edge. The county could do what they wished with this information after we saved the child.

I took Jake to the ranch, and three weeks later, sure enough, in my ranch driveway sat motorcycles, lots of motorcycles. There in the center of these "middle-aged bad boys" was Jake's father. They sure looked out of place in my driveway. A few of the ranch hands arrived to see what all the noise was about; one thing I did not need was an old-fashioned fistfight. I sent my ranch hands back to work.

Jake's father came up to me and asked to speak to whoever was in charge. I said in a strong voice, "I am in charge and am happy to visit with you about your son, provided we speak in private. I paused a moment, "My office is this way."

As we headed for my office, I told one of the counselors to give the motorcycle riders something cool to drink. This let the men know I was open and not prejudging them and, it was hot that day. Psychologically, it showed I was not afraid. One could only hope that my guardian angels were not napping this day. (I always figured in my profession there must be more than one angel looking after me.)

When we were alone, he got right to the point, telling me he would burn me out and he wanted his son right now, "Or else, you will suffer the consequences."

I politely listened while he had his say, and then I spoke, "I have given you five minutes of my time to listen to you, I am asking only for equal time. I spoke as directly as my voice would allow.

"Looks like we have ourselves a situation here; however, there is a solution. You see, I heard you were going to do something like this, so I figured I really needed to find out more about you. I did; you have quite a negative background."

"You were convicted of murder and spent time in prison, and you are on probation. I also did some research and found you have three outstanding warrants in the state of California. I don't hold to the idea of sending anyone back to prison. So this is the deal. You, sir, leave California right now. I never want to see you on this ranch again. I keep Jake and you keep your freedom. He started to interrupt. I held my ground holding my hand up, "Jake is in a good home here I will raise your son as my own and give him the love he so deserves. That is something you, with your lifestyle, cannot give him. You have my word on this."

I was quiet and waited for his response.

He stood in front of my desk for what seemed a very long time and then spoke. "Lady," he said, "you have the balls of an elephant! You are crazy. I could kill you or have it done."

By this time I am standing, "That's what you will have to do to get Jake. I am keeping him here at the ranch." I think having God as a partner, you have this inner strength that simply comes bubbling out.

Here before me and my one hundred and twenty pounds was a bearded man wearing black leather, with all kinds of chain paraphernalia hanging over and around the leather clothing. He stood about five feet eight inches and weighed about two hundred and fifty pounds, maybe more, most of which was in front. Long unkempt hair and an unruly beard did nothing for his appearance.

He returned to the bikers and shouted he would be back. He and another gentleman, stretching the word gentleman considerably, were arguing over something, and the other gentleman walked toward me. If I thought Jake's dad was big, this guy looked to be six four or better. I whispered, "Well, Lord, you can step in any time," and amazingly, He did. When the man began to speak, his voice was soft; "I too was raised by a wonderful man who lived in the country and ma'am, we will not be back." He thanked me kindly for the ice tea and they left.

Later the probation officer said my reverse strategy must have worked. Jake's father went to Oregon where he knifed someone and went back to prison. The good Lord does answer our prayers in the strangest ways.

Jake's entire story flooded my memory as I stood on the driveway with Chuck and the surprise visit from Jake.

"Chuck," I said, "take these darn handcuffs off this boy!"

Jake was trying to hug me with the cuffs around his wrist. The cuffs were removed, and Jake fell into my arms crying and begging me to take him back. He would do anything to come back to the ranch. When you have one of these boys for more than a year, the bond becomes as close as if he were your very own son.

Jake, happier times at the ranch

Jake stayed at the ranch for two and a half years, and then I lost him to the state of California because his "time" was up.

Seeing him now in handcuffs, as a fifteen-year-old looking thirteen, was heartbreaking.

Jake thought I could fix it where he could stay at the ranch. The last day at the ranch, he kept looking at me and asking, "Can't you do something, Mom, so I can stay?"

For those who have no idea about laws regarding wards of the state, please allow me to give you a brief education. If a child is doing well on his program and has stayed a certain amount of time, the state enters the picture and will move him to a foster home. That is what happened to Jake. The state ordered his placement in a foster-care home. The judge and I fought it, but the law was clear. There was nothing we could do but let him go.

Jake lost his horse, his dog, and a paying job at the ranch where he was receiving two hundred and fifty a month. AND, he lost all his friends at the ranch. It destroyed him. He lasted two months at the foster home. Jake ran away stole some things and went directly into hard core lock-up. A prison for juvenile delinquents, and this time no one was there for him. What do they learn there? The young ones learn how to further their education in becoming an adult criminal. All this we owed to "state-run programs."

Boys ranches do work, and there are many people with the right intentions to help children, but for the most part they are governed totally by government regulations and based upon funding restrictions, not the child's needs. Privately funded programs are great. They are licensed by the state to protect the children, but the program itself is run by the private entity, making it possible for the child to stay until he or she is grown.

When Jake received a phone privilege, he telephoned Joe, his best friend. The two boys arrived at the ranch two years before, and the two became inseparable. When Jake had to leave it was a heart breaking moment for everyone. For Joe it was like losing a brother.

One day after one of these phone calls, Joe came into the office, extremely upset, and began talking; "Jake has been raped in lockup." I could see Joe was upset and had been crying. We started to talk, or rather; I began to listen, while Joe talked through his turmoil. Joe wanted answers as to how this could happen.

"Did Jake do something bad at the ranch?"

"No," I replied, "I really would like to come up with an answer to your question that makes sense, but I have none. The ranch is a federally funded program, which sets the regulations as to how long a boy can stay." Joe knew he was taking a lot of my time; I simply offered an understanding smile and told him, "I have all afternoon just for you." There were times at the ranch when a boy needed my undivided attention.

All these memories came rushing back as I stood there in the bright afternoon sunshine, my arms wrapped tightly around Jake whose life was so full of sorrow.

I held him as long as I could. Then Chuck shattered the moment when he spoke, "We'll have to be going on down the road. There are people waiting for Jake."

When he pulled Jake from my arms and put those handcuffs back on my son, it was one of my worse days at the ranch—and in my life, for that matter. I knew I could not take Jake back. As the van drove out of the driveway, I could hear Jake crying for me to help. I thought to myself, someday I will do something to change this injustice.

I turned and headed for the horse barn, telling one of the ranch hands to saddle my big roan. I needed to ride.

That evening, I rode all the way to the lake, a Journey of seven miles one way. Needless to say, God and I had a long conversation during that ride. I did not get back until two o'clock in the morning.

As I rode up, the lights were on in the barn. I got off my big roan horse, Gentle Ben (G.B.), and there in the shed row of the barn was Tom, a tower of strength at six foot two inches tall, two hundred and twenty pounds of professional in-shape cowboy. He was sitting in a chair leaning against the shed-row wall with his cowboy hat tilted over his eyes. Raising his hat, he looked up and said, "Did you have a good ride?"

He knew I rode to relieve stress, hurt, and the heartaches that came with this profession. I said, "Yes." He began to unsaddle my horse. As I walked around my horse, he grabbed me by the shoulders and turned me around. He pulled me into his arms and held me very close. I thought the ride had handled the heartache I was feeling, but when he held me and wouldn't let go, I began to cry. I cried and cried some more.

I really think in the few years we had been together, Tom had never seen me cry. It wasn't that I hadn't felt like crying, but the ranch program needed a constant show of strength to succeed. I had to be that strength; there was simply no time to cry.

As Tom stood there holding me tightly, I knew this was definitely the time to cry.

~ Chapter 2 ~

THE PURCHASE

Oakdale, California, early 80's

The first time I saw the property, it resembled the old ranch house on *Green Acres*. The thought occurred to me, "Forget the remodeling and simply bulldoze it down." On closer inspection, the brick ranch house had no cracks in the brick veneer. The old house was solid in structure; it just needed some old-fashion hard work and clean-up. Regardless of the condition of the property it was all I could afford.

The owner's neglect was obvious. The yard, from the lack of water and mowing, stood knee high in yellow grass and weeds. Trash from recent storms laid scattered next to the house as though the house was shouting, "Anyone, anyone at all, please help me before I am buried."

The next day I called the realtor listing the ranch property and asked permission to deal directly with the owner. Permission was granted. I called the owner and began the conversation; "Ben could you please sit in your most comfortable chair because the offer I'm about to give you might be a little unsettling." I was aware no one had turned in an offer. So I presented my first offer to Ben by offering something I knew he would hate.

"Well Ben," I continued, with as much straight forwardness as I could muster, "I really would prefer a straight lease option for a year with no down payment."

This statement was followed by dead silence.

I paused for just a moment and then continued, "Or I could just buy you out for one hundred and fifty thousand."

Ben was asking much more for his ranch. I stayed silent waiting for his response. It took him only a minute to accept the direct buyout. My strategy had worked. The seller was divorced and in dire financial need. In the field of real estate this seller was referred to as a "co-operative seller," a rather cowardly terminology to describe someone who is down on his luck.

I knew the seller through my association with the rodeo world. He and his former wife had the usual family: three children, a few cats and dogs, and some fair quarter horses.

The next day, Ben called to confirm the offer and asked me; "Rene' could you please bring the offer by the house tomorrow; I am leaving town and would like the contract signed on the sale of the ranch before I leave?"

Since I had my real estate license, I replied, "Ben I have no problem with coming early tomorrow. We can discuss the details and closing of the property."

I arrived the next day at his ranch with real estate on my mind and knocked on the kitchen door, where a sign hung; "This is it, Entrance." I heard a voice say, "Come on in; the door is open."

I found Ben setting at the kitchen table fidgeting a little. He immediately opened the conversation, "Rene' sit down and have a cup of coffee," and pointed to the chair by the kitchen table. Before I could inform him I drink only tea, (except in the mountains, and who can refuse old fashion mountain coffee.) he was pouring me a cup of hot coffee. I opened my briefcase and put the contract on the kitchen table. Then Ben began to give me more information than I needed.

I am going to tell this story because it is a great lesson in the old cliché, "What goes around comes around." This story might make someone out there who reads this think twice before doing what Ben did with his life. It may just save a marriage or two.

Ben started telling me about his divorce before I could discuss what I was supposed to be at this meeting for—the purchase of his ranch for my boys' ranch and the signing of the contract.

Ben seemed determined, as though he felt it necessary to tell me his side of the story, so I just sat back and politely listened.

Ben at that time was the director of Steer Wrestling for the Professional Rodeo Cowboys Association (PRCA) and could rope and dog steers with the best of the top hands. Ben ran with the upper professional cowboys. Every year "The Who's Who of Rodeo" went early to the National Finals Rodeo and told their wives it was because of "all the board meetings" going on the first week of the National Finals. This, of course was an outright exaggeration of the truth. They did have a few meetings, but the main purpose was the parties. Ben acquired a reputation for being a player. For the first four days of the National Finals, which were held in Oklahoma City at that time, Ben partied with any and every female who would participate, and there were always plenty of participants. The parties continued through the night. I believe these young party females are called "Ladies of the evening." There is another term that Rodeo families used—they called them "Buckle Bunnies," known to follow rodeo cowboys from one rodeo to the next. These buckle bunnies all came with "Rounded Heels" on their boots, for if a professional rodeo cowboy touched them on the shoulder, they instantly fell to the floor ready and willing for that horizontal conversation. Most of these so-called young ladies knew nothing about rodeo, cattle or which end of the horse to feed, and most had no standards or morals.

Ben played this game until the fifth day. This is the day his lovely family arrived in the city. Ben showed up at the rodeo looking like the perfect family man, wife and children in tow. I might take this time to tell you that not all rodeo men are this way. Today the rodeo world is big business and most people involved are professionals who set great standards for our young people to follow.

Ben, getting up from his chair asked, "Would you like some more coffee René?"

Before I could say "No, I actually prefer hot tea"; there he was again topping off my coffee, not noticing the level in the cup had moved very little, all the while continuing to tell his side of the story.

In the spring of the year, usually in April, the little town where Ben and his family lived hosted the Team Roping Competition. Ben paid his entry fees and roped with the rest of the locals.

Leaning over the table to create a bigger space, he continued his story, "You know what happens after an Oakdale roping, we all go to the cowboy bar downtown and have a few beers. Me and my roping buddies drank well into the late afternoon. Before I knew it, I looked at my watch and it was 9:00 PM. I was to call my wife before I headed home. This meant dinner would be late. Really late!"

Ben noticed the concern his roping partner had for him about going home with liquor on his breath and continued telling his buddy, "My wife was not happy the last time this happened. Why, I stayed in the dog house for two months."

Thus began the "Cowboy Way" of solving the whole situation.

Sid, as we shall call him, was full of advice, "Ben, you should use a different approach on confronting your faithful wife of many years. I suggest that you enter the house mad as H—, slam the door behind you as hard as you can, then look straight into her eyes and yell, "'You bitch, you cheating bitch!"

Sid's wisdom continued, "Man, you can't lose with this strategy. It catches them completely off guard. Your wife is so busy explaining that she has never cheated on you; she forgets that you are really the one who is at fault. And then, what makes it really great is that the wife spends the rest of the night making up to you."

Ben had never spoken to his wife in this manner, but thought about this strategy and decided it would work with his faithful wife of eighteen years.

As he entered the house through the kitchen door, there sat his wife peeling potatoes for their very late dinner. Ben slammed the door and yelled, "You bitch, you cheating bitch!" He looked at her startled expression and was thinking to himself, "Wow this is really working;" Until she began to speak.

She dropped the potato peeler and began to speak with some shock in her voice, "How long have you KNOWN?"

Although somewhat confused, Ben was able to come up with a reply, "Since the very beginning."

His wife looked even more shocked and said, "You have known for two years?"

Ben, weak in the knees and becoming very sober, managed a reply, "Yes."

It seems his wife and a wealthy farmer had been seeing each other for quite some time. What followed was the divorce, plus Ben had a nervous breakdown, and his hair turned snow white.

Ben told me this story with all the emotion and sadness that only a cowboy can deliver. I could not help but feel sadness for this man, but I already knew the whole story. His wife and I had lunch a few times before the divorce. She had invited me to lunch after the divorce to tell me her side of the story. She told me how very happy she and the children were with her new marriage and that she knew all along about Ben's infidelity that had continued for years; although she tried unsuccessfully to correct his infidelity to no avail. In both stories, his and hers, they did not mention any concern for the children. A year later two of the children ended up in my youth counseling program.

Ben signed the papers on the ranch, and I was polite and managed not to offer my opinion on Ben's sad tale of woes. It did not take a genius to analyze the whole picture. It became clear the cowboy roping partner, Sid, knew of her cheating, but did not want to lose a friendship or a roping partner, or come right out and tell Ben and take the risk of getting punched in the nose. A cowboy is not going to chance losing a roping partner or a friendship, especially when his roping partner and he are making money and winning. In Sid's defense, I do not believe Sid thought it would cause a divorce. He was only thinking about his situation.

I decided to put this little story in because perhaps someone considering cheating on his or her partner in life may decide it's not worth the cost. If you have been married a while, your wife or husband has probably learned to read you pretty well. Lack of communication is one of the major reasons marriages fall apart. It is my professional opinion; his infidelity does not justify her actions. Believe me, two wrongs of this nature, for goodness sake, does not make it right

I saw Sid and Ben team roping a year later and they were still winning money and the best of friends.

The ranch purchase closed without a problem and I had my property for the boy's ranch; along with all the headaches of a start-up business.

Dear Lord, please forgive us for our indiscretions in life and guide us towards a more productive set of standards for family and our youth.

~ Chapter 3 ~

THE REMODELING

Oakdale, California 2005

The two-lane road followed the river and led toward the old ranch. While on this business trip to Northern California, I decided to visit the place that I once owned and had my last boys' ranch. As I drove up the paved road, I looked ahead to see a faded old four-rail fence, the fence post pushing at the ground to keep from falling. It once stood straight and gleamed white in the California sunshine from the many times one boy or another was assigned to paint the fence as a restriction. Looking at it today, I could see the years of neglect had taken its toll. A strong wind could blow it over. As I drove a little farther, there stood the old ranch house. The yard was a mess, and the paint on the old house looked as bad as the fence. To say the ranch suffered from lack of care was an understatement. It was almost like reliving the first time I saw it with dreams of visions that came true.

I slowed down and turned into the long driveway leading up to the old ranch house. Yes, this was where it all started. It took sickness to remind me how lucky and blessed I was and how rewarding my life's Journey has been.

I moved away a few years ago, and here I am now getting out of my pickup and walking up to a house that held so many memories, good—no, they were great memories—of children laughing and the good Lord blessing me each day with his guidance. He helped me to understand these children needed so very much to have that last chance to become productive adults. We called them "at-risk" children, which simply meant they were teenage boys whose opportunities of becoming productive adults were slim or next to none. "Throwaways" was another term used, because their so-called parents had done just that—threw them out at a very early age, some as young as eight years old, literally kicking them out on the street to find their way. I imagine it is hard to believe there are adults of this nature, for you are probably reading this in the warmth and comfort of your home. Well, you have my word on it. This reality does exist in our society today.

I knocked and introduced myself as the former owner and got permission to wander around the old ranch. As I walked around the corner of the house, visions of my boys and loving memories of the past jumped out at me. I could see Joe climbing out of his bedroom window in the middle of the night to meet Jake out behind the barn, only to find me waiting there. The memories that were running through my mind gave me a warm and fuzzy feeling.

Looking around this old ranch, I wish I had been able to keep it a little bit longer. I had pneumonia four winters in a row, and my doctor said it was time for a well-deserved rest. The timing was right because most of my boys were ready for reunification and/or graduation from the program. I sold it to a wonderful African-American lady who had been helping children in the Bay Area. A big corporation had tried to buy the place, and not once had they asked about the children—they just wanted to see the accounting books.

The very first thing she asked, "I want to meet the children and see their rooms." So I sold to someone I felt would continue my work. She did for seven years and then died of cancer. Her family had been bad managers and lost the ranch, and now it really needed remodeling again.

There, still standing in all its glory, was that fabulous old giant of a walnut tree. Its big branches hung over into the arena making the same shade where many a rope horse stood after a session of hard riding and roping cattle. After I got comfortable under the old tree, moments of tranquility set in, and I silently reminisced about my life and the boys' ranch. For the first time in years, I felt at home.

Early eighties

My first day at the ranch was rather overwhelming in nature. Everywhere I looked, there was either something to clean up or something to remodel. That night, sitting in the quietness of the old ranch house, I took a moment to say a little prayer. "Okay, now what do you want me to do? You've guided me into this mess and I don't know where to go from here. How do You, the Great Creator, expect me to do all this stuff?" A moment of silence followed and then he answered, as if he were right there in the room with me.

I heard the familiar warm voice in my mind saying, "My silly child, use the capabilities I have given you. I have done my job; now you do yours."

I found Ben, the owner, had left a lot of paraphernalia lying around. So I held my first garage sale. I then found myself participating in everything that might be beneficial to my project. I gave speeches to organizations informing them of the boys' ranch. It wasn't long until my remodeling project took off right before my eyes. Local organizations, such as the Chamber of Commerce and Junior Chamber, donated lumber and paint and sent volunteers to help out on the weekends. However, this help did not last long.

The nearby town of Oakdale was a quiet place nestled in the foothills not far from Yosemite National Forest. It was located just sixty miles south of my hometown of Sacramento, California. The population appeared to be blessed with old-fashioned, down-home values. I forged ahead, doing what needed to be done: remodeling and old-fashioned scrubbing and cleaning.

Over the next few weeks, I found myself having many discussions with God (my silent partner). What interesting conversations we had. I chastised him: "You have simply created too many black widow spiders." Sometimes I got into what I call my "pity-me parties," especially on occasions when I thought he had definitely overloaded me. Can you imagine how "brave" I was, questioning God? He, on the other hand, was so very patient with me. That familiar, loving voice brought me to my knees. "My child, you are the one I have chosen to do this. I will never give you more than you can handle."

The pity-me parties left immediately, and by the next day I was my old "workaholic" self, fully convinced I was a one hundred and twenty pound Wonder Woman. It was just after such a scenario that I took on texturing and painting with a new meaning.

There were some things I had to admit needed more than two hands to handle, for example, the repair of a broken window in the living room. Naturally, I hold the record in ownership of the most "how to" books on remodeling. After thumbing through the *How to Repair or Replace a Window* book, I decided to fix the broken window in the living room and save some "real money."

Please understand, once I made up my mind I can do something, there is no stopping me. I see something I think I can do, and before you know it, I've convinced myself that I am an expert. I took the old window out with no problem. The window stood approximately three feet off the main inside floor and five feet to the ground outside. I proceeded to take the broken window out. Not a problem! Just zap and it was out. I had the new one sitting right there ready to lift into place. Funny, when two burly big men unloaded the darn thing, it didn't seem that big or that heavy.

After much maneuvering and two hot tea breaks, I finally set the window in place, with the help of a neighbor, or so we thought. The neighbor questioned my expertise in window replacement just before we set the window in the empty space. I informed him that I had read the book on this matter and did not need conversation. I did not consult my silent partner on this project. That was a big, big mistake.

Oh, what a sense of humor God has. I was thoroughly entertaining Him on this project. As we, this neighbor and I, set the window in the empty space, it seemed to fit perfectly, so we naturally turned it loose. It stayed just long enough for us to step back two steps, and then watch helplessly as it fell out the other side to the ground, breaking into smithereens. As I stood there looking at the broken glass, I heard God laughing uncontrollably.

I was outraged! I looked up at the heavens and yelled, "I just want you to know up there—this is not my funniest foolishness." I went to bed that night with a smile on my lips and a chuckle in my heart. The thought entered my mind, "perhaps it was pretty funny after all." There would be other days and other remodeling projects.

One day, I noticed some of the acoustic was flaking off the ceiling in the den. I began checking on what needed to be done and how to replace it. I sought advice from the salesman at the local hardware store. I presumed he knew what he was talking about concerning the repairs. I listened for a minute and thought to myself, "I can do this!" I'm such a trusting soul, and asked what tools I needed to do the job. This salesman happily fixed me right up with "everything." The thought did not occur to me that this kind-looking, sweet-talking gentleman worked on commission. I left the store with the full knowledge I had the right equipment, and I could do this simple little job of spraying the ceiling. If I remember correctly, the cost of the assurance he gave me was around four hundred and fifty dollars.

The next morning I got up eagerly, anticipating the job that lay ahead. The first job at hand was scraping off the old acoustic texture on the ceiling. I put on a female-looking baby blue pair of neatly starched and ironed coveralls. My hair covered, I was ready to begin this "little" ceiling project. As I scraped this unusually flaky stuff (popcorn acoustic) off the ceiling, I couldn't help but notice that it was falling like snow. It was falling all over the floor and all over me! Oh well, so I made a mess, and I would look a mess—no one ever came by during the day.

Really, the only person in the area that knew me was a dear friend, Harlan Madison. He stood six feet four inches tall, weighed about a hundred and ninety-five pounds and kept himself in good physical shape. Actually, I thought of him as more than just a friend. He had been married so many times, to what I refer to as "whatever's," that I really did not want the relationship to go any further than my secret thoughts. I guess I should explain what a "whatever" is. It is simply a gal who will follow the cowboys anywhere and, I might add, do anything to please them, whether it is vertical or horizontal. They are better known for their frequent horizontal activities. This, of course, is my own definition, for I never could find a name that quite fit this type of female. I just decided to label them "whatever's." In later years Harlan did get it right, by marrying a wonderful lady who married him for the man he is, not for the rodeo titles he carried. They were happily married until his recent death.

Back to the story...

By noon, I was really a mess. Stopping for a lunch break was out of the question. I did take a moment to realize my blue coveralls were now grayish white, along with my cap that covered my hair and pretty much everything else in the room. I had the ceiling completely scraped and was now ready to spray with the machine I rented. The kindly-looking, sweet-talking gentleman at the hardware store told me I should remember to adjust the velocity, or power, or something. Of course, I forgot exactly what he said. I turned the machine on then climbed on the ladder, and began to spray the ceiling with a few adjustments to the velocity switch. The white new acoustic came shooting out of the thing, spraying here and there, spraying everything but the ceiling. I could barely control this wild thing much less hear the doorbell.

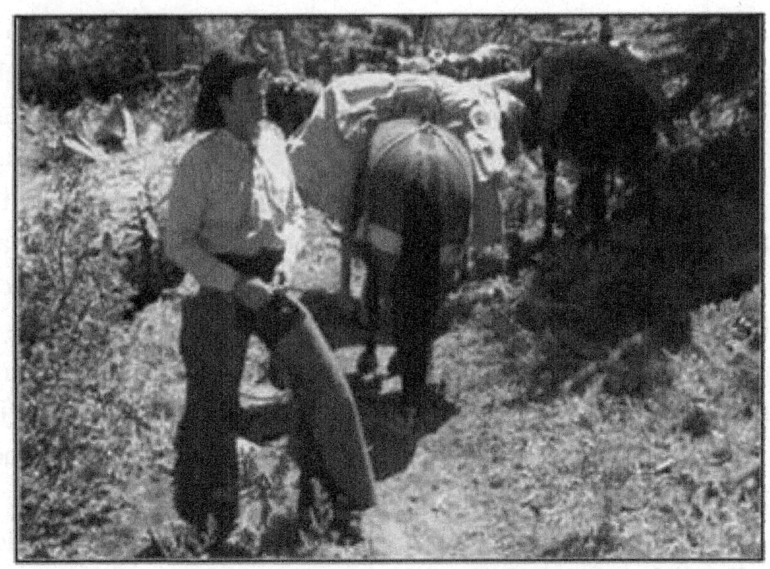

Tom on the trail

The absolute last thing on my mind was company. Since I did not have the door locked, the company just came on in. Suddenly, a voice said "hello." It took me totally by surprise, and I turned with sprayer in hand, spraying Harlan white. It was a struggle just to stay on the ladder. Harlan was not only a world champion in rodeo circles, but he always looked sharp, except, of course, for right this very minute. He informed me he just wanted to visit and see how I was doing on the remodeling.

Now that I look back, it was a pretty funny moment. He looked at me and said, "Well, I was going to ask you what you were doing, but I see you are spraying the ceiling, yourself, and anyone else that happens by." I think it was about this time I lost my balance and started to fall. Harlan, being such a gentleman, made an attempt to catch me. For just a second I thought I was saved, but we both crashed to the floor. You see the wood floor was pretty slick from all the spray. He too had a sense of humor; he started to laugh and said, “René, you really are a mess.” We both broke into laughter.

Did I finish the ceiling? I hired a carpenter by the name of Tom Monroe to finish this job. Tom was the very picture of a cowboy. He was in his mid-forties, six feet and two inches tall with a well-developed frame. He was quiet, with a western manner that was unmistakably cowboy, and very masculine. This carpenter became a main part of my life and the boy’s ranch.

The town of Oakdale was not used to seeing all this work being done by a little pip-squeak of a gal. The old ranchers stopped by from time to time to see how and what I was doing, and before they left, every one of them asked about my partner. It became a private joke between God and me. When ranchers asked, I simply said, “Well, I really don’t want anyone to know, but I do have a silent partner that’s helping me.” This statement alone seemed to feed their curiosity and convince them they were right all along— a woman could not be doing this big project by herself. When they left, God and I continued our discussions and I continued working.

About four months into the project, I was getting really tired. It was easy to do a sixteen hour workday. One night before retiring to bed, I had my usual cup of tea. This became a nightly ritual. I thanked God for the day and discussed plans for the next day’s agenda. This time, I happened to mention I was getting tired and could sure use some help—in the human sense. I surely didn’t want to hurt His feelings by implying He was not helping. After this bit of clarification, I went to bed.

The very next day, my phone rang. The voice on the other end was so familiar, yet I had a difficult time placing the voice with the person. It sounded somehow so familiar and yet so grown-up. It was Helen, a young girl whom I helped raise. She had married a young man who had worked for me in the early years. They told me I had a godchild, and they were moving back to California. I was so excited and, after further conversation, found myself asking them to come live with me at the ranch. Needless to say, my silent partner had come through for me again. I now had help, human that is, to complete the project of remodeling the boy's ranch.

Mickey at four years old with René

When they saw everything I was doing and what I still had to do, they pitched in and things really started to fall into place. One of the things they noticed right up front was no television. I had not been able to afford one and truthfully had not missed the darn thing. So we did other things in the evening hours.

One activity that I enjoyed was playing and scuffling with Helen and Paul's four-year-old child, my godchild Mickey. Every evening after dinner, Mickey and I got down on the floor and literally scuffled with each other. I was very lucky to have received only two black eyes from his little boots. After the second black eye, we made a new rule—he could not wear boots during "playtime." We even taught his dad, Paul, how to be a bucking horse. Paul got down on all fours, and when spurred properly, he bucked like a real horse. This playtime with little Mickey is such a special memory of mine. With this special family at the ranch it took us only two more months and we were fully licensed and ready to operate as a working boy's ranch.

I experienced this special bonding with my own parents when I was little, for we did not own a television either. It seems that bonding is missing in so many children's lives today because parents are so busy making a living. Very few parents have the time to play with their little ones at that beautiful young teaching, learning, and bonding time. We simply have forgotten to "remember the why."

Ask children today when their last playtime was, or better yet, when they last remember having a conversation with Mom or Dad. They will give you a blank look and seem to be lost for an answer. They probably can tell you more about the latest video game. How very sad that family bonding is being replaced by video games and computers. Remember the why: remember why you had these children in the first place. You had them because you wanted to bring a person into this world that would be a part of you. You are not only the parent but also the example, the teacher, and the provider. If you, as a provider, give them only TV and video games to keep them busy, don't be surprised when one day you realize you have no idea who or what your teenager is like. You lost the control and respect a long time ago, when you failed to give them the attention they so desperately needed. It's so simple if you "remember the why."

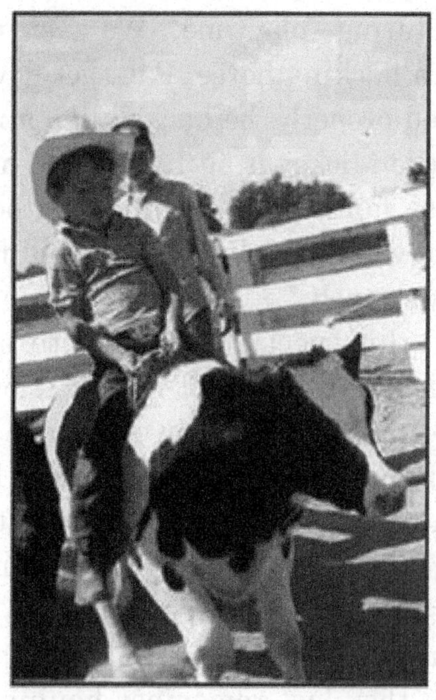

Mickey at six years old on his first steer

~ Chapter 4 ~

MY FAMILY

Coming from a financially poor, and I do mean poor family, we were unable to hire help so my older sister and I were encouraged to do things ourselves. As a matter of record my mother–God rest her soul–was a workaholic, and there was little she felt she could not do. This "I can" attitude I'm sure, is why I always felt I could accomplish so much in my life.

My mother had this remarkable outlook on doing things. First, you never, ever, said that awful word, "can't." It just simply was not allowed. And the tools—it amazes me when I think about the tools we used for remodeling the houses she bought for resale. Basically, in her eyes, if you had a hammer, pliers, screwdriver, and a cutting saw, you had enough tools to accomplish anything. If you had two or three of any of these items, you were abundantly equipped.

I remember one of my favorite sayings as a teenager, "I'm never ever going to see my next birthday." She played along with me by asking why? I replied, "Because you are going to work me to death!" She would laugh and then we continued whatever remodeling project we were doing, except with a smile.

I was blessed with two wonderful parents who, both in their own way, contributed to my success in life and with the boys ranches. When I was thirteen years old, they divorced and I lost my best buddy, my father. My mother would not allow him to visit. It easily ranks as one of the worst experiences of my life.

My father, God rest his soul, was the most positive-thinking person I have ever known. He could find something positive about any situation. We were very poor, but loved.

When I was in the first grade, a classmate asked me if my family was rich. The question threw me. I was a first grader. I did not know the answer.

That evening when my father came home from work, I asked, "Daddy, are we rich?" He smiled his wonderful, knowing smile, took me by the hand and led me outside. Then he asked me a question, "We have chickens, but look at our next-door neighbors. They don't have any chickens, do they?"

"No, they don't have any chickens," I answered, a little puzzled.

He asked me, "Do you see the neighbor's outhouse?"

I replied, "Yes."

"Well, do you see how far he has to walk to his outhouse?" He has to walk a very long way. "Do you see our outhouse?" he asked.

I said, "Yes," not yet understanding.

He continued, "It's closer to our house; we don't have to walk as far. Well, Sis, I would say we are very rich." With that statement, he took my very little hand in his very big hand and we walked back to the house. As we walked back, he looked down at me and said, "God loves us, and we love you; and that, Sis, makes us very rich."

I still remember the warm feeling that came over me. I was small for my age and my father stood very straight and tall. He was six feet three inches and weighed about a hundred and eighty-five pounds. I just knew my father had to be some kin to God himself, because when he spoke, it was with such sureness. As a child, I did not question anything my father said. If he said it, it had to be true. So the next day when I saw that little classmate, I told her we were very rich. For the next couple of years, I told everyone we were rich because according to my father's way of thinking, we were.

As I grew up and went through the usual growing pains, my mother had to correct me when I did not go by the rules, which was an everyday occurrence. My psychological theory as a child was "maybe she won't catch me," but she was always there, looking over my shoulder and appearing out of nowhere. I remember thinking how strong in character she was and how my father was just that very quiet-spoken man. I never really knew his strength until he became ill with cancer. I would call and ask how he was doing, he would reply, "I'm feeling just great!" or "I'm finer than a frog's hair." Every morning, for the last six months of his life, he walked a mile around the neighborhood with his little white dog, even if it was bad weather or bitter cold. He never complained that during the last months of his life he could not eat. A liquid vitamin in a can was all he could keep down.

He had one surgery, and then the doctors told him he needed another. He simply told them, "If you couldn't get it right the first time, what makes you think you can get it right the second time?" Dad sure wasn't going to give them the chance to mess it up again. When his doctor told him without surgery he would die within months, he said, "I think you are the wrong one to be telling me when I'm going to die." He thought God was the only one who knew when his Journey was over. My father lived another two and a half years. He most definitely had an inner peace, with God shining through as a very quiet strength.

I look back and marvel at my parents' insight in teaching me what I know today. So with this background, I had no doubt I could do this project and remodel this dilapidated old ranch house because of the strength and knowledge my parents instilled in me.

My ranching background did not come from my parents, but rather from my great Uncle. Unc owned a cattle ranch in Northern California. Aunt Chunky took care of the chickens and the pigs, and Unc took care of the rest of the ranch, which consisted of taking care of the cattle. I was, literally, his shadow.

All the valley ranchers respected Unc, who contracted with a mere hand shake to cut, rack, and bale their hay. Unc permitted me to watch—but not talk—during their business deals. Dates to bale the hay were made according to the yearly almanac for the following year. Unc then gave the old fashion hand shake and sealed the deal by entering it in his big black book, which he forbade me to touch.

When I was about four years old, Aunt Chunky gave me my very own room at the ranch. From as far back in my childhood as I can remember, I stayed at the ranch whenever possible. It was such a great time in my childhood. I rode with Unc on the tractor when he went to the fields to bale hay.

My parents lived within a few miles of the ranch and sometimes my mother drove the tractor for Unc. They often had shouting matches, and then she would quit and not go back to the fields for a few days. After they got over their mad spell, Unc hired her back. Their frequent disagreements continued through the hay season and, for that matter, through my young life.

Unc was so great. As he drove the tractor, I sat in my little chair he had welded beside his; my job was to watch for baby bunnies and baby pheasants. If I saw one, Unc stopped the tractor, and we ran down the furrows in hot pursuit trying to catch the darn things, having a great time; the rest of the hay crew yelled at us, madder than heck that we were holding up the line. My mother would be shouting the loudest. Unc would just grin and tell me, "Don't worry about them. I'm the boss, and if I want to take the time to chase bunnies, then we will chase bunnies."

In Great Unc's eyes, I could do no wrong. I loved the outdoors and the livestock but went absolutely crazy at a very young age over horses.

On Wednesdays, when we weren't going to the fields to bale hay, we went to the local cattle sale together and had one of those great, old-fashioned hamburgers, you know the kind. The smell of grease coming from the kitchen and the smell of cattle coming in through the windows, ah-h-h, it was heaven. Even today, I still order everything on the hamburger, just as Unc and I did long ago. The only real difference is, now I get heartburn, reminding me I am no longer six years old.

Unc had me convinced the ranch could not run without my help. I totally bought it. At the age of six, I often played sick to get out of school, so I could help Unc with the roundup. Mom finally gave in, and on roundups at the ranch, I went straight to the ranch instead of going to school. On

Saturdays when Unc wasn't in the hay fields, we watched all the old western films on television. Roy Rogers and Gene Autry were our favorites.

Unc was also the head of our whole family. This meant no one in the family bought a car or made any decisions about money unless we first had a family meeting with Unc. At one of these family meetings, my mother wanted his permission to purchase a new car. Unc realized she could not afford this vehicle on her income and told her so. My mother purchased the car and, when she fell behind with the payments, he refused to help her save the car. They did not speak to each other for months.

One day Unc invited my mother to the Wednesday cattle sale. Needless to say, I was not pleased. She made me sit still through most of the sale. Back then, once in a while, a local rancher would run a horse through the sale, and it simply made my day, week, and month. This particular sale had three local horses which we looked at before the sale started. When they ran the second horse through, Unc bought him and looked at me with a grin and said, "He's all yours."

I couldn't believe it! WOW, what a feeling of shear joy. Mom was furious at him; they had another shouting contest, and I had my very first horse. In my childlike mind, this horse looked just like Gene Autry's Champ, so naturally we named my first horse Champ.

Years later, I was given this picture of Champ from my great aunt's album, and here in that old picture was absolutely the ugliest horse you could ever imagine. His head looked more like a long-headed mule than a horse. His ears were longer than most horses' ears. He was a no-butted, big-gutted, long-legged, big-headed nothing of a horse. Yet, in my child like mind he was simply beautiful.

René age six and Champ

The picture shows a little girl sitting on her first horse, with a smile a mile wide. It was winter and Champ had clay-mud balls on his belly. The saddle was an old iron army saddle and looked as bad as the horse. This picture, today, remains one of my favorites. Unc never let on that Champ was an ugly horse. He allowed me to believe in my child's imagination, my horse truly looked just like Gene Autry's horse.

Everyone thought Unc and Aunt Chunky worked too hard, and they did. I cannot remember Aunt Chunky ever talking back to Unc or having a cross word to say about anyone. But their love was yet to be tested. Three months after their fiftieth wedding anniversary, Aunt Chunky had brain surgery for a tumor. It was not a successful surgery and left her totally bedridden. My uncle sold his beloved ranch and devoted the next ten years to caring for her. He rarely left her side. He even developed a device that was attached to the ceiling to lift and turn her. He had to feed, change, and bathe her, as well as do the laundry and the housework. In general, he had to do it all.

A few years into her convalescence, we had a family meeting and told him he was just too old to continue taking care of her. Unc let us all have our say and then proceeded to show us to the door. For the following years of her life, she was always clean and smelled so very nice after each bath. He made sure he used the same perfumes and bath powder she used throughout her life. Then one night she died in her sleep—much loved and very peaceful. This is the greatest of loves. When Unc was tested, he was not found wanting.

When my mother divorced my father, my teenage years were taken from me. I had to work and go to school to help my mother support us. She informed me I would be handling the bill paying and put this responsibility on my shoulders at the young age of thirteen. My sister had left home when she turned eighteen and was lucky enough to have both parents there to see her through those years.

My mother became more and more abusive as her inner bitterness increased with time and hardships. By the time I was sixteen I could no longer cope with her physical abuse and left home in the summer. I finished my high school education by holding down two jobs and graduated in January. (If you qualified, you were eligible for early graduation, meaning you had earned enough credits. The degree was called a high senior graduation.) I think this difficult experience contributed to my understanding the hardships these boys experienced. It is a social misconception that all runaways do not finish school. I lived with my dad until graduation night, leaving the next day and moving to San Francisco. I turned seventeen that summer and finding a job in a big city was not easy.

The family set the best morals and standards for me to live by, creating a path for my future success. I feel these morals and standards are missing in our society today.

~ Chapter 5 ~

THE POLITICS

Working with the federal and state government, politics enters the picture, whether we want it to or not. The children's programs, and the monetary rates providers received per child, proved again that it's "who you know, not what you know." I experienced this political red tape up front and personal with the boys' ranches.

So I thought this special little part of my story should be told. Who knows? After reading this book, you might decide you want to participate in a children's program of some kind. If so, I hope it is a privately funded program so you do not have to experience the full extent of the redirect in politics.

I presented everything the government agency required to qualify for state licensing and the rate on my ranch, only to be introduced to "a hurry up and wait" policy. This "hold your horses attitude" was not what I needed. I made several trips to Social Services office about my rate and the budget package I had submitted, only to find that it was on Miss or Mr. something another's desk and had to go to another desk, because he or she was in a meeting or out of town, or on vacation, or, or, and or.

It did not take a genius to see I would need some politicians behind me. So, being very naïve about the process, I just assumed I would simply make an appointment, go to the State Capitol, and the state representative or senator would be waiting there, glad to see me. After all, I helped pay their salary.

I figured as long as I was going to have to see someone about my children's program and rate, I might as well see a senator, as my philosophy has always been, starting at the top of anything is better than working my way from the bottom. You never know when they just might say yes at the very top.

During this time my attorney was trying to tell me in a polite way that I was wasting my time. We ended up in a bet as to whether or not I would succeed in this little venture.

Three weeks later, after the initial phone call and appointment, the day arrived. I dressed in a dark blue suit accompanied by a dress hat, and drove to Sacramento, the state capitol of California, to visit with the senator.

I arrived at my destination in high spirits and carrying a politically naïve but positive attitude. As I entered the manicured park-like setting surrounding the capitol grounds, the roses were in full bloom, with the sweetest scent in the air. Ah, what a wonderful day this was going to be.

I had to get directions to the senator's office and on the way took in the magnificent interior of the State Capitol of California. So this was democracy, and I was a part of it. WOW, what a great feeling. I entered the senator's big waiting room and informed the secretary I was there and took a seat. Not only was I on time, but early.

Two hours passed. People came and left his office, and I continued to wait. Twice I walked over to the secretary's desk and asked if there was a problem. Each time she informed me there was no problem; however, the senator was running late today because he had an important bill he was trying to get passed the following week. I would just have to wait, but that he would see me. I was sitting close enough to the door I could hear some of what the senator was saying. On one occasion a gentlemen leaving his office turned and replied, "Three o'clock will be fine for our golf game tomorrow."

I waited another hour. It was now five o'clock, and I was the only one in this rather large waiting room. The secretary walked over and informed me, the senator could not see me today, but if I would care to make another appointment, which would be another three weeks, then he would see me. I hesitated for just a moment, smiled lightly through gritted teeth and asked which bill he was working on because WESA, a national woman's organization, was interested in backing him on the bill, but I really needed the number and more information. She was more than willing to give me all the information. I thanked her and left.

Was I really interested in this crazy darn bill he was working on? Of course not! Was I happy about waiting in his office for three hours while he failed to honor my appointment? "Not."

I have two types of mad: the first is giving my opinion rather loudly, and the second is what I refer to as past mad, extremely silent.

In this case it was the latter that was driving me. At this time in my life I was the Northern California director for WESA (Woman Educational Service Association). We were senior executive women teaching and tutoring junior executives and young women fresh out of college how better to succeed in business and career. It was a wonderful organization. Most of us were from the old school. We still liked our doors opened and loved and admired the old-fashioned morals, standards, and values that made this country strong.

That night back at the ranch I phoned several members of the organization and asked if they would meet me in three days at the state capitol to protest a bill the senator was trying to pass. I needed a couple of days to study what I was protesting. I informed them of the rudeness I was met with at his office and thought we needed to receive a little more respect as tax payers. Most were eager to participate, and they too made phone calls in my behalf.

Three days later we were gathered on the porch steps of the state capitol protesting, you got it, his very important bill. Surprisingly we were paid a visit by his assistant who invited me to his office where we could speak on the matter in private.

Amazingly after this meeting and my creative soap box protest, I was able to see not only the senator, but anyone else in the capitol. We discussed my rate, and within two weeks I started getting results. Another senator became involved and loved my ranch program so much he continued writing letters in my behalf. Other politicians became interested in the ranch program, especially around election time. Nothing gets votes like the backing of a children's ranch program.

I won the bet with my attorney, and his respect for accomplishing something he thought impossible, especially for a country girl. The average down-to-earth, everyday, hardworking, naïve, but "determined" and educated country girl, can achieve greatness, conquering the politicians at the state capitol.

Three years later the boys ranch planned a trip to the State Capitol. The boys complained about the educational trip the whole sixty miles; that is, until we got there. I was amazed at the teaching tool this provided for my streetwise boys. I informed them, "This is where you could be as an adult making a difference in people's lives." They began to listen to the tour director, taking everything in from the art on the wall to inquiring where the bathrooms were located.

About politicians, there are good ones and bad ones. The good ones will help you find the solution to your problem, and the bad ones—well, I just say NEXT, meaning, "Don't give up, go to the next politician." If you are thinking about doing a government program, try looking into a privately funded program; remember you must let the female tenacity to succeed kick in; do not give in to bureaucracy bull-ca-ca. I'm sure the reciprocity (political term for getting even) took over my emotional side, and it worked.

Politicians are in a category all their own. The good right along with the bad trickles down and into the very system it is sworn to protect. The problem lies in the fact most laws are written for the masses and blanket the subject matter in such a way that there is no common sense factor involved, especially when it comes to children.

One such law I personally experienced when a social worker paid me a visit unannounced. The first thing she asked me as she was sitting down was if I received her memo regarding regulation so-and-so on showing emotional affection (hugging my little ones), toward my boys. I had to think a minute and asked if she could refresh my memory on the subject matter at hand.

It was mid-afternoon and my little nine and ten-year-olds were due home from school. When the children arrived from school to the ranch, the boys were to come to my office and tell how their day went---bad or good. They would usually come running through the office door, hug me, and proceed to tell me all about their day.

The social worker began to explain that this particular rule concerned touching the children. I was still in the dark and asked her what she meant by this statement.

"Well," she replied, "You are not to touch these children at all, for it might be construed as sexual child abuse, and that includes hugging a child."

By this time I had been in business a year and a half and had established myself as having one of the better ranch programs in the country. As the Good Lord was my shining light in this matter, I felt extremely safe.

"Wait just a minute, you mean hugging a child, and goodness knows these children need hugs more than most, is now not allowed?" I said.

She replied, "Yes," sitting across from my desk without a show of any kind of emotion. Do they train these people to act this way, which is not to have any common sense in regard to feelings or emotion? She continued, "According to rule such and such, and so on and so forth...." I just sat there in disbelief as to her lack of understanding and feeling.

About this time my young ones, three of them, came running through the door. I turned to face the boys as they jumped onto my lap. I was sitting in a very unsteady old but comfortable swivel office chair. There in front of Ms. Rules and Regulations we all went over backward falling to the floor. My feet went flying up into the air, including the boots and spurs I was wearing, normal dress for the ranch. The boys were laughing; I was laughing; the social worker had her mouth open.

I informed her that this was their time and if she did not mind waiting, we could finish our talk after my little ones told me about their day. This only took about five minutes; they gave me a big hug and left. With a quick "Sorry, Mom," they were out the door as quickly as they appeared.

When the boys left, she informed me of such and such rule I had just violated, and I informed her I had no intentions of changing how I ran my boys ranch, and that included hugging my children.

I asked her if she had children. "Yes," she answered. I have two. "When was the last time you hugged your child and said, I love you?" She did not answer me, but left in a huff, informing me I would be hearing from her supervisor.

Nothing ever came of this threat because of whom I knew in politics and because the politicians knew my reputation, my background, and my high regard for morals and standards. I simply made a phone call, and the subject was dropped.

A week later I had Tom make a sign that said: "Hugs Are Free." We hung it behind my desk, up high for everyone to see.

~ Chapter 6 ~

DANIEL'S NIGHTMARE

Most Americans live in a relatively tame environment. For the most part we are raised by loving and caring parents, live in a decent neighborhood, and have been sheltered from the harsh reality that street children experience. We see telethons and advertisements that tell of starving children around the world.

What we don't see or just don't want to see are the starving children in our own towns and big cities. There are children thrown out on the street at a very early age to fend for themselves, eating rodents and other people's garbage. This wealthy country does not have soup lines for children.

Sure, we have shelters such as churches that offer a place to eat and sleep, but these shelters are so under-funded that the children can only stay a short time and then—you guessed it—back on the streets they go, only to be preyed upon by street gangs and pimps. This reality I saw from the inside out.

If they end up in the system that is supposed to protect them, they are "evaluated" and then put on prescription drugs to correct their behavior. Prescription drugs seem to be the "in thing" for a child who may only need some old-fashioned understanding and patience.

Today, this behavior has all kinds of names, but Attention Deficit Disorder (ADD) is the most popular, with bipolar running a close second. If we don't understand what's going on we're inclined to order a pill and zap the child. A pill seems to be an easy solution and the parents have something other than themselves to blame.

As a child I was very energetic, bouncing around the classroom until I drove the teacher mad. My behavior was handled by a simple phone call to my mother who showed up at school, took me outside, and gave me a "pep talk" on just what she expected me to do. I was to sit down in my seat and listen to the teacher, or my backside would be a bright red. She returned me to class and what do you know? I became an avid listener—without drugs of any kind.

I had nightmares over my recent medical diagnosis, but these nightmares were mild compared to the nightmares of the children placed at the ranch, especially Daniel.

When Daniel came to the ranch in the early eighties, he had the most defiant look in his eyes, as if the world existed only to punish him. Daniel was a full-blooded Native American boy with beautiful dark skin and thick black hair. His two front teeth were noticeably missing. His file was handed to me in lockup, just before my interview. It was thick, similar to that of an adult, and included a felony assault on a police officer. He was only eleven years old.

I don't know whether or not it was my Native American background that said yes to his placement at the ranch. In all honesty I could not imagine an eleven-year old with a felony assault conviction on his record. This conviction made no sense to me, and, personally, I could feel his pain.

A week later, when Sue, the probation officer, brought Daniel to the ranch, they were shown to my office. "Good morning, Sue," I said as the meeting began.

"Daniel, please come in and sit down." She unlocked the handcuffs, and they both sat down across the desk from me. Sue told me everything I needed was in the folder and that she had another appointment. "I'll get in touch with you later in the week," she said. As she stood up to leave, she handed me a copy of Daniel's file that was supposed to have his complete history and background. A sack containing a number of prescription drugs was handed to me.

I had interviewed Daniel the week before and told Sue I would like to find out why a child was so messed up at the ripe old age of eleven. Glancing through his file again, I came across the felony charge against Daniel filed by a police officer.

"A felony assault on a police offer, come on, at eleven?" I said out loud as I read the report. I couldn't understand how a trained police officer could consider an eleven-year old boy a bodily threat. It bothered me so much I called the police officer named in the report and talked to him personally. I started the conversation with the police officer by asking if he was four feet tall and under a hundred pounds.

He said, "No, I am six one and weigh two hundred and twenty pounds."

We both laughed. Then I asked, "How could this little boy become such a threat?"

Sue and the police officer found Daniel living on the streets and picked him up for his own safety. But as the system fails most of our street children, it had also failed Daniel. They did not have enough charges against Daniel to hold him long enough to get the help he needed. The only possibility was to take him back to Social Services where they would place him in yet another foster home, where Daniel would simply run away again.

On this particular day, the police officer received a call from the school concerning Daniel. The principal's informative conversation was concerning Daniel's punishment for acting out in class. Daniel rebelled, being Daniel, ran from the principal, and somehow ended up on the roof of the school. What made this problem worse, the roof was one of those rock-covered roofs.

Daniel proceeded to throw rocks at the principal and everyone else within target range.

The police officer tried talking Daniel down, but this tactic was not working. So there was nothing else for the police officer to do but go up on the roof and bring Daniel down, physically. As the officer approached, Daniel picked up a plastic pipe he found lying on the roof. Daniel swung the pipe, hitting the police officer on the knee, thereby creating the opportunity to file a felony and assault charge on a police officer to qualify him for a program like mine. Sue hoped if I interviewed this child, I would not refuse him. She knew of my psychological-behavioral modification program; she had placed a boy with me before.

After blowing placement after placement, Daniel, with the felony charge, qualified for my ranch program. The problem started when he was six, but the history of the child contained in the report I received started at eight years old. This meant that two very important years had been left out.

The nights during the first six weeks with Daniel at the ranch were long and terrifying. He had nightmares almost every night, talking in his sleep.

Every new boy under twelve years old slept in the bedroom next to mine until he adjusted to the ranch life. During this time, I also wanted these children taken off as much medication as soon as possible. I felt most prescriptions were unnecessary. All children on medications were monitored by a doctor on a daily basis. The doctor believed as I did, instead of medication, children needed the opportunity to be children.

A child who is overly medicated becomes zombie like. Yes, they are quiet. Yes, they do not cause the parents trouble. And yes, they sit in front of a television, hour after hour, until you call them to dinner. But make no mistake about it; they are not developing their minds as children. Their minds are literally asleep.

The nightmares Daniel was having told me a lot about this troubled little boy. I could hear him thrashing about and yelling, which meant very little sleep for me. I sometimes sat with him for an hour or more after waking him from a nightmare. We discussed his nightmares at length, and I stayed there until he fell asleep.

Daniel's nightmares involved lots of blood and how he could not wash it off. He screamed at the top of his lungs, "No, no, no!" and then talked of blood again. These nightmares, coming from a child so young, gave me chills just to listen. Imagine what this child must have gone through. Meanwhile, I continued searching his history file, but nothing shed light on his behavior. I knew there had to be more to his background.

In one nightmare, he shouted, "Don't, don't shoot my mommy."

The voice I heard coming from Daniel was that of a much younger child. I knew at this point we were dealing with much more than just a child's defiance. The only information available about his parents included their Native American ancestry and their time on a reservation. The last known address was the reservation. His father was in prison, and his mother was deceased, but the history did not indicate why.

As time passed, Daniel became a little more settled at the ranch and with the other boys. We found things he liked to do. One day I asked Daniel, "Would you like to go see the horses with me?" He said, "No." I asked, "Do you like horses? He said, "No."

By the end of the first month, I insisted Daniel go with me to the corrals to look at the horses. He saw a medium-sized brown-and-white-paint horse that made his eyes light up, but said nothing. Most Native American children like horses—it's just their nature—they have a natural ability to ride and bond with horses easily. This negative response from children when they first come to the ranch is normal. They are protecting their feelings toward anything that might be used to hurt them. So I tried to listen to the boys with an open mind. My job is to turn negative feelings into positive ones.

So Daniel and I simply went to look at the horses. I started talking about the different horses and their problems. "See that brown bay; people abused him, and when he arrived at the ranch, Jake was the only boy who could catch him." Or "See that palomino horse; he is Joe's assigned horse. He also had a lot of problems." And "That old paint horse, well, he's not assigned to anyone yet. He sure needs someone who really cares about him. None of the boys want him because he is not a roping horse, and so he is just here at the ranch waiting for someone to need him and take care of him."

"What do you have to do to get him assigned to you?" Daniel asked.

"Well, he needs an awful lot of care, so I would probably be willing to bend the rules a little just so he could have someone to take care of him."

By this time I was thinking, "René, you have just manipulated this young child. You should be ashamed of yourself." And it worked!

Daniel was so excited I immediately gave him a halter and helped him lead the horse out of the corral. Daniel spent the rest of the afternoon with that horse; and the next, and the next. One afternoon I looked out the window, and there was Daniel, without anyone telling him anything about riding, sitting on the horse bareback with natural ability. Oh, what therapy animals of any kind can be for a troubled child! Daniel now had something he liked and something that needed him as much as he needed the horse. It was, I thought, a good beginning.

In one of the private sessions, Daniel began talking a little more. I asked about his father. There was no response. When I asked about his mother, I got nothing. No response. I immediately changed the subject and continued on to a new subject.

I used relaxation methods with Daniel. This was working to achieve positive flow regarding the activities on the ranch, but fell short of going deeper into his troubled mind.

In one of the many sessions we finally reached a breakthrough. Daniel said, "I have a grandmother, but I lost track of her in moving around from foster home to foster home." He missed her. This was a good sign, so I began research to find her. I asked if he would like to see her. He said, "No," another negative response to protect his feelings.

I thought finding Daniel's grandmother would put everything into perspective and perhaps help the boy through these difficult times. I really needed someone to fill in the blanks, especially about his mother. Daniel was still having those awful nightmares, not as frequent, but they were still happening and there was no clue in the file to explain his problems.

After a few weeks, I was able to locate the grandmother in the San Jose area. I called her on the phone, and what a conversation we had! She had lots of things to tell me about Daniel, and so I invited her out to the ranch to pay a visit.

Daniel did not want to see her. It again was another way of protecting his feelings. He knew if she came to the ranch I would learn the truth about his past. I had simply told him he did not have to see her and not to worry. I would handle it for him.

This is the story the grandmother told me:

At six years of age, Daniel watched his father come home in a drunken rage and shoot his mother with a shotgun. Daniel was sitting on the old broken-down couch, and his sister of three was sitting beside him. The father opened the front door and began to cuss and yell at the mother who was in the kitchen. As she came into the living room, she stopped next to the couch where the children were sitting. The father reached for the shotgun on the wall, turned, and shot her twice at close range. She was standing so close to Daniel her blood from the first shot literally splattered on Daniel and his sister, with Daniel getting the worst of it. Daniel then turned to protect his sister, with his back to the mother. When the second shot hit her, the mother's blood went all over Daniel's back. Daniel was literally covered front and back with his mother's blood.

The father ran out the front door, and a neighbor who heard the shots came running in only to find this very gruesome sight. The two blood-drenched children had not moved from the couch and were locked in each other's arms.

Daniel's little sister had not spoken a word since the shooting. She had been through all kinds of therapy, and after five years, she still was not able to speak. The grandmother tried to raise them but could not cope with all their problems. When the two children were turned over to Social Services, they were immediately split up and sent to different foster homes. Not only did they lose their parents, but because of the Social Services and the state laws, they lost each other.

After hearing this story, I thanked the grandmother, and she agreed to stay in touch with me. She wanted to raise Daniel and definitely loved him. However, she knew with his problems, she could not help him and sincerely hoped the ranch could succeed.

When I confronted Social Services with this information, they were more than happy to update the file, which they had failed to research properly in the first place. Now with this information, I felt I could help this child.

Shortly thereafter, he was brought to the office by one of my counselors for fighting one of the older boys.

"What is this about?" I asked Daniel when he was escorted into my office.

"He called me an Indian."

Daniel took this as an insult, and the fight was on. Understand that this little boy would fight for any reason, but being called an Indian was no reason to fight.

I looked at the older boy and asked if this was true. He replied in the affirmative, "Yes," I paused and said, "The older boy is right. You are an Indian."

I continued, "Let me get this straight. You are fighting because someone called you an Indian? Could you explain to me why that made you want to fight? You are an Indian and should be proud of this fact. Was your father a full-blooded Indian?"

"Yes," Daniel replied.

"Was your mother a full-blooded Indian?"

"Yes," he replied.

"Then, son, you should be proud, and stand tall. Because you see, I'm what they call a half-breed, part Cherokee and part Irish. And I am proud of my heritage, especially my Indian heritage. Just think about some of the advantages we have. We don't ever have to worry about sunburns, and we have beautiful skin tone that other people would die for."

He began to look at me in a different way. "Did you ever get called names in school?" Daniel asked.

"Of course, I did. When I was in elementary school, the other kids called me 'Blanket Ass' So much that I just started looking at it as a compliment."

Daniel was puzzled. "But you have blonde hair."

"Yes, but when I was young, I looked like this." I reached into my desk drawer and pulled out a picture of me exercising one of my racehorses. I had very long dark brown (almost black) hair.

I explained, "Like my mother's side of the family, my hair started turning gray when I was only thirty-five. Since I was not ready to become gray, I dyed my hair blonde."

Daniel and I started to bond during the second month. He wasn't cussing me so much, but still cussing, so in the third month, we had an old-fashioned cussing contest in my office, which seemed to solve the problem.

Sometimes a boy just needs to shout at an adult, and the adult needs to shout back. It was rare for me to resort to such measures, but sometimes it worked. No one was allowed to interrupt me during these sessions.

Daniel left my office that day to tell the other boys, "Mom can really cuss when she wants to."

Boys sometimes use cussing as a way to intimidate adult females, but they usually never meet a woman who can intimidate them. Daniel still cussed every once in a while, but basically with me, he stopped.

On the grandmother's second visit to the ranch, Daniel met with her. Daniel began to open up more. I knew what was causing his very deep pain, and now we could begin to deal with his nightmares. We continued meditation for relaxation. These sessions, which included creative visualization for positive energy flow, were very successful for children with behavioral problems.

There was something else that happened about this time that created a big difference. The big brother I chose for Daniel was John, a Native American who was proud of his heritage. John was sixteen and became very protective of Daniel. Between having John for his big brother, the little paint horse, and many, many sessions, some at two o'clock in the morning, and trips to the High Country, Daniel began to heal. He was also off all medications and looking like a normal and healthy boy. Yes, he was active, and yes, he was mischievous. He was a normal boy doing boy things. I could see a big improvement in Daniel after about five months. The ranch program was working: the combination counseling methods combined with the horse project, good food and a loving hug when needed made a remarkable difference.

His grandmother began to visit Daniel every month. When she showed up at the ranch, she always brought something homemade, like cookies, for Daniel to share. The other boys started asking Daniel when his grandmother was going to visit again. Cookies and cakes were always welcome at the ranch.

Within a year and a half, Daniel was released from the program and went to live with his grandmother. For the next six months, she and Daniel came back to visit us as I requested in the psychological report presented in court. I really looked forward to her wonderful visits and our conversations about Daniel's progress. She sent me the following letter while he was still on the program, which I keep among my treasures.

Dear René and Staff,

I am writing this letter in regards to my grandson Daniel, who has been with you for the past year. I would just like to thank you for his care and the big improvement in his state of mind.

I got him when he was six years old and couldn't deal with his problems, but you have made such a change in him (for the better) he is so well behaved and is so happy there with you that it has even made my life so much happier. I never saw him smile so much in all his life. Thank you for everything. I wish there were more people like you and your staff and I wish Daniel would have had you five years ago. I know he still has a lot to deal with, but I am very confident in you and I know he'll grow up to be normal and proud because of you. I love him very much and I love you and your staff for all the hard work and love you have given Daniel, and for taking time with me when I visit.

Thank you again. And God bless you all, Ramona.

Not always do you get this kind of thanks for making a difference in a little boy's life. It is nice when someone takes the time to thank you for a job well done.

~ Chapter 7 ~

THE INVESTOR

This part of the boys ranch story needs to be told because without this wonderful gentleman, the boy's ranch program probably would have failed for lack of funding. I started remodeling after having a few garage sales to get the money I needed. That money was now gone. I could see I needed an "investor," and not just any investor—I needed an "elephant."

This is common terminology among people who are self-employed. How can I as a lady refer to the terminology of the elephant investor and still be a lady? Well, I'll try to explain so you can get a more visual picture—it refers to a male elephant's lower anatomy.

That means someone who can make a decision without questioning everything. He just knows what you are doing is what he wants to be involved in and he believes in you. He can read people and is not necessarily a reader of words, but rather a reader of people. He is usually a very down-to-earth man. I had heard Max a real estate friend of mine, use this term in his real estate office.

At the end of one very busy day when things seemed overwhelming, I prayed for God to send me an elephant. The next day, I called Max. He knew everybody who was anybody in Sacramento. I asked him to help me find an investor. He was aware of my work at the boy's ranch. He said, "Give me a little time René, and I probably can find someone."

I said, "Okay."

That was around ten o'clock in the morning. I did not really know what an investor was or what to expect, but I had a vague concept he or she would give me money to finish the boys ranch and make it a productive working entity. I had no idea of what a "little time" meant—surely it would only take an hour or two. That's how naïve I was.

At three o'clock that afternoon, you guessed it, I was on the phone to Max: "Well, where's my investor, and how do I get in touch with him?" Since I was very straightforward and knew I needed this money for a good and productive cause, I just assumed everyone should be a phone call away and of the same mind-set.

Max had done some business with me in the past including a partnership in a mortgage company and knew I was serious; therefore, I expected him to produce. He laughed, joking with me, and said, "Since you have given me all this time, I'll try to have someone for you by five o'clock." Sure enough, I had a phone number by that afternoon.

The next morning, I was on the phone with a perfect stranger telling him my life history in the short form; of course, this for a female is sometimes very hard to do. I was talking so fast about what I intended to do and what I needed from him. When I took a breath, he interrupted me with a simple response, "Young lady, I will be happy to meet with you, but in all your explanation, you have left out your name." I had a slight giggle in my voice as to the embarrassment of this important point of conversation and immediately apologized. He accepted my apology and wanted to meet with me the following week, and I said, "Sir, I don't mean to sound disrespectful, but you sound like the investor I need. However, sir, I need to meet with you now, and if you are as excited as I am, and really want to invest in what I am about to do, then you'll meet with me now."

I was quiet, and he was quiet—extremely quiet. It seemed like an eternity before he answered. Finally he said, "You're right, but it has to be at nine o'clock tomorrow night because that's the only time I can fit you into my schedule."

"Great, I'll see you tomorrow night." It sounded like he was trying not to laugh but otherwise had a wonderful, masculine voice. "Don't you want to know how to get here?" he asked.

In a small voice, I said, "Yes, sir," thanking him again for finding the time to see me. I wrote the address down without checking to see where it was located. The investor finished our conversation by telling me the things I should bring to the meeting. In short, a business plan.

I hung up and proceeded to do the Snoopy dance as if I could hear the happy jazz theme from the *Peanuts* cartoon.

I sat down and diligently began to write out what I thought he needed. When finished, it was three pages, written in longhand—I had no computer. That was the day I discovered I was not a business plan writer. I just wrote what I knew I was capable of doing and what I needed to make the boys ranch program work. I left out the fluff.

There is something about investors that I have since learned. "Real" investors are not readers, and readers are not investors. The real investor can read people, and they listen closely to what you are saying. A real investor is a good judge of character.

The next evening, I dressed in one of my business suits, every hair in place, and finished the look off with a pillbox hat. I have worn hats all my life, it's a way of setting myself apart, owning the room, a terminology used by self motivated people. In my rush to leave the house, I left the handwritten business plan on the table, and naturally, I did not realize this until I was almost to Sacramento, sixty miles from my ranch.

As I drove closer to the address, I saw a dark, spooky industrial area with rows of huge buildings designed exactly the same with large roll-up doors. The slivered moon provided little comfort and light to supplement the burned out streetlights. Uneasiness caused my mind to work overtime. Surely Max would not get me involved with a serial killer! Immediately, I began to recite Hail Mary prayers, without the rosary.

As I drove closer to the designated address, a thought crossed my mind; I realized this might not be the smartest thing I had ever done! I really needed this investor, now! So I continued ahead. Finally there was the address right in front of me.

The investor had instructed me to press the button next to the small door and then wait. A large industrial door would open automatically, but I was *not* to step through the door. He cautioned me to wait for someone to meet me. In my excitement over achieving the interview, I forgot the small details and parked my vehicle, walked up to the rather large door, and rang the bell. When the giant industrial door opened and a dim light came on, I walked in, setting off a blaring security alarm. Simultaneously, Godzilla the second appeared out of the dark shadows walking toward me. "Hail Mary, full of grace, for goodness' sakes," I muttered, I needed to get the Lord beside me immediately. It looked like a David and Goliath situation. This guy was huge and looked even scarier in the dim light! I really shouldn't be scared, after all David faced Goliath with confidence and won. Where was my faith? I remembered Max making the comment that I was not afraid of anything or anybody. Well, if Max could see me now!

Thirty seconds went by, and then my fear vanished when I heard his gentle voice. "Are you René?"

In a meek little voice, I managed to say, "Yes."

He said, "Paul is expecting you." All the while, the alarms were still blaring. I followed him through three offices where there were bags upon bags filled with all kinds of cash. Numerous money counters sorted paper money in stacks of ones, fives, tens, and twenty dollar bills. Coins of nickels, dimes and quarters were everywhere. Never had I seen this kind of money up close except in the movies. I just kept walking until this giant of a man stopped and said, "Go through to the next office. Paul is waiting to see you."

I swallowed hard and took a deep breath. My imagination was spinning off wild scenarios of gangsters and corruption. I tried to focus, thinking if I survive this, I am going to bring bodily harm to Max.

Finally, I was face to face with my potential investor. He really needed a shave, was wearing a short-sleeved, Hawaiian designed polyester shirt, and was on the phone. He looked up and acknowledged my presence and continued with his phone conversation. His business like firm voice indicated total control of the situation. When he hung up, he must have sensed my fright because he spoke softly and said, "I have one more phone call to make and then we could talk." His voice and mannerisms conveyed a deep sense of composure and wisdom. He pointed to a chair in front of his desk and I sat down.

The phone call was to his wife informing her he was going to be late and not to worry about warming his dinner. His softer tone and concern for his wife put me at ease.

When he hung up the phone, he got right to the point and asked to see my business plan. I said with as much conviction as I could muster, "Well, sir, I forgot it. However, you have the real investment sitting here before you. So you ask the questions, and I will answer them."

Paul looked directly at me for a moment, and then he spoke. "Tell me what you are doing. What is the total project about, and how much money do you need?"

I thought to myself, "This man and I, what a match—right to the heart of the matter. Yes, oh, yes."

In the next fifteen minutes, I told him exactly what I planned to do, what the project was about, what the projected profit and loss figures were, and how much money I needed.

He asked me what kind of payments and interest he could expect to receive. I looked at him as if he were from outer space and shouted in disbelief, "PAYMENTS? You expect PAYMENTS? There will be no payments! If I could afford payments, I wouldn't need you for the money!

He sat there for a minute with this stunned look on his face and then asked, "Just how am I going to get my money back, or do you even plan to pay me back?"

"Oh, yes, sir," I answered. "I plan to pay you back when the property sells and/or shows a percentage profit. Your money will be secured by the property. When the ranch sells, whenever it sells, you will receive fifty percent of the profit on the turnover. To sell a boys ranch, you have to sell to the right individual; it has to be what we refer to as a "true caregiver." I'm a workaholic and will probably suffer burnout in five to seven years."

Paul smiled and said, "Well, darlin, when do you need this money?"

"Yesterday" I replied!

Paul smiled again and said, "Meet me tomorrow morning in front of the bank."

"Oh, sir, one more thing," I said as I was leaving, "I will probably need more money in the first year, and, sir, I don't know how much that figure will be. But, sir, I will be conservative, and I am honest. Besides, the money I borrow comes off my side of the fence when the property sells. So you see, sir, I will be conservative."

I waited to see if he was going to run backward at this point. He paused for just a moment and then said, "I will see you at the bank tomorrow, and if it's not too much trouble, could you please bring me something in writing for the money?

This was a man amongst men. I had met my "elephant."

I simply said, "Yes, sir," and turned to find the gentle giant standing there to walk me to my truck.

Did I sleep that night? Of course not! My mind kept coming back to all that money lying around. Was he some kind of gangster? And then I thought of his soft voice, the warmth in his voice when he spoke to his wife, and his remarkable ability to relate to me in my hyper state of mind. Nevertheless, I had to be absolutely sure he was one of the good guys.

I called Max the next day and asked, "Max, what does this gentleman do for a living?" Max laughed at my suspicious mind. "He is an honest businessman and has a good reputation."

I mentioned to Max seeing all that money lying out in plain view.

"René, he owns one of the largest vending-machine businesses in Sacramento, and that's why the money was there."

I was so excited I arrived at the bank early; he was a little late. With my high energy level, it just seemed like it was longer than ten minutes. At last, there he was, and he walked over and handed me a cashier's check. I thanked him and told him what a great thing he was doing and gave him a big hug.

He allowed me to rattle on and on about the project; all the while, he said nothing. Finally, when I took a breath, he asked, "Don't you have something to give me?" In my excitement to meet him, I had once again forgotten to bring the contract regarding the percentage and the payback.

I looked at him and handed the check back. He said with a great deal of kindness in his voice, "I know, you forgot; it's on the kitchen table." He continued, "Darlin', I don't need the money back. Just when you can fit it into your schedule, please get me something in writing and send it through the mail."

And that, my friends, was the beginning of a long and lasting relationship. Through the next years, we developed a deep, platonic friendship. If I had a neighbor complaining about my boys ranch, I simply called Paul, and we bought them out.

He called Max one day and laughed about my honesty. "One thing you don't want to do with René is ask a question if you can't handle the answer." Paul was referring to a conversation we had at the beginning of the week. He had called to ask how we were doing.

I told him we were short for the month by five thousand dollars. The state had lost two of my boys checks, and I needed at least two placements to break even. I think he was expecting me to butter things up a bit to make the boys ranch look better. He was quiet, and I knew he was thinking—then he told me not to worry. "If you need more money, just call."

Thanking him for his generosity; I told him things would work out by the end of the month, and I really did not want to borrow more money, and sure enough by the end of the month everything was back to normal.

This was, indeed, an elephant of the biggest kind. I have not had the privilege of meeting such a person since. Paul had more class in his little finger than most people I have met. Yet I never saw him in a suit—just plain old polyester. He was the very best at reading people and situations. He had a special common sense way of looking at things. To me he had the wisdom of a saint, without which, I could not have accomplished as much as I did. He was my strength and not just in money, but in supporting me mentally.

By the way, during all the years as my investor, he never said my name. He just called me Darlin. I knew he was a devoted husband and family man, and meant no harm. He was not an educated man, but he had a PhD. in common sense.

I shall never forget him and the many boys he helped by supporting the ranch with his unquestionable generosity. I thank you, my kind and gentle friend, for allowing me the opportunity to live some of the most memorable and productive years of my life.

~ Chapter 8 ~

THE COOKS

The cooks that worked on the ranch were as much a part of its success as any of the people we hired. My mother, being from the old school of learning, believed a woman could not amount to anything, much less get married and be a good wife, unless she knew how to cook and clean. Mother never finished the fifth grade, and to her way of thinking, she wanted us to finish high school, a common statement of hers was, "So you can get married and give me grandchildren." Mom never discussed higher education in our house because sending her two daughters to college would be a waste of money, which we didn't have anyway. And I went on daydreaming about the things I wanted in life, such as college and a career. Learning how to cook at a very young age was to satisfy my mother.

I learned how to cook by the age of ten, often by standing on a chair to reach the countertop and stove. I much preferred my horse and outdoor chores. Learning how to cook, clean and mend ranked low on my chart of pleasant activities and high on the list of things to avoid. However, my mother refused to hear any nonsensical negative rebuttals from me. "No" to my mother was considered talking back.

When Mother was teaching me something, regardless of my age, she'd say, "You're never too young to learn. Just pull that old kitchen chair up to the stove and watch and listen to everything I do and say." She knew how to put the fear of the good Lord in me. She had me believing that if I did not learn how to cook, I could not become an adult, much less go to heaven. I am very grateful for that teaching; I have used this special talent throughout my adult life.

In the early years of the boys ranch I prepared most of the "home style" meals. The boys loved to sit down to the big old-fashioned dinners with gravy and biscuits, fried chicken, and lots of home-grown vegetables. I became an expert at making sheet cakes and six to ten pies a week. I loved cooking big Sunday and holiday dinners, with lots of ham and turkey. The boys came into the kitchen anytime they wanted. Unlike other children's ranches, the refrigerators were not off-limits. The ranch did not have locks on the refrigerator doors; the knives were not locked up either. These rules proved to be a big problem when I needed to hire a cook.

When I fried chicken, there were more than the usual amount of gizzards and livers. My little ones sure had a nose for fried chicken. As they came through the kitchen door, I would hand them a fork with a gizzard or liver on it. They would go out the other door, and pretty soon, they were back for more.

When I baked my pies, my little ones wanted to help. Children reach a certain age where every other word is "can I help?" Of course, this is at an age when they are too young to help, and by the time they become teenagers and they can help, they don't want to help.

David, Willie, and little Shawn were nine and ten years old when they wanted to help me make pies. I let them be the official "taste testers." When I made the filling, I made enough to put some in three little bowls; their job was to let me know how it tasted. "What do you think, maybe a little more sugar?" Of course, this meant they each needed another sample just to make sure I got it right.

Pie-crusts offered a pure feed for fun on the ranch. When the aroma of the first pies reached the boys nostrils, they rushed in the kitchen, straight from their mud puddles. I insisted they wash their hands before "helping." Have you ever in your life watched a nine-year old wash his hands? It's done as if they were going to a fire, very fast. The speed necessitates the soap be omitted, the most important part left out entirely. The speedy lads turned the water on and ran their hands under the faucet, then grabbed the towel and the dirt came off on the towel all in a single motion. You could always tell the towels that my little ones dried their hands on because those towels were the dirtiest.

Back to the pie-crust making.

The boys came into the kitchen ready to dig their dirty fingers into the pie-crust. With my natural desire for hygiene, I concluded they needed to make their very own pies. I found some small individual pie pans—very small but just right for the occasion.

While David and Willie progressed with their pie-crusts, Trevor, one of the older boys, strolled in the kitchen and instantly noted David and Willie's dirty fingernails. He whispered in my ear, so as not to hurt the little ones feelings, that he was not eating any of the pies if "they" were helping. I thanked Trevor for his discretion and informed him that I baked for the entire ranch while our little chefs baked only for their own consumption.

Trevor's mind at ease, he sauntered out of the kitchen, pausing just long enough to dip his grubby finger into my pie filling and giving me that million dollar smile to let me know it tasted great.

Trevor's discretion occurred as a result of systematic teaching techniques. I taught the boys never to be intentionally cruel to their little brothers. The older boys understood my point because of the approach I used. I reminded them by saying, "These little brothers, had a similar background to yours, and came to the ranch because of serious abuses. As we are a family, we care about one another." I also initiated a big brother's program, which the older boys took seriously. If an older brother made some remark that resulted in tears in the younger ones, I enacted certain kinds of restrictions. I reminded them of their abuses when they were younger. Amazingly, the older boys loved taking care of their assigned younger brothers.

The little ones offered some of their pies to the older boys, but there were never any takers. The older boys rubbed their stomachs and would say things like "Gosh, I'm so full!" or "I just don't like apple (or whatever)."

As the ranch program became more and more successful, the demand to expand my boy's ranch was inevitable. The expansion created a dilemma I had not prepared for. I needed to hire a cook, surely a simple matter of running an ad in the local newspaper, interviewing a few applicants, and then hiring the best choice, who would naturally be available to begin working in a matter of days. Wrong!

The first ad I ran simply read: "Cook Wanted for Boys Ranch" and gave my office phone number. A nice gentleman called and said, "I have been a chef for a well-known restaurant chain," He informed me he made most of their breads and desserts. But his specialty was pancakes. He showed up for the appointment nicely dressed in casual clothes and showed a great interest in the job. So I hired my first cook.

He worked a week, and things were not bad—just not good. The boys complained. My new cook was late with the meals and altered the planned monthly menu that was essential for the ranch. I thought it was because he was new to the ranch. This man was in his late forties and so very thin, although he did pass his physical. We required a physical for all potential employees before they could work at the ranch. His skill in meal planning wouldn't pass muster on a trail drive. He established no rapport with the boys.

Two of my little ones came into the office one day and asked why the cook smelled funny. Their question should have given me a clue. The next week was not much better.

Finally, one evening I called over to the main ranch house and asked if he would come to my office—we needed to discuss some things. No sooner had he opened the door until I smelled what the boys had smelled—the smell of hard liquor filled the room. Needless to say, I fired him quicker than he could flip a pancake.

I hired cook number two, an educated girl whose attempt at teaching school turned out to be less than the pretty picture painted in her mind. I asked her point-blank if she could cook, and she assured me that she cooked extraordinarily, and created all kinds of "special dishes." I emphasized the necessity of on-time meals because the ranch program operated on a timetable of sorts. She assured me of her abilities and pleaded with me to give her a chance. I hired her on the spot; after all, not every ranch employed a nicely dressed thirty-something educated cook.

The term "special dishes" should have given me a clue. We had little time for cookbooks at the ranch. All meals were prepared by taste the old fashion way. Things happened so fast; when lunch was over, we started the baking, and then it was time to prepare dinner.

The first dinner she served was a casserole and a large bowl of green salad. This was simply one dish set on the table to feed eighteen hungry boys, as well as staff, most of which were hungry cowboys.

She was not accustomed to yelling and language problems. I informed her during the interview my boys were street-smart boys, and this was, after all, a boys ranch. By the third week, she came running into the office crying. It seems my little angels had put plastic spiders in her bed, and then there were the real dead flies in the mashed potatoes at dinner one night. In retaliation, she put up a "No Boys Allowed in the Kitchen" sign, and the little ones hated her.

The coup de grace that brought her into my office crying for the last time, they had stolen her cook books, and this she said was the last straw. She resigned, stating, "The boys are too much for me." I fully agreed with her. I replied," Is that all you have to say to me." "NO I quit!" she said, and left in a huff.

I held a group meeting that evening and asked if anyone wanted to tell me why she quit. One of the counselors said she cried a lot. I made a suggestion that all the cookbooks be returned by morning to the kitchen table. Sure enough the next morning several of her cookbooks were on the kitchen table.

Of course, every time a cook quit, I became the overwrought cook, preparing all the meals. The boys loved it but I was wearing out.

The next ad read: "Old-fashioned cook wanted for out-in the-country boys ranch. Familiarity with country lifestyle preferred." I interviewed about three ladies and decided on one that looked the part. She was a grandmother-looking German lady who said, "Homemade biscuits are not a problem." She asked for Wednesday evenings and Sundays off to attend church.

The first week was great as far as I was concerned. She was a good cook but the boys still did not like her. They complained about everything she fixed until one day I called for a group session in my office. "Boys, if you cause this one to leave, you are going to be doing the cooking on this ranch by yourselves."

The sign "No Boys Allowed in the Kitchen" was still above the door. I told her she could take the sign down, but she did not respond; nor did she smile. The sign remained. Understand that this was a very busy boys ranch. Things were happening all the time.

Joe, an eleven-year old, joined a wrestling team at school. I encouraged Joe in playing sports, and it made a difference in his attitude. The sport actually helped him grow and develop physically and mentally. But since no one would practice with him, I volunteered.

He would hide from me, and as I walked through the house, Joe surprised me by jumping on my back; and we wrestled each other to the floor. We played this silly game over the next couple of years. No—this wrestling was not approved by the state-licensing agency, but it was fun. It served three purposes: it kept me in shape and alert; it made him feel big that he could attack Mom, and we both had fun. Keep in mind that everyone at the ranch knew about this—that is, except for the new Dutch cook.

When Joe first came to the ranch, he was small for his age, and jumping on my back was great, but as Joe grew, Tom became concerned that I might get hurt. Truthfully, I was getting concerned because it was getting harder to win the match.

So one day I called Joe into the office to tell him the fun and games were over because he had grown too big, and I had, well, had too many birthdays. He grinned at me and said he fully understood, but there was a twinkle in his eye that told me this was not over. Joe was just one of those kids that pushed the envelope to the limit.

The cook seemed to be working out pretty good—the food was great, and I liked her whether the boys did or not. She was in her late fifties and was "full figured," with her hair pulled back in a bun. The only thing that bothered me was she just cooked and paid no attention to my boys. She never smiled.

One day, I was coming through the sliding glass door that entered into the den area. There was Joe behind the curtain, and as I came through the door, he jumped on me from behind; and we both went to the floor. We rolled through the den area, tumbled around on the kitchen floor, and then rolled into the living room where the flat rock stone fireplace was located. Remember this was not a fight; it was just something Joe and I did. To give you a better picture, the fireplace had square corners on the edges, and they were very sharp.

I could hear two of my other boys shouting, "Pin him, Mom; pin him."

As Joe threw me over to pin me, my head hit the corner of the fireplace, and I felt a very warm liquid flowing from the back of my head. Dazed I could hear voices far in the distance. "Mom, are you hurt? Mom, say something." I thought I heard crying, but it sounded far away; I saw shadowed bodies weaving in and out through the confusion.

The cook had been fixing dinner and came over, looking down at me to see what was happening. The boys were yelling at Joe, mostly words that were not allowed. Joe told the cook to stop her whining and get a f——n' towel for Mom's head. "Can't you see Mom's hurt?" When I came to, the boys were cussing Joe, and Joe was crying and talking at the same time. By this time the shadow of Tom and his voice was calming the room, the sound of ambulance sirens far off, and then I was out.

The cook quit the next day and stated, "This ranch is a zoo and you are the zookeeper." Oh well, I've been called a lot worse.

I responded by saying, "Perhaps you are right, but I have a very happy zoo."

I ran another ad, and this time, the job description was a full paragraph. The first sentence read: Must Love Children.

Three days later, I interviewed several people, a few absolute no's and a maybe. I asked the counselor if there was anyone left outside, and he said, "Yes, ma'am, Aretha Franklin," and got this silly grin on his face.

"Tell her to come in," I said. Sure enough, she was a rather heavy-set, but jolly, sort of individual—an African American named Bertha. She had a smile that melted my heart. She was widowed and in her fifties, and all her children had moved away. For the next hour, Bertha and I sat and talked about our families and her grandchildren and my boys ranch. I don't recall asking a lot of questions about her background, except "You can cook, right?" One of the little ones came into my office asking a question. She smiled at the boy as though he was one of her very own.

This kind, jolly lady loved my children and loved everything about the ranch, including its country location. I told her that if she had ideas about changing things for the better, just let me know. "I appreciate anything that will make this ranch run smoother." A few days later she called me and said, "Miss Rene' I need to tell you something because I cannot handle this any longer."

I was prepared for the worst. She begin to talk, "If you will come to the kitchen, I will be happy to fix you something cold to drink." At that time of day, it was more than welcome. With each step from my office to the main ranch house, I was thinking of some really tough restrictions if my boys had caused this one to quit.

I asked if she would say what was on her mind. "Well," she said, "I have been breaking the rules here, and I just can't do it anymore. Yea see, ma'am, I really like the children, and they have been coming into the kitchen, and well, helping me; and that sign says, "No Children in the Kitchen." I've been so worried about this and needed to tell you.

I sat back for just a minute and looked at this sweet lady. I have never smiled as big as I did after that statement. I knew we had our ranch cook, and that wasn't all we had—I knew my boys had someone who truly loved them.

I told Bertha this was "her kitchen," and I was in full agreement if she wanted to take that darn sign down. I thanked her for the ice tea. As I left, I heard the sign being torn off above the door. So began a friendship with this wonderful Christian lady who helped us through many hard times.

When I first introduced her to the children, she just looked at me and said, "Hum-m-m, hum-m-m, what a voo-riety!" She meant, of course, all the different nationalities. Her friendship became so valuable, and the kitchen became everybody's favorite hangout, including mine.

~ Chapter 9 ~

HEALTH ISSUES

The first year of my tenure at the ranch was an education and a half on what NOT to do. I do believe my inexperience with children gave me more of an open mind in setting rules for the ranch; for instance, they could speak their minds openly and freely to me. At first, the boys simply did not know how to talk to me because they were afraid of the female gender in speaking their minds. I felt this had to be corrected immediately, so I simply told the boys, "Speak to me as though I were one of you. Be relaxed when you need to tell me something that is troubling you." So they began to relax more, and in turn I learned more about their problems and their fears. However, this did cause them to be a little more blunt spoken than I imagined.

Health issues for instance; occurred on a regular basis especially in the winter. Just imagine when you as a parent experience the flu with, say, three children. We, you and I, were probably having the same thoughts about whether these flu and cold sessions would ever resolve themselves or we would simply die before we cured our children.

With ten children running around the first year with the flu or colds, I finally went to vitamins C and D. (The following year I had eighteen boys.) This seemed to work for the boys and me, as I felt much better and more positive about the children's health issues in the winter. I do believe it kept my boys from catching viruses at school. I later learned to separate the sick child from the rest of the children, and sometimes this actually worked for the betterment of all the children and staff. On occasion, the colds or flu would still spread like wildfire and again my sick boys and I would have little sleep.

Early-Eighties

"There's nothing to it!" I replied to Willie's question. I continued, "I'll tell you what I will do to make this whole thing more acceptable. I have never asked any of you to do things Mom would not do, so I will go through the same experience you are going through after you have completed this minor task."

David and Willie came bursting through the door with the fear of God on their little faces. Willie who usually let David do all the talking blurted out, "Do we have to get those physicals that the older boys are talking about?" It seems the older more experienced boys with this procedure had literally scared my little ones to death by exaggerating the truth into an outright lie.

What started this whole business of physicals with my boys was Social Services had sent me one of their many letters requesting that the boys should have their physical reports in their files to meet the state's requirement for the coming year. Naturally, upon closer examination of my files, I noted that only two of my boys had received physicals and qualified for this requirement. The rest would have to comply, receiving their physicals.

David spoke up about this time, "Mom, Trevor said the doctors cut out our testicles, you know our balls below the belt!"

Willie joined in and added, "Mom, they told us they would grow back and not to worry 'cause it only hurts for a little while." But me and David think Trevor lied about the hurt-en, cause' we think it's gonna hurt "a whole lot."

David chimed in, "Mom, I like the ones I have and we don't want to lose them. Can't you do something?"

I immediately corrected this over-the-top rumor. "David," I began, "first of all, the older boys told an absolute lie about your below the belt extremities."

David jumped up and began asking, "What's that extreme---, ah word mean, Mom? Is that the same as our balls?"

"David, yes it's the same, but rather a different terminology. Oh for heaven sakes, I will discuss this later in the afternoon at group session." I had not yet mastered the common terminology that was simply required for the boys ranch. As they left my office, they were in full conversation about wondering if this included "everything below the belt."

I immediately called for a group session. I had no idea the house parents, without knowing the harm they were doing, let the cat out of the bag about the physicals and the older boys decided to do their thing with my younger ones.

In the year or so that I had been director of my boys ranch, I experienced language of all types, most of which were profanity. Nothing they could say would surprise me. I taught all to speak straightforward, and they thought this freedom was a grand idea. In many ways it let the boys be boys and say what was on their minds. So David and Willie were simply telling their little problem to me in their own words. They had heard me use the term "below the belt" before, so naturally they felt this usage fit their situation. And it did! And on my side of the fence I felt an accomplishment of sorts; they were talking to me freely in their own words.

That afternoon all the boys at the ranch were required to attend this meeting to straighten out this mass confusion regarding yearly physicals.

"Boys," I began, "there is nothing scary about getting a physical! There is nothing to it, and there is NO cutting below the belt or for that matter anywhere on your body. I myself have had several physicals and they are not painful. I have told the younger ones that Mom will be receiving one right after you boys get yours."

About this time John, my serious fifteen-year-old spoke up and informed me of something I had neglected to take into consideration. "Mom, in your examination, do they check your below-the-belt parts? This one remark brought home what the boys were in an uproar about totally. It did not enter my naïve mind that they too would be examined in their private areas. "Yes, son," I replied. "And to my knowledge no one has been hurt by this procedure. However, I will check with the doctor to see if there is some way to make it easier for you."

After checking with the doctor, I did not like the setup. The nurse would be there watching the doctor perform the exam, but the boy would be in the room by himself. My children had been through so much before they came to the ranch that I felt it my responsibility to protect them as much as possible.

I proceeded to call my old doctor that came to the ranch for many of my boys health needs. He agreed to do the physicals at the ranch and they could be done in my office behind a screened in area. The boys felt safe with a nurse they were familiar with from previous visits. The children felt a sense of relief with this arrangement. At another group session, the old doctor came to the ranch before the physicals occurred to explain in very plain English what would take place and why. He did a great job, explaining their genitals were examined for the betterment of their growth in this particular area. David interrupting the doctor asked, "You mean you can tell how big we are going to be down there? "Well young man we can tell whether you are developing right in your growth pattern for your age." Ignoring the older boys laughter in the back ground. The kind doctor's gentle manner was a welcomed sight.

Sometimes females fall short in explanations of some things. I had asked some of my male adult counselors to explain this procedure, but none volunteered for the job. They did volunteer some information, like it did not hurt and they had been through this procedure when they were young and in their adult lives as well, and were still healthy as a horse. This contribution seemed to help; especially coming from the cowboys.

A week later all the physicals were completed and all went fairly well with some outburst occurring with my little ones. Both David and Willie refused to have the nurse seeing "everything." I supplied the nurse with a black sleeping blindfold, and they finished their little physicals. Hugs were given to the young ones, and homemade cookies were accepted as one by one they received their physicals.

At the next group session, the boys reminded me of my commitment to schedule my appointment for my yearly check-up, and they wondered if they could accompany me on this visit. Being very naïve, I agreed that I could take six of my boys and suggested taking my little ones, who all agreed. The meeting was adjourned.

WOW, the ranch had made it through all the boys' physicals and the requirements were met. There was, of course, my physical to contend with, but as I had given my word, so be it. I scheduled my doctor's visit for my physical. The next week, six of my nine-and ten-year olds were on our way. We entered the doctor's office with my chatting all the way about the proper behavior I expected, which basically included, "Sit in the chair, be quiet, don't visit with strangers, and absolutely NO cussing. And, yes you may read the magazines."

"Mom," David began, "Where's the. . . ." I interrupted, "David, the restrooms are that way," pointing in the direction of the big sign on the wall. I sat with the boys for just a moment, and then the nurse called my name. My older doctor had retired and frankly this younger doctor I was seeing was recommended to me by a friend. Well, all I needed was a renewal of my estrogen. It was always a yearly ordeal when my older doctor just asked if I was O.K. I would say, "Yes." The old doctor renewed my estrogen and I was out the door until next year.

They put me in the examining room next to the outside waiting room where my little darlings were sitting. I thought this to be a great idea as I could hear if there was a disturbance of some kind.

A few minutes passed as I sat fully dressed waiting for conversation and the meeting from this new young doctor. Because my body was low on potassium, I had experienced some cramping at night in my legs, but for the last few days I had been free of such nonsense.

Enter the new young doctor! As he asked his questions about how I felt, I informed him, "Everything, Doctor, is fine. I just need my estrogen refilled to keep me happy and running smoothly. You know doctor, the "homes in harmony" prescription." This required a shot in my backside, which I had been giving myself for many years. Usually the vial contained a few shots, whereby, I simply called the local drugstore and they refilled the vial every few months until the year had expired.

This doctor replied with an almost grin on his face, "That is not a problem; however, we will need to do a pelvic examination. If you will be so kind as to remove your clothing, I will step out for a moment and will be back for your pelvic examination." "Ah---doctor, the "Play pen" is fine." I repeated, "I have no female problems! If you will just look at my chart, it will tell you I had a complete hysterectomy in 1970. I have nothing to make problems!" He simply smiled and said as he was leaving the room, "I will see you in a few minutes." The nurse handed me the typical white gown spit up the back and a white sheet to go around me. The nurse more or less repeated the instructions of the new doctor.

So here I was in my "W,s" (wranglers) and undressing dutifully while mumbling to myself. I had these examinations through the years, but always when there was a minor problem. Oh well, this young doctor was trying to be thorough, so one must respect this part of the procedure.

The nurse and the doctor entered the examination room. The nurse first checked to see if I was prepared to spread 'um like a percheron horse. Naturally they did not use this old- fashioned terminology. The nurse politely asked me to lie down and put my feet in the stirrups, which were attached to the examination table. Under normal circumstances, this was not a hard thing to do!

I am going through this explanation just in case there is someone out there who is not familiar with a physical examination for a female, and as I said before, it is not normally a complicated thing to accomplish.

As I raised my feet to put them in the stirrups, I felt a darn cramp coming down my right leg. About this same time the doctor was preparing to do the exam. As he bent forward with his hand covered with a basic glove and seated on his swivel chair that rolled rather easily underneath the sheet that covered me, I yelled, and he jumped back rolling the chair backward. I came off the examining table jumping around the room trying desperately to relieve my cramping leg. The young doctor looked startled. I immediately began explaining, "I have a bad cramp in my right leg. I am so sorry, but I cannot stand this pain, let me get my leg feeling a bit better and we, I am sure, can proceed." Sure enough in a minute or two the pain and cramp were gone, so I dutifully climbed back onto the table and put my feet back in the stirrups. The doctor began the examination, and just about the time he began to touch some very private area's on me, the cramp in the right leg hit me as though a lightning bolt had taken place, and again I jumped up with the doctor moving backward with the speed of a professional reining horse. I yelled again as the scene unraveled taking place with another yell, grabbing the sheet that covered my knees up in the stirrups, as my feet hit the floor.

The boys about this time heard the yelling and David said, "That's our Mom," and the boys came bursting through the door of the hallway looking in the rooms for their mom, causing a bit of confusion with the nurses and one patient. Thank goodness I was in the second room they looked! All six came running in my room and shouting, "Are you all right, Mom?"

Trying to gain some composure with the hospital gown and a sheet wrapped around me from the shoulders down was somewhat difficult to manage. There stood my young ones ready to tear into the person who was responsible for hurting their mom's backside. About this time nine-year-old David saw the doctor with the plastic glove on his hand. I assumed he connected this doctor with the doctor who did his physical with the gloved hand. David kicked the innocent doctor on the shinbone with his cowboy boots, and all six joined in with the nurse trying to no avail to control the boys.

The scene was total chaos, with the doctor trying to hold off the boys, the nurse getting pushed to the floor, and me hopping around yelling about the cramp. I tried to tell the boys, in between my yelling, I was all right. Finally I yelled, "Time Out!" To my boys this meant stop, and they did. By this time my leg had stopped hurting long enough to tell them, "My leg is creating all my pain." I looked down at their little concerned faces and began to speak in a very soft voice, "This kind young doctor did not hurt me. I simply had a cramp in my leg. The doctor needs an immediate apology from you boys."

David looked up at me as though he were listening but still not ready to leave me with this doctor. Speaking straightforwardly, he apologized, and in the same sentence asked, "Can we stay, Mom, kind ah like you stayed with us?

"No, but I am sure the doctor won't mind if you stand outside the examination room by the door." My leg by this time with all the confusion seemed to be over its cramping spells. I could not believe in all these years and at the exact time of the doctor's examination, my leg would pick this time to cramp. I really do not know who was the most embarrassed, the young doctor or me; we were both a little red faced.

With my little ones outside the door, the doctor gave me one of the quickest pelvic examinations I had ever experienced, which delighted me. The boys were still giving the doctor a dirty look as they left. They were extremely protective of me as this doctor's visit became all too clear. I thanked him for his patience in this matter and wished him well on his shin recovery. On the way home I had to stop twice and get out of my truck and walk around a while to relieve the cramping. This little social educational experience told me it was not necessary to invite my boys along on every trip.

Dear Lord, I hope as I continue my Journey in life for you, I will be less entertaining and more productive.

~ Chapter 10 ~

ROMANCE

There were two wonderful men in my life during the early years of the boys ranch. At first, I was so involved in developing the boys ranch and making it a success I failed to notice all the practical jokes these two gentlemen played on each other. As time passed, I found I was the reason for all the fun and games. Harlan Madison and I had been long-time friends, way before Tom Monroe came into the picture. It was a good friendship, and I must say Harlan remained a true gentleman.

One day after I purchased the run-down old ranch, Harlan pulled up in front looking like he stepped out of a western wear catalog. Neat as a church mouse, he asked, "What in the world are you doing working in the heat, operating a weed eater?" You see, most cowboys are not into manual labor, and there I was cutting weeds in the hot sun. A cowboy's logic, if you can't do it horseback, then it's not worth doing.

A weed eater is a properly-named, but funny-looking tool. The weed eater's line spins around, cutting weeds or grass only to fling the debris all over the operator and anyone else foolish enough to be standing close. Of course, there is nothing in the instruction manual to warn the operator of the miniature self-created dust devil, other than a suggestion to wear safety goggles, long pants, and closed-toe shoes. Harlan was familiar with the process and continued talking to me from a respectful distance.

He told me, "You know you can hire someone to do this."

"Yes, Harlan", I stopped the weed eating for a moment to visit. "I would be happy to hire someone to do this job if you want to pay the bill." I continued, "I need the money I have for remodeling the boys' ranch. I could not afford to keep my horses. In fact, I had to sell my good horses to help pay the expenses on the ranch." With that bit of information, Harlan went back to his truck and drove on down the road.

A week later, Harlan showed up at my place. He unloaded two of his roping horses and asked in a gentlemanly manner if he could keep them at my ranch. He said, "I would consider it a favor if you would ride them for me as I am going to be busy the next few months. I will be putting on some rodeo clinics in Australia, and they should be ridden while I'm gone. I will not be here to exercise them." I stood there with my mouth open, only barely able to respond "yes" to his request.

As he was leaving he commented, "Oh, and about the feed, I'll furnish the feed while they are here at your ranch and pay you so much a month. Is one hundred a month plus feed all right?" This kind gesture was Harlan's way of helping me through this tough time. Anyone who has ridden horses all of his or her life can sympathize with a person who is doing without one. A horse is something that is true therapy and so very much a part of the inner soul. He knew, being as independent as I was, I would never borrow or permit a borrowed horse on the ranch. He had to make it look as if I were doing him a big favour.

Harlan and I are both half Native American, and there was surely a kinship from the beginning. He admired how hard I worked, and I had a great admiration for him. He had done more with his life than just rodeo. Most cowboys who traveled the rodeo circuit at that time did not think of anything else except going to the next rodeo, and the next, and the next.

The definition of a cowboy before they increased the rodeo prize money they have today was "Someone that has a very shiny belt buckle and a very flat pocketbook." Of course this is just an ol' fashion saying, because the rodeo prize money today has made many a cowboy a millionaire. Most still possess their old fashioned values whether they're professional cowboys trying to earn a little extra money or making a professional career out of it.

Harlan, on the other hand, had accomplished more than most and had more than most. He ran a successful real-estate business. With the help of many wealthy women, some of whom he married, Harlan became more than just a cowboy. His masculine looks, which were easy on the eyes, made him popular among the ladies.

I had lost count of how many times Harlan had been married. He was the most marrying man I had ever met in my life. "Oh well," he would say, "they asked me to marry them, and what's a fellow to do but say, "Yes?" I never did figure out which made him the most money, the real-estate business or the wealthy women he married. Harlan won the world steer-wrestling championship three times way back when and had been smart enough to capitalize his blessings into marketing himself as a public figure.

He was great at marketing himself, and who could fault him for that? I, too, was always trying to better myself. I believed working hard for what I wanted and not marrying some guy just because he had the money was more satisfying. I guess I'm just old-fashioned. Now that I have arthritis in my shoulders from all the hard work I've done in the past, I wonder if maybe his way had some merit after all.

Tom Monroe came into the picture while I was remodeling the old house. He stopped by one day and asked if he could board his horse at the ranch. I had some bad experiences with cowboys and did not trust any of them when it came to money, my horses and my tack. In a contemptible voice I asked, "You DO have a steady job?"

He smiled and said, "Yes, ma'am, I'm a carpenter, and I drive a cattle truck."

"Okay," I said, "here is how it is going to be. The rent is one hundred dollars a month, and it's due on the first of every month. If you are late, your horse will be tied to the outside fence next to the highway. Is there anything that I have just said that you do not understand?"

He said, "I understand, and I will not be late with the payment."

"Oh by the way, one other thing," I continued, "The gate to the barn does not start at my door, but through the gate to the barn area."

The next day, he brought his horse to the ranch, paid me his rent for the month in advance, and left by way of the barn gate.

That evening, I went out to ride and found his saddle and gear in "my tack room." Cowboys have a way of using your tack and keeping it when they leave. I phoned Tom and asked him if he would come to the ranch, as it was important that I speak with him. He asked if his horse was all right, and I said, "For the moment, yes." I wanted his undivided attention right away.

When he arrived at the ranch, I told him the one hundred dollar fee did not include his tack in "my tack room." He asked if he could remodel the stall next to his horse, as he really needed a place for his gear.

I thought about this a long time and wondered if he were using me. I thought to myself, "If this were the case, it will cost him dearly." I said, "You may use the stall next to your horse, but it will cost fifty dollars more per month, and you must promise to put the stall back in its original condition when you leave." Tom agreed to these conditions.

Harlan called me the next week and said, "René, you're getting a reputation for being a real bitch."

"Well, Harlan," I told him, "as a friend, please spread the word. Then maybe these darn cowboys will stop bothering me."

Tom remodeled one of the stalls and continued to leave me alone, except on the first of every month. He took me at my word and was never late with the rent. Tom's new tack-room door looked good and had a lock on it. I started locking my tack room, just in case he decided to bring his cowboy buddies around. After a couple of months, Tom offered to help on some of the remodeling.

By this time, I knew I needed to hire someone, but I also knew I could not afford a "real" carpenter that wanted union-scale wages. I told him, "I need to see some of your work before hiring you"

He said, "I don't have a problem with that," inviting me to go to the barn so he could show me some of his work. When we walked out to the barn, he unlocked and opened the door to his tack room. Wow! What a tack room; it put mine to shame. Tom put in a nice wooden floor and covered it with twelve-inch squares that looked like real wood. Two of the walls were covered with plywood, resembling planks. On the other two walls, he hung sheet rock, taped and textured, and painted it a light tan. He added a small dark brown trim, and horseshoes used as hangers for the bridles and halters. It was simply gorgeous.

He looked down at me with a twinkle in his blue eyes and said, "Of course, when I leave, I will tear out everything and put it back to a dirt stall, just as I found it."

I hired him, and he helped with the carpentry I felt I could not do.

When I left on business, Tom took care of the ranch and fed the livestock. What a wonderful gentleman, and a pretty good hand with a horse. Of course, I paid him for the chores he did. It's amazing how wonderful men can be when they think you have money. At that time I did not have that much money—I just had more than he did.

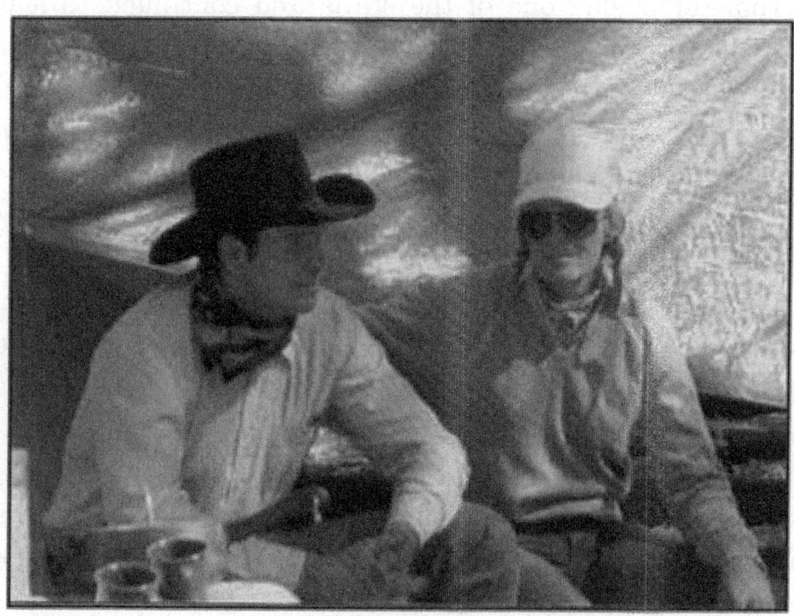

Tom and René in the High Country

Finally, the boy's ranch was licensed, and the boys began to arrive. Tom came in handy. I could see the boys related to Tom's western manner; his natural ability in relating to the boys caught my attention. I hired Tom as my vocational instructor; thus began a personal and professional relationship that lasted eight years.

When Harlan heard I was dating someone, he called and asked if he could come over for dinner or a visit. He frequently gave me his advice on whomever I was dating.

Harlan was not one to butt into other people's business; however, I think he felt a need to protect me. Harlan basically told me to watch my backside with Tom. I replied, "I hired Tom as the vocational instructor for the boys ranch and he seems to be working out okay." What's that saying? "We were just friends." Thus began an interesting sequence of events that can only be described as "little boy games" from these two grown men.

Harlan left his horses on the ranch in my personal section of the barn. By this time I had purchased my own horses; I kept my personal horses separate from the other horses. Harlan dropped by every evening to feed his horses when he was in town, and if he were out of town, we fed his horses for him.

One day, Tom stormed into the office with a red face that reflected his Irish temperament. Normally, Tom was a laid-back easy-going guy but today was different. He growled at me, "I've had enough!" As I sat back in my chair, wondering what had upset him so much, he unfurled his growing resentment. Harlan was watering his horse and turned with the water hose in hand and soaked Tom "accidentally." Naturally, he apologized immediately, trying to stifle his grin. Tom's irritation had been festering because Harlan had developed a habit of driving through the main gate, passing

Tom's vocational workshop, honking the horn and waving vigorously just to get Tom's attention. Tom's vocational shop was in plain view of the outside gate. He explained the ongoing issue.

We let several horses out in the afternoon to feed on the grass between the vocational shop and the outside gate. This meant the gate had to remain closed, or the horses would get out. Harlan picked this time in the afternoon to leave, opening the gate, driving through, and leaving it wide open. Harlan's mischievous behavior forced Tom to race to close the gate before the horses got out.

I asked Tom, "How long has Harlan been doing the gate thing?"

Tom answered, "About two months."

I decided to solve this little problem, whatever it was, before it got out of hand. I invited both of them to dinner without telling the other of my plans. This seemed like a good idea at the time. My intentions were simply to ask Harlan to please close the gate when he left the ranch, and that would make Tom feel better.

Sometimes the forest got pretty thick for me, and I just simply could not see the trees.

Keep in mind, I was knee-deep in the boys ranch and really did not have a clue as to what was happening before my eyes— that is, an old-fashioned case of jealousy. I knew that I could smooth over this little misunderstanding between these two professional cowboys. They simply needed time and a congenial setting to know one another and get acquainted. The dinner would solve the problem between them.

What a dinner it was! I fixed a nice roast with all the trimmings and threw in an apple pie. My boys and house parents had rather a smooth week, which meant I might not have too many interruptions during dinner.

Harlan arrived first. He was dressed in a pair of top-of-the line western slacks and a Panhandle Slim shirt, tailored to fit. The man had class. About fifteen minutes later, Tom showed up in his creased Wranglers and a nice work shirt. Tom was not a world champion but did carry a PRCA card and enjoyed the same event as Harlan, steer wrestling. I was setting three plates on the table as they came into the kitchen. Each man greeted the other coolly. I began talking about the upcoming rodeos, and they picked up the conversation. They talked about which rodeo was going to be the toughest, how high the entry fees were going to be, and who had the stock contracted for which rodeo.

I backed out of the conversation and let the two of them talk. They were both good men with good, old-fashioned manners. I still had not picked up on the jealousy because they were incredibly civil to one another.

I put the meal on the table, and they sat down on opposite sides of the table. My phone rang, and I had to leave for a few minutes to go out to my office and get something for one of the house parents.

As I came back through the den area off the kitchen, I heard Harlan say to Tom, "You should at least wait until the lady of the house sits down."

I did not know what had taken place. When Harlan saw me coming back from the office, he passed the roast to Tom and said, "Dig in." Harlan had set Tom up, and for the remainder of the meal, snide comments continued between the two men. I brought the closing of the gate up during dinner, and Harlan said something along the line that he had not realized Tom was so "out of shape"—so he would try to help Tom out by shutting the gate.

Tom, fifteen years younger than Harlan, said something about how he realized Harlan probably wasn't getting out of his pickup because of his "old age and bad knees." Finally, I had had enough of their sarcasm and told them both, "For my sake, I want you both to be friends." I picked up the dirty dishes from the table and offered them apple pie for dessert. Tom told me to sit down; he would wait on me for a change. He began to cut the apple pie, and I thought, "*What a nice thing to do.*"

It wasn't such a nice thing. He cut the pie and served mine first with ice cream on top. Tom asked Harlan if he wanted his pie cowboy style. Before Harlan could answer, Tom set the piece of pie in front of him. I had no idea, nor did Harlan, what Tom was talking about until he served Harlan's pie. Tom had poured hot sauce over the apple pie and then put the ice cream on top with jalapeno peppers in the ice cream. Tom could eat those darn things like candy. Harlan, on the other hand, did not like spicy foods of any kind. Tom told Harlan to "dig in," and Harlan, not wanting to back down, dug in.

I told them I had an early meeting in the morning. In bringing the evening to a close, I stressed how important it was they remain friends. I insisted they shake hands, which they finally agreed to do, but it turned out to be more of a gripping match to see who was the strongest. I finally broke them apart and walked Harlan outside to his truck.

The next day, I called his office to visit. Betty, Harlan's secretary, said, "René, Harlan is sick with some kind of stomach problem and is staying home for the day." It was obvious the "cowboy pie" had not settled well.

Things returned to normal for a while. Then out of the blue, Harlan called and said he really needed a favor. He was shorthanded and wondered if I would send Tom over to help him with his arena. I heard Harlan was building a new arena on his ranch; I told him I did not think Tom would mind and to consider the “favor” handled. Tom was not thrilled about the idea but said if I had given my word to Harlan he would help “as a favor to me.” I should have figured Harlan was up to something.

Tom came in late that night. It was summer, and the sun was just setting in the west. Tom was covered in mud from his shoulders all the way down to his boots. He looked at me and said he needed to talk to me in my office—“NOW!”

When Tom arrived, Harlan had rented a “two-man” posthole digger to break up the hardpan in the arena, which is a type of soil that’s common to the area. On one end of the posthole digger, he hired a man who worked for some of the ranches in the area, and he put Tom on the other end. Harlan had flooded the arena the night before preparing it for the use of the motor-driven posthole digger and needed two good men to run it.

Harlan, standing dressed in his usual neat style, just drove off leaving them to do all the work. He led Tom to believe he was going to jump in and help. I had assumed the same, but Harlan left supposedly to show some real-estate property.

Tom was past mad! He was so red in the face that the Irish was showing through all the mud. I tried very hard not to laugh. This was not a good time for my off-the-wall sense of humor to kick in. Tom said, “René, do not ever again volunteer me to do Harlan’s dirty work.” This was not a fair thing Harlan had done, so I took it on myself to even the score.

A month went by, and then one day, I took the boys out, and we worked driving stakes into the ground for a new fence line. The old fence line, made out of wire was falling down. We needed a new one and decided that we would build a four-rail two-by six fence along the outside of the main property and down the east side. The boys and I drove some fifty wooden stakes into the ground. This meant the same amount of postholes had to be dug. I rented the same two-man posthole digger that Harlan had rented, and it was time to "call in the favor."

I should tell you a little about favors from one ranch to another. You never asked for a favor unless you could repay it. That's just how things are among the ranchers; the big foundation ranchers still live and do things this way, as their ranching fathers did before them. If you ask for something, you give something back!

I called Harlan early the next morning, "Harlan, I need that favor returned. Could you please show up in some old work clothes after lunch because I'm desperate for some help?" I did not mention Tom's name.

I waited until he told me he would be there and then got off the phone as quickly as I could. I did not want him to ask me anything about what he would be doing. Sure enough, after lunch, Harlan showed up, and I wasted no time in taking Tom and Harlan out to the motor-driven two-man posthole digger. They were both in amazingly good shape. To rodeo and be serious about the sport, you have to be in shape, or you do not win; and if you do not win, you do not make any money. Today, cowboys who rodeo, are for the most part family men, making a tremendous living by continuing the tradition of their forefathers.

Harlan and Tom both were grinning at each other and thus began a hard driving afternoon with both men trying to outlast the other.

I also had the whole town surprised and talking. No one had ever seen Harlan do manual labor before. When the word spread he was doing manual labor, two professional team-roping friends of both men went home and brought their cameras and began taking pictures. It turned out to be a pretty eventful day. I did what I could to settle the score between these two very competitive men. Plus that afternoon, I got all the postholes dug and wore out two very competitive professional cowboys.

The National Finals rodeo is held in Las Vegas in December. I looked forward to attending the various events and seeing old friends again. The conversation was always the same subject matter; who had the best performance horses and who made it to the top ten to qualify for the National Finals in professional Rodeo; and so on and so forth. It was also cowboy-market time, an indoor extravaganza featuring the latest in leather goods, from new saddles to leather clothing. Anyone who had anything to do with the western lifestyle knew this was the place to be. Harlan and I always made it a point to save one evening for just the two of us to go to dinner.

One night over dinner, I mentioned to Tom that I bought my ticket some months earlier; this led to the subject matter as to whether I was going and could leave the ranch unsupervised. The staff was, by this time, well trained and the boys seemed to be settled at the ranch; things were going along pretty smoothly.

"I really wanted to go." I said

Tom smiled and then replied, "I can handle things," and insisted that I go.

I thought about it for at least two seconds before saying "Yes, yes, yes, thank you, thank you!"

Tom and I had gone to dinner a few times, and at this point, neither was obligated to the other. He was aware Harlan would be at the National Finals. Tom was, however, on the payroll as the vocational instructor. I was beginning to have some real feelings for this man. We had developed a trust between us, and that was changing my life for the better.

The National Finals came and went. Harlan and I went to dinner and talked about the coming year and about Tom. Harlan was concerned Tom was more interested in my rather high income. I assured Harlan I had that situation pretty well handled. Tom was on a salary only—and had no access to the corporate funds.

The biggest problem I had with Tom was his social drinking. Tom never drank around the ranch, but just the thought of being with someone who liked to drink was a big threat to me. Tom actually drank very little, but with the boys ranch everyone that was employed was under a microscope of sorts. I know first-hand how much damage drinking can do to relationships, families, and friends. I did not want this in my personal life. It was the reason for my divorce from my ex-husband several years before.

When I returned home from the National Finals, Tom asked me out, and we went to a nice place to eat and dance, during which Tom had two mixed drinks. Was I counting? Of course I was, because a staff member's drinking could affect my boys' ranch.

We arrived back at the ranch; I invited Tom to come into my home for the first time. He was all smiles until I told him I would not be dating him anymore. I decided we should keep our relationship strictly professional because of his social drinking.

A couple of times over the next three weeks, Harlan came to dinner, and since I lived on the upper part of the ranch and Tom lived on the lower part of the ranch, he could see when I had company and who the company was; so he knew Harlan and I were seeing each other on a pretty regular basis. What he did not know is the visits were about a young girl Harlan was planning to marry.

One morning, the doorbell rang, and there stood Tom. He did not say "hello," or "how are you?" or anything else. He just began talking; "I am a social drinker and I have given a lot of thought to our conversation about drinking and I have decided to quit, just for you." I listened to Tom's statement and replied, "Tom, you are quitting for the wrong reasons. I suggest you go back and think about the right reason for quitting. The right reason should be quitting for you, not for me."

He left in a rather distasteful manner. It was another two weeks before he came back, asking to visit with me over dinner. Again, we went to dinner, this time there was no drinking. Afterward, I asked him in for coffee. He told me he had thought seriously about his reason for social drinking. The conversation that followed included the magic words—he was quitting for his health and a better tomorrow. And yes, he stayed for breakfast.

~ Chapter 11 ~

THE LANGUAGE

Present Day

I set under the walnut tree at the old ranch; it was such a magnificent day to be alive. I drifted off into deep thought only to be interrupted by two young children arguing—using words you hope Momma and Daddy don't hear. They probably belong to the family renting the old ranch.

They were cussing at each other, throwing that four-letter word around, occasionally mixing it with the usual cuss words. These two looked to be in the early stages of puberty, eleven or maybe twelve years old.

They sure couldn't hold a candle to my boys. Of course, my boys probably had more cause to use such language. Friends told me I must have the patience of a saint; they had no idea my favorite daily prayer was "Please Lord let me see these circumstances as gifts from you."

The boys who qualified for my program had the roughest vocabulary, second to none. During what I refer to as the honeymoon period, which usually lasted four to six weeks, the language was pretty bad. I was called f—n bitch so much those first few weeks I actually caught myself answering, "Yes, what do you want?" Eventually, I found ways to control these unpleasant outbursts, but it did take some ingenious thinking on my part. Most of the boys could not complete a sentence without that little four-letter word. I developed different methods through trial and error to handle this problem.

One method was to have the offender write several times the definition, which was very long, from the Webster's great book of knowledge. The dictionary defines F— as "For Unlawful Carnal Knowledge." The definition deflated their interest in using the word and almost made it polite to use. This word is used on a daily basis in England by English lawyers in the courtroom. We abbreviated and Americanized the expression, and when using it here, it has an entirely different meaning.

There was another method that worked with the young ones, especially the nine-and ten-year-olds. I had a full view of the roping arena from my office window. With the window open, I could hear everything that was said. I simply gave these "potty mouths" ten laps walking around the arena. This probably does not sound like much of a punishment, but they had to stop at each fence post and yell out at the top of their voice that famous four-letter word—the punishment worked. This did three very important things. First, the boys were tired when the walk was over. Secondly, they had no desire to say this little four-letter word, at least for a while. Third and probably the most important, it allowed the child to release a lot of anger, eventually resulting in a polite and mannered child.

We actually witnessed the remarkable changes taking place. They went from "I want to hurt any and everyone" to "I want to go to school and church, and I even like myself." Of course, this did not happen overnight. But it did happen.

There was a drawback to this particular punishment. Ten laps of constant vulgarity was not my idea of a quiet afternoon at the ranch. However, it did work. The child became quieter after about the fifth lap. At this point, I had to inform him I could not hear him. You see, if I could not hear him, then the laps simply did not count. By the time the tenth lap was completed, "Yes, ma'am," flowed rather nicely, and for a while, it corrected the situation.

All did not go smoothly with this particular solution. One day, I had a ten-year-old by the name of Shawn doing his laps with a voice louder than the Jolly Green Giant. I heard a knock at the office door. In walked the local ladies' church group, hair pulled back in old fashion buns, faces purged of any makeup, and the demeanor reminiscent of Salem Puritans. They were uninvited and unannounced; the ladies assumed they did not need an appointment. I offered them chairs, and the three ladies sat down. Meanwhile, Shawn continued exercising his lung capacity to the fullest. I figured my best strategy was to ignore Shawn, but he seemed to be getting louder by the minute. The ladies took the same approach, so we talked about the weather and how nice the summer was this year. Just imagine trying to have a conversation with these ladies while Shawn continued to pepper our polite conversation with a booming delivery of the queen mothers abbreviation of all four-letter words. Two of the ladies were handling it pretty well. Finally, the third lady simply could not stand it any longer and asked, "Are you hard of hearing! Do you intend to stop this sinful boy from saying that awful word?"

"No ma'am, I am not hard of hearing!" (and I wasn't then) I guess about that time, the neatness of their protected world and the reality of what this little boy of ten had been through got the better of my good disposition. Before I could stop myself I was telling them what the real picture was like. Most people never see the real picture. And so there I was, telling it all. I stood up and looked straight at this "oh so proper" lady. I leaned over my desk and began to answer her question with the basic facts.

"The fact is this boy was molested by his grandfather, at the early age of six." My voice became louder. "The fact is his mother stood by and let this take place time after time. The fact is she was an alcoholic. She locked this little boy in the closet for two or three days at a time; he went without food and water, while surrounded by his body waste matter. Then one day while she was sleeping, he set the bed on fire. Then and only then did someone pay attention to this little boy!" By this time, my Miss Congeniality award was out of sight; I had lost all control to hold anything back. "My hope is, ladies," as I gritted my teeth, "by allowing this little ten-year-old the opportunity to shout that four-letter word, he is able to release his inner anger. This little ten-year-old has a problem; you see, ladies, he cannot cry. If by the end of his laps, with God's help I will hug that little boy hoping against hope he is able to cry and that he hugs me back; and that is what we are trying to accomplish here. For, I do not have Boy Scouts at this ranch. I do have boys that, if reached in time, may go on to someday be great kids and productive adults. Then and only then will I have done my job."

"And to answer your question, no, I have no intentions of stopping him. Do I think he will go to Heaven? If I were a betting person and was left to choose between that little boy and you three ladies, my money would be on the little boy" I happened to know the lady doing the complaining was sleeping with the preacher. This was to come to light three months later, when both couples divorced, and the preacher was fired. I continued, "Furthermore, this is their ranch, and you were not invited!" As if my voice had tolled a bell, a counselor entered my office and I informed him, "The ladies were just leaving. Will you be so kind as to escort them out?"

Another one of my favorite cures for this particular language problem was a trip to the High Country. In my younger years I spent a lot of time there, including a few summers as a guide, not knowing how valuable that experience would be in developing my future Journey. The back wilderness area of Yosemite is some of the most beautiful scenery in the United States. It is some of God's best work.

Sometimes, no matter what I did at the ranch to correct the language, nothing worked better than a trip to the High Country to clear trails with a two-man saw. This of course was for the older boys, the teenagers. Once I took in three placements at the ranch at the same time: Trevor, Harry, and Joe. All three were mouthy and streetwise. Trevor was the oldest, but far from the smartest. He and another boy had stolen his neighbor's car only to run out of gas three miles from the house. Trevor was caught when he refused to leave the stolen car along the side of the road unattended. His supposed friend left immediately, leaving Trevor to face the music alone.

When Trevor's probation officer called, he said, "You have to come and interview this kid." There was a slight laughter in his voice as he revealed the charges from the incident. This boy's logic was not typical of a teenager with problems. For goodness sake, he was a caring teenager.

When I finally located the mother, she was still having horizontal conversations for a fee. Trevor was abandoned at an early age and in and out of foster homes with a great deal of abuse along the way.

First, he steals a car and it runs out of gas; then he won't leave it because someone might strip it. I could not stop thinking how funny this logic was because obviously here was a truly caring teenager without a sense of direction. The probation officer knew I could not refuse this kid.

Harry was from an abusive background. His mother died a year earlier of cancer. His father was an alcoholic, who beat Harry repeatedly and, to make matters worse, blamed the boy for his mother's death. I could not refuse this messed-up kid either.

Joseph was small, wiry, and very intelligent. He had no traceable parents so he basically lived in foster and group homes most of his life. I liked him from the word "hello." I had just violated one very important ranch rule: only one new boy per month placed at a time to allow the boy to get through the "honeymoon" period with our full attention focused on that one child. With three new boys arriving within the same month, we found ourselves overloaded with constant emotional outbursts. The situation was my fault and my counselors reminded me of that fact. I just could not decide which one not to help. I assured myself I could help all three. Thank the good Lord for his guidance and understanding. After three weeks with little progress on the program, to keep my counselors from an all-out protest and keep my head attached on my shoulders, I knew what I had to do to get the boys attention. We gave them a short lesson in horsemanship, and off to the mountains we went. I headed into the mountains with one ranch hand as a packer and three uncontrollable boys. I might add that I was never alone. There was always a presence, just as though God was making every trip right by our side. When I consider God's inner primal energy as our creator, then I know I am never really alone. I still am a believer of this principle. The inner God power or inner strength is within us all; we just have to feel it. It is an inner strength that I constantly draw from. It is there to strengthen our weaknesses. How do I know God's presence exist? After all the trips to the High Country with the boys, most of whom came from the cities, none of the boys were hurt on the mountain trips, not even a cut finger. There is no way I could have done this alone. There was definitely a higher power with us on every trip, for this was the rugged back wilderness country of Yosemite. Experienced hikers and tourists with a multitude of injuries are carried out of the back wilderness area of Yosemite every year.

These three boys had been telling me, with their four-letter-word vocabulary, just how tough they were. So we would see just how tough "tough" was.

Before we entered the High Country, we circled the horses and asked the Good Lord to allow us safe passage through His country. This was my ritual—asking God to protect my boys, mainly from themselves. Following this invocation, I made a short talk about how the boys were going to control their language. It went something like this:

"Mom has packed lots of good food and I am a real good cook. I have packed steak, potatoes, and things to make biscuits and gravy. However, I have also packed cold sandwich meat. If I hear one cuss word from you, it is cold sandwiches for dinner for all of you. If I hear a lot of yes ma'am's and see in general good manners, then you will have the best home-cooked meal you have ever tasted." The first two days were as tough on me as it was on them. I did not look forward to eating a hot cooked meal in front of my boys but from a psychological point of view, it worked.

On the third day, we had our first great home-cooked meal. After that, I had—without a doubt—the best-mannered boys in the High Country. After this experience, I decided to take some of the older boys along on these trips to help me with the newer ones. The older boys would tell the new boys what was expected and remind them of what would happen if the older boys had to eat cold sandwiches for dinner.

If the work was completed early in the day (and I made sure this occurred) the boys could swim and trout fish the rest of the afternoon. I wanted their trip to be enjoyable too.

We stayed ten days; this is a picture of the boys as we headed home. Only Joe, Harry, and I are shown in this picture. The boys are bent over their saddles, tired to the bone. I'm in front and you will notice I am sitting straight up. All three boys came off this mountain trip oh so polite, with newfound respect for others as well as themselves.

Above timber line, back wilderness area of Yosemite National Park

Rene' on the trail

The trips to the mountains became a privilege that helped strengthen the ranch program. Once the boys made the trip to the High Country, they could not wait to go back.

Thank you Lord, for the solutions you give us that are so very simple in structure, and yet so very successful when put to use.

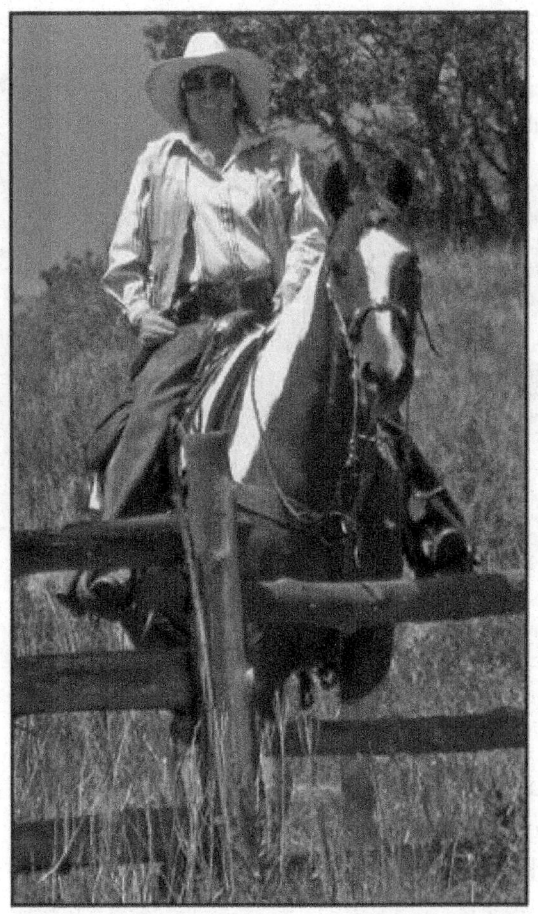

Today, author's favorite mountain horse, Jack

~ Chapter 12 ~

HIGH COUNTRY MOUNTAIN DISASTER

In the summer the boys began packing for one of our many trips to Huckleberry Lake. Our twenty-mile arduous Journey consisted of nine boys, two cowboys, and lots of horses including one obstinate, pig-headed mare named Molly.

I refused to allow mares on the ranch other than for breeding purposes. The old foundation ranchers thought mares to be dangerous and totally unpredictable around children as well as adults. Mares gave credence to the old cliché "in the wrong place at the wrong time." Most mares were kept on the big ranches usually in the back pasture for breeding purposes only.

A few months earlier Tom and the boys attended a horse sale to purchase more horses for the ranch. Molly was in with a group of four geldings Tom wanted to buy. A ranch sometimes will run a group of horses together to make sure they get rid of the one that won't sell. Molly epitomized the unsellable mare. Tom brought her home and informed me of the situation.

Her pintsize stature made her unfit even for breeding, so I vociferously objected, assuming everyone would understand. Never assume anything with children. The little ones instantly fell in love with her because of her pintsize stature. Being an educated person and assuming I was in control of the situation, I called the nine and ten-year olds together in my office; everyone else at the ranch seemed to follow. I explained the reason for NOT keeping the mare on the ranch. David one of my nine-year olds kept raising his hand through all of my logical explanation. Finally I said, "Yes David" which he replied, "Mom, can we just vote on whether we keep her or not?"

I could see I faced a monumental, uphill battle so, at David's request, I called for the democratic vote, believing the cowboys, house parents, and older boys understood the uselessness of this very small mare. In a case of this nature everyone at the ranch had the right to vote, from the house parents to the ranch hands to the boys. The democratic ballot would take place the next afternoon. The next morning I awake to the sound of cow bells ringing and an abundance of little voices outside my bedroom window. David and Willie had made signs and were using their rights as young citizens to make their point. The signs were short and to the point read, "SAVE MOLLY." One went so far as to state: "SAVE MOLLY FROM THE KILLERS." I indisputably lost the vote.

The boys won and named her Molly, so Molly had a home. I would look out my office window toward the arena and see Molly surrounded by four or five of my little ones who were playing in a fantasy world all their own. Sometimes she would be their sick little horse and the boys were Molly's pint size vets, topping their look off as veterinarians with Tom's big white shirt. One day I looked out and the boys had two burlap feed sacks thrown over her back leading her around. Molly's place on the ranch became clear. The cowboys at the ranch began to work with her and she became one of our packhorses. For a while, it seemed like maybe this would work. I personally know of ranches that have roundups and will not allow a mare on their ranch during the calf branding. Geldings are just more dependable and trustworthy for working ranch horses.

A few days later, we left for the High Country. We loaded horses, the motley crew from the ranch and drove some one hundred and twenty miles to our unloading point. After resting for a while, we mounted our horses and formed a circle for prayer and God's blessing before starting into the high-mountain range.

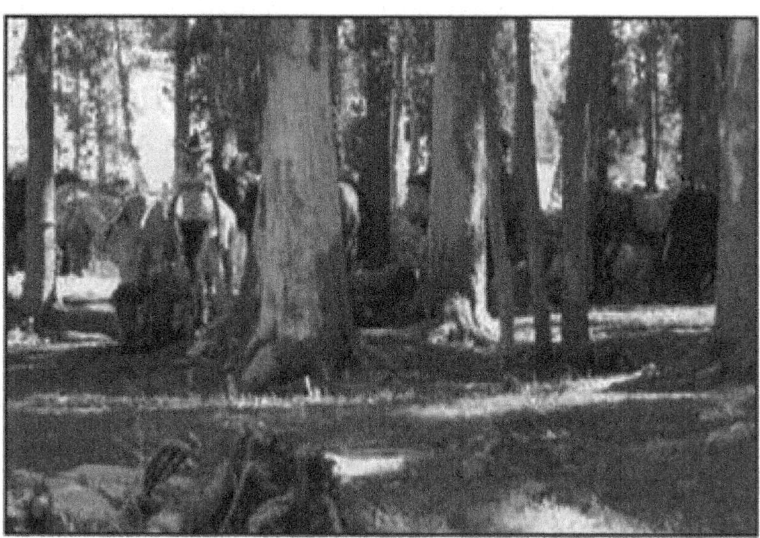

Main camp at the lake with ten head of horses in background, all geldings except Molly. Molly is the little white horse behind Harry

Yosemite National Forest allowed by law only ten horses at a time on the trails. Our twenty-one horses required that we split into two groups with a gap of two hours between each group. Our extra horse stretched the law a bit. Tom and I took the older boys and left two trusted ranch hands in charge of the younger boys in the second group. I purposely led the older more experienced boys to keep a promise to show them two high mountain lakes, located in a rugged area, too dangerous for the little ones. The older boys earned the privileged trip.

Oh but how my boys and I loved the High Country! My personal feeling about the high country: **It's the only place on earth that I know you can actually go to Heaven without dying.**

We headed to Kibby Lake to rest for the first night to acclimate our valley horses to the High Country air. The trip of five miles to Kibby Lake usually moved along pretty well, except on this day.

Molly was in her heat cycle. I assigned Joe, a fourteen-year-old boy, to lead her behind his horse, a good-looking yellow palomino gelding, and medium in height but stout in stature. Joe was small for his age and he and the horse fit together like a hand in a glove. The yellow horse was level-headed, bonded to Joe, as good horses will do. This special bond probably saved Joe's life and saved the horse from going over the cliff.

Molly created all sorts of problems for Joe. She kept pulling back from Joe, which made the horses behind her pull up. I finally took her and dallied her to the horn on my saddle, and after a little schooling, her disposition changed for the positive. I handed her back to Joe, and we continued on up the trail. I told Joe not to loop-tie her. This tie is a loop attached to the back of the saddle. Then the lead rope is weaved through and around, with the end of the lead rope being held by whoever is in the saddle. Some packer's tail tied their packhorses, but with the children, I felt the loop tie was safe, because it is designed to break lose should the pack horse pull back.

We were about a mile from Kibby when Molly kicked Mouse, the horse behind her, in the chest. The horse's chest swelled up like a grapefruit. He was named for his mousy-looking color, but was one of my better geldings. We walked the gelding around a little, and he seemed to be okay except for the knot on his chest. Put one mare in with sixty good geldings, and she will figure out which one is the best gelding and kick him. Meanwhile, I voiced my opinion again on how worthless mares are as I stomped around pacing back and forth in the grass. To be fair about the mares in this country today, I have friends who show and compete and say they are great performance horses. Horse trainers say they are easier and smarter to train. I am speaking about large ranches and old foundation rules of ranching and, of course, my own experiences and beliefs.

That night in camp when the other group arrived and heard about Molly, two of the younger ones came to Molly's defense.

"Molly," one of the boys said, "she just accidentally kicked Mouse." The boys had such worried looks on their faces.

I went over to Molly and stood beside her and the boys, my younger ones with their apprehensive faces looking at me for some kind of response. I began to stroke her talking in a soothing voice. "She probably just needs some TLC."

The boys went to bed that night satisfied Molly wasn't in trouble. Call it ESP or women's intuition, I just wished Molly was not on this trip. I felt uneasy and vowed when I got back home Molly's destiny as a productive workhorse was over.

She loved the boys attention just as they loved her, so they could keep her as a pet—preferably a corralled pet.

The cowboys took care of the horses, taking them to the grassy meadow where they could graze and bed down for the night. I started supper for the crew and the boys, who by this time were giving me more help than normal. They were hungry as a coyote during a drought and knew if they helped by gathering the wood and peeling potatoes, they could chow down a lot quicker.

We had just begun to eat when we heard a noise that sounded like the horses were in trouble. The hands and I dropped everything and made a run to the meadow. Horses are either hobbled or line tied in the High Country. Line tying is simply a large rope tied between two trees across the meadow. This rope has loops spaced six feet apart so that each horse is tied with the lead rope, which is left long enough for the horse to reach the grass. Molly was line tied, and she had tangled herself in the lead rope with the horse next to her. She and the other horse were fighting. She had the whole bunch stirred up.

Meanwhile the boys had made it to the meadow and wanted to know if Molly was all right. I assured them, grinding my teeth, Molly was okay, and we all returned to main camp to finish eating supper.

Tom and I went for a long walk down by the lake, and when we arrived back in camp, the little ones had cleaned the main camp, including sweeping around the campfire. The boys were taught that keeping a camp clean in the High Country was a matter of pride. Brush with leaves makes an excellent sweeping tool, and the boys had done a really good job.

David asked, "Mom did you notice how clean the camp is."

I said, "Yes, I noticed, and it looks great."

This response was not good enough for David. "Is that all you're going to say to us, Mom? We worked really hard."

I responded, "Well, thanks for cleaning the camp. You did a great job."

"Is that it?" This was my David.

I looked him square in the face. "David, In the real world, to give someone too much praise for something that you should have done in the first place—well, it's just like bubblegum— you can chew it, but don't swallow it."

The next day, everyone was up early and making ready for the trip to Lord's Meadow. The boys were packing their gear in camp. The hands and Tom saddled the packhorses and checked all the horses and their gear to make ready for the day's ride ahead. Lord's Meadow sits between Kibby Lake and Huckleberry. Our next stop from Kibby was the springs, the midway point to Lord's Meadow.

We mounted our horses and started out on the trail. Joe was leading Molly behind his horse; Molly set back on the lead rope and nearly pulled Joe off his horse. One of the cowboys rode back, took Molly and wrapped the lead rope around the horn of his saddle and we continued on our way.

This silly mare was making me a nervous wreck. We stopped for lunch at the springs before we started into the canyon. The ride from Kibby Lake to the watering hole at the springs was not that bad. Six Pack Canyon is considered the most dangerous part of our trip and lay heavy on my mind. Once we started into the canyon from the springs there was no place to turn around. The trail was one switchback after another, six in all that were bad, carved out of the side of the mountain made of granite, with loose shale rock running down in numerous places. Six Pack Canyon was just ahead of us.

I announced it was time to go with everyone checking their gear and the packhorses. The boys checked their saddles to make sure they were tight. If the saddle came loose going over this pass, a rider could lose his or her life.

When we mounted our horses to leave, I did not notice that Joe was leading Molly. If a boy was assigned to lead a packhorse behind his horse, it was his responsibility to take care of that packhorse for the entire trip. Joe took his responsibility seriously.

We started over the pass and down into the canyon. I was in front leading two packhorses single file, followed by Harry, then Joe leading Molly; Chad and Trevor with Tom leading two packhorses bringing up the rear.

We were in the third switchback when Molly began throwing her head trying to pull back. I yelled for Joe to keep talking to her, but it was obvious Joe could not hear me.

In the next switchback, it happened. Molly pulled back and started to lose her footing on the steep rocky cliff. Joe was in trouble. My worst fears were happening before my eyes; Molly was about to go over the side taking Joe and the little palomino horse with her.

Molly was small, weighing maybe eight hundred pounds. The palomino horse weighed around a thousand pounds, with the packs on her back weighing one hundred pounds. The yellow horse struggled to pull Molly back up on the trail. She slipped on loose tiny shale rock, and her hind feet were losing ground on the edge of the narrow ledge.

G.B., my big stout roan horse weighed almost fifteen hundred pounds. He had always given me whatever I had asked and more. He was without a doubt the best horse I ever owned.

I turned loose of the two packhorses, turning the big horse around, trying to get back to Joe. I rode past the packhorses I was leading hitting them on the butt so they would continue on down the trail I rode along the cliff shelf, taking my knife out that hung on my side. The big roan and I worked our way back to Joe. The small loop tie behind Joe's saddle; Joe and I discussed not using the day before. The boy had simply forgotten.

In case of a wreck, this light tie loop behind the saddle should have broken, but it did not give way. It had to be cut, and be cut immediately. Joe was in the fight of his life, and all he could do was try to pull Molly back up. He and the stout little palomino were losing the battle. Under normal circumstances, the palomino could pull her and correct the situation. This was not a normal circumstance; this was a wreck of the worst kind happening right before my eyes. Riding along the edge of the cliff, my big roan worked hard not to go over the side and fall, taking us both to the bottom of the canyon. I was forcing him to go uphill against gravity to reach the boy. When close enough, I yelled to Joe, "Get off Yeller on the high side of the cliff." Joe refused to leave his horse. I knew if I did not reach them soon, they were all going over the side.

I kept talking to G.B. to steady him. He was losing his footing. We had to keep going and I prayed I could reach them in time. The big horse sensed the urgency and kept moving forward as I asked more and more from him. I reined him in alongside of Joe's horse and aimed my knife for the loop attached to the back of Joe's saddle. My knife hit the loop the first time and cut Molly loose. Joe and the palomino regained their footing, but Molly, who had been pulling back, went over the side. She and the packs fell to the bottom of the canyon. I thanked God that the little ones were two hours behind my group and did not have to see her fall.

However; our troubles were not over yet. G.B. was trying to keep his footing on the shale but was losing the battle. I could only turn him down the mountain toward the canyon and hope we stayed upright. When I turned him downward, he sensed what I was doing, and we began to slide and jump over small protruding rocks and brush in our path. I held his head up trying to give him as much support as possible. I knew if his head dropped too low, we would go end over end.

God's angels finally intervened. Suddenly, there was a break in the shale rock giving way to the large ledge where we could catch our breath. My horse found enough footing to stay on the ledge, and I thanked the good Lord for his timing in the matter.

I sat there a minute and looked down into the bottom of the canyon. I could see Molly. It was a pathetic and gruesome sight. The fall had not killed her outright; she was still moving. I had to get to her before the boys discovered what had happened. Meanwhile, on the trail, my older boys and their horses moved on down the canyon to safety.

The big roan and I had slid halfway down the mountain. The ledge went around the side of the mountain and became wider as we worked our way down. It wasn't the best trail, but I appreciated having a way out. It looked like it continued on down to Lord's Meadow, appropriately named for its beautiful grassy meadows, our camp sight for the night.

Tom sent his horse with the older boys down the canyon to set up camp. Then he carefully worked his way on foot back to me. The ledge at this point was wider, so I got off to look at G.B.'s legs. He had just saved my life and almost lost his in the process. His legs were scratched and cut from the rocks and brush. He was not putting weight on his right front leg and was bleeding from his knees down on all four legs.

When Tom reached me, I handed G.B.'s bridle reins to him. Tom looked at me and asked, "Do you want me to do it?" Tom knew, as well as any good cowboy would know, Molly would have to be put down.

I said, "I can handle it, will you take care of G.B?"

I watched for just a moment as Tom led the big gelding down the mountain. Sure enough, he was hurt badly. I just prayed it would not be too bad. I was starting to get teary eyed. This was not a time to cry. With a disaster like this, it was my responsibility to handle the situation, not to let the situation handle me. The boys needed my strength. I had to take care of Molly now before the next group of boys rode down Six Pack Canyon. I needed to do it for Molly, too.

I skidded as I struggled to make it down to the bottom of the canyon. As I approached, she saw me and raised her head as if to say, "Help me." Molly struggled trying to get up but couldn't, which meant she had probably broken her back.

On closer look, I saw she was bleeding from her nose and had broken her front legs and one of her hind legs. A large gash on her side exposed her ribs. Cut marks covered her entire body—a bloody mess to say the least. I figured she probably punctured a lung. I had to put her out of her pain and suffering. It is not like you see in the movies where the cowboy takes his gun out and shoots the horse. In the High Country, we are not allowed to carry a firearm of any kind. The national forest service strictly enforces this rule. I always thought this rule was written in favor of the bad guys, because the bad guys never read the rules.

I've carried a ten-inch big buck knife for many years in the High Country. I cooked with it and skinned deer with it, but I had never been in this situation before. I had hunted most of my life and cutting a deer's throat to bleed out was common place. I took off my jacket and covered her eyes and head. Then I took out the knife. I knew my knife was sharp enough to do what I had to do, which was cut her throat. There just was no other way out. She was suffering, and I knew she had to be put down. I took a deep breath and asked the Good Lord to make the first cut a good one.

I knelt down on my knee and talked to her a minute trying to make her as comfortable as I could. She quit trying to get up as if she knew what I had to do. I made the cut quickly, and it was a good, clean cut. I sat down and put her head in my lap and stayed there, petting her, until she gasped her last breath. Cutting the throat of an animal and watching it die by bleeding is not pleasant, but it's far worse to watch one suffer a slow and painful death. Cutting the tack cinches followed. I began to cut brush and covered her so the little ones could not possibly see her. It was a long way from the bottom of the canyon to the top where she had gone over the edge.

She landed not far from a small stream that ran down to meet the river in the canyon. I washed the blood from my hands and some of my clothing so as not to look too bad when I arrived in camp. I stood straight up throwing my hands and arms into the air, looking up to the heavens; I let out a yell trying to release my sadness. It echoed down the canyon.

I knew my younger boys would be coming over the pass anytime now. I finished covering her and headed on down the mountain into camp. Halfway down the mountain I looked up and saw the second group coming through Six Pack. I knew at the rate the boys were traveling, they would be in camp at Lords Meadow ahead of me.

By the time I walked into camp, "dark thirty" fell as the sun disappeared behind the mountains. Tom and the boys were cooking supper. My little ones immediately came running up to ask, "Is Molly okay? Did you bring Molly back?"

I called the boys around the campfire. Then came the difficult part—telling them Molly had been a good horse and that she now was resting in God's heaven for animals, where good horses go when they have finished their work here on earth. The younger ones started crying and shouting at Joe, who already blamed himself for Molly's death. If the death and loss of this little horse was anyone's fault, it was mine.

Joe ran off into the meadow. I told the boys, "It's no one's fault, especially Joe's. God just needed Molly more in Heaven than we needed her on earth."

I took time to tell the two ranch hands, "At first light go back up the cannon, set fire to the brush over Molly and take the shortwave radio to tell the forestry service what you are doing, "after" you take care of Molly." They gave me a questioning look, "If you encounter trouble, I will pay the fine. But see that Molly is taken care of, she deserves a decent burial." Molly had landed in a rocky area with no close trees and very little brush near her, so I knew the fire danger was minimal.

I went looking for Joe who was sitting by a rock crying his heart out. I thought he needed some time alone, but now it was time to put everything back together. I walked over and sat down beside him, and for just a minute, neither one of us said anything. When boys are fourteen, they feel like they are too old to be hugged; I needed to figure out what Joe was feeling and take it from there, letting him lead.

Joe stopped crying and looked at me. He told me how sorry he was; that he knew it was his fault. I let him talk and then said, "Joe, it was not your fault, and you can't blame yourself. If anyone is to blame, it would be me. I knew she was not acting right at Kibby, and I should have sent her home."

He was relieved by what I said. "You, son, only did what you were taught at the ranch. You were assigned this horse to lead her for the duration of the trip. All you were doing was what you were supposed to do, being responsible for your assigned packhorse. I am so proud of you for a lot of reasons. Today you made very grown-up decisions and, with those decisions, showed you are definitely growing into quite a young man."

"Do you remember today," I continued, "when I shouted at you to get off old Yeller? You stayed with your horse. That decision could have cost you your life, but you did not 'spit the bits out. You stayed with your horse and that showed loyalty and strength. Today you grew towards manhood."

"Mom," Joe said, "I just couldn't quit him. He has been my best friend and my assigned horse for a very long time, and I couldn't let him go over the side. I really tried to save Molly."

"I know you did, son," I answered.

By this time he had turned and was looking straight at me. Suddenly, he stood up. I followed his lead and stood close to him. Then the little boy came bubbling out, he never said a word. Joe hugged me, letting the tears flow like a faucet. The fourteen-year-old boy emerged again, and he let go. When he was able to control himself, we walked back towards camp with neither of us saying a word.

Almost back to camp, he stopped, looked at me, and asked, "Do you think Molly is really in heaven?"

I answered, "Yes, son, I do believe there is a heaven for animals just like there is for people."

Arriving back at camp, Tom walked up to me and asked, "Have you checked on G.B.?" My stomach turned when he asked that question. I had been concentrating on the boys so hard that I had forgotten about G.B.

I was almost afraid to ask, “Is he all right?”

Tom looked down at me and said, “He will heal to chase another steer, but it will be awhile.”

I went back to the meadow and looked for G.B. When I found him, his legs were swollen from the knees down. I stood there thanking him for saving my life and then led him to the river that ran through the canyon.

Standing the horse in snow melted cold water was the best thing I could do. It would ease the pain and reduce the swelling in his legs. I led him close to the water’s edge and then gave him a slap on the rump. He walked in up to his knees in the cool running stream. As he stood in the water, I began my much-needed conversation with the good Lord.

“Well, Lord, this has been a rather trying day. You teach us, Lord, you will never give us more than we can handle. Today you cut it pretty close; that said, I just want to thank you for saving Joe and taking care of me. My guardian angels appeared to be napping. They did save me, but they sure took their sweet time in doing it. Oh, well, thank you for the things you did do: for not letting Molly suffer too long and for giving me the strength to endure life’s tough decisions while I continue in my Journey on earth. And, Lord, knowing full well you have done your part today—but if you could do one more thing for me—take care of G.B. and make his legs as good as new. Well, Lord, that’s about all for tonight. I would appreciate your visiting with those guardian angels of mine and tell them not to go to sleep on the job. Thank you again, Lord, for watching out for my boys. Amen.”

I took G.B. out of the water and stood there next to this wonderful gentle giant of an animal, so trusting and so loyal.

I leaned against him and hugged his neck. The big gelding knew when to stand still, allowing me to lean against him as the events of the day overwhelmed me. It was a good time to cry.

~ Chapter 13 ~

THE COUNSELORS' PROTEST

The state required my counselors to attend continuing-educational classes every year. One particular class lasted two and a half days, starting on Friday morning and ending Sunday afternoon. The classes, held in San Francisco, required the counselors to stay through the entire weekend, leaving the house parents and me with all the boys.

The counselors left Thursday afternoon. Friday afternoon, the boys returned from school and came running into my office, wanting to know, "What's short sheeting Mom?" I smiled, wondering what I was going to do to entertain my boys for the weekend. I now had my answer.

Being the biggest kid on the place, naturally, I couldn't just tell them about short sheeting. I explained, "Short sheeting is simply taking the top sheet and folding it back halfway on the bed. The unsuspecting victim tries to stretch out his/her legs to no avail." But I felt they needed to experience short sheeting up close and personal. The next day the boys and I proceeded to go into each of the counselors' rooms, where we short sheeted all their beds. A good time was had by all! The boys were laughing, and before it was over, we even got a little creative with the whole thing.

The creative part is putting salt in between the folds of top sheet and pepper in the pillowcases. If you have taken a shower or bath and you get into a short-sheeted bed, your feet, instead of going to the end, only go halfway down the bed. If there is salt added and you are "just in your underwear," the salt will stick to your skin. My cowboy counselors considered pajamas and underwear unnecessary pieces of clothing.

After you figure out what's happened and you put clean sheets back on the bed and take another shower, you crawl back into bed. Thinking the joke is over, you put your head on the pillow and try to sleep. It usually takes a few minutes before you start sneezing, and then it takes a little longer to figure out there is pepper in your pillowcase.

The boys and I had a ball playing this prank on the counselors. I loved watching the boys have fun and laugh, with me right in the middle of things.

When the counselors arrived home late Sunday night, they took their showers and went to bed. That night, we sure found out who had sportsmanship and who didn't, or in other words, who was going to last at this ranch and who wasn't.

First thing Monday morning, you guessed it; I had an office full of unhappy counselors. Simultaneously, they told me all about what the boys did to them. The cowboy counselors were included in this practical joke; however, they did not even bother to come to the office.

One of the many rules at the ranch: a resident could not enter a counselor's room without a staff member present.

What the counselors did not realize was my participation in this matter. I let them tell me about all the broken rules, such as the boys coming into their rooms without an adult present.

When they calmed down a little, I broke the news to them, holding back a giggle, "I was simply teaching the boys how to accomplish a task by participation." Some of the counselors laughed, but two who did not think the prank was very funny insisted on speaking with me privately after the meeting.

And we did talk. One counselor asked, "Just what were you trying to teach these boys about behavior?" I observed his expression for a moment and then replied, "You are the counselor. You tell me, what YOU think I was trying to teach these boys?" Neither could answer this question.

I answered for them, "This is teaching at its very best. A child must have fun too before he can learn from you."

In allowing them to have fun, they were learning this isn't such a bad place to be, and I, being the director, could be someone other than the one handing out rules and regulations. I could be fun. The ranch could be fun, and most importantly, it was okay to have fun and to laugh—something I knew four of the boys had not experienced, especially with adults.

The two angry counselors refused to see my point, and I could see they were not the kind of counselors I wanted at the ranch. I did not have to fire them because they both quit.

A week later, I came home from the monthly grocery shopping trip late at night, totally exhausted from being on my feet all day, only to find my bed had been taken apart. The bolts lay neatly in the floor, beside the rails, and the mattresses, carefully stacked against the wall. The sheets were tied in a number of knots, not too tight, but just enough to make me work. I called Tom to come up to the house and help me put my bed back together. He made me literally beg him. I'm not exactly sure, but he was probably behind the counselors and cowboys doing this little trick.

The next day, everyone was asking me if I had a good night's sleep.

Lots of practical joking occurred at the ranch, and the boys loved it! The ranch had a program I developed for counselors' in college; however, not all fit the program at the ranch. One such counselor came to us right out of college. I showed him around, ending the tour at my office to talk. I sat down in my chair, and he sat down on the chair in front of my desk.

Sitting on the chair was a box. I had not put the box there, and as he moved it to sit down, out jumped a big bullfrog. Bullfrog jokes were common occurrences at the ranch. If you were used to the frogs, you just laughed and went about whatever you were doing. But if you were brand new to the ranch, the frogs were always a surprise.

Well, the box went flying into the air, and the poor old frog went flying the other way. The young man looked at me, and I was laughing so hard I nearly fell out of my chair. It seemed the boys knew about my interview with the new counselor and had decided to play a joke on him. I could see right up front this young man did not have a good sense of humor and probably would not last long.

After he calmed down and I regained my composure, we began the interview. "Have you had much experience with children?" I asked.

"Oh, yes," he replied. "I have been a Boy Scout leader and a Sunday school teacher at my church." Being the Sunday school teacher was good experience, but there were no Boy Scouts at my ranch.

I suggested he work at a smaller facility, perhaps a family foster-care facility would be a better situation. He thought I was being unfair and said, "I really want the chance to work here, because it's a ranch."

I did not want to be unfair and gave him a thirty day probation period where he would be able to prove himself. I would pray for this one nightly as I figured his tenure was going to be sad to watch. My boys would take bites out of this one, and there really was not much I could do except sit back and be entertained.

This young man had little beady eyes, stood about five feet four inches tall, and wore big thick glasses. He was book smart, knew computers, and carried a 4.0 GPA all through college. I respected him for his accomplishments and his academic knowledge. I knew I would not feel right if I turned him away. His parents had paid for his education, which meant his experience to the real world was lacking. He saw himself doing all these cowboy things and sincerely wanted to help the boys. He simply was on the wrong page as to the streetwise boys at the ranch.

He knew nothing about ranch life and looked absolutely ridiculous in western clothes. The boys wasted no time. The first night at the dinner table, they launched his initiation. The dinner table had very long benches, one on each side. I always sat at the head of the table with the boys sitting on each side. The person sitting at the end of the bench needed to eat being alert. If you were not alert, you could find yourself on the floor. I heard him ask one of my boys, is there a certain place at the table I am to sit. Sure enough, the boy smiled and told him he had to sit at the very end of the bench. He started to eat when all the boys stood up at once. The bench tipped upward landing the counselor on his backside, both legs flying into the air.

The boys laughed and sat back down. The young counselor kept waiting for me to say something, but I was laughing with the boys, so he sat down again. I could not believe he went back for seconds! But there he was again being thrown into the air landing on the floor. The boys had done it again!

This time he asked me if I was going to do anything. I told him I was not the object of this practical joke. "You are the counselor, and you need to find a solution to this little matter."

He excused himself and came back with a clipboard in his hands. He wrote down all the boys names and gave them a three-day restriction. A new counselor on probation could give a restriction, but I usually questioned the restriction and then suggested an alternative solution.

The boys looked at me, and I looked at this counselor and simply gave him the solution. "You sit in the middle of the bench between the boys, and there will be no three-day restrictions."

The boys had an absolute field day with this one. They put baby power outside the door of his room, which has a tendency to make the hard wood floor slick. Three lizards showed up in his room, and of course, nobody knew how they got there. Then the final straw broke when they stole his clipboard for writing restrictions. This counselor lasted only twenty days, which was ten days longer than I had figured.

All counselors were on a probation period and were not officially hired until the probation period was completed. The probation period gave me a chance to see first-hand how they interacted with the boys before they were hired.

One of the many things I repeated over and over in training, "Children have not read the same books you read in college. You must look at each child as an individual person. The key is to make friends first, but not to be phony about it. Children, especially the type of boys living at the ranch, will sense phoniness and then you have not only lost their trust, but you have also lost any chance of reaching them. Most important is to learn how to have fun with these kids. If you don't have fun with them, then there is NO WAY IN H— you are ever going to teach them anything."

Do you remember when you were in school and your teacher was so caught up in teaching "what she knew" that she simply bored you to death? Well, it's the same at my boy's ranch.

When I first opened the ranch, I had no one to teach me anything. Of course, I knew I had God on my side and He, without my really knowing, had given me a wonderful tool. I call this tool "readability." Simply put, it means I can read a child's needs through his expectations, instead of the child coming up to my expectations. This tool actually has nothing to do with academic skills but is a God-given talent.

Boys at my ranch were not punished for playing jokes or having good old-fashioned, clean fun. Why? It is learning and growing experience of the best kind.

At my first boy's ranch, I had been open about three weeks, when the "old snake in the drawer" joke showed its ugly head. The boys being boys, before group session had put a little bull snake in my top drawer. When the afternoon group session began, I still had not opened my top drawer. One of the boys said he needed a pencil, knowing the pencils were kept there. I continued talking on the subject matter at hand as I opened the top drawer. I did not see the snake at first but felt his presence with my hand. Thank goodness I was a tomboy growing up, or I would have been screaming my head off. (When I was nine years old, my first horse died of sleeping sickness. What I wanted was another horse, but what I got was a doll. I did not want that darn doll so I lynched it with a rope. And yes, my mother gave me a good talking to on my backside.)

I calmly pulled the little snake from my desk; we talked about how cute he was and I asked the boys to name him. Thus began the rule about practical jokes and sportsmanship. No one could be punished for a truly good practical joke. However, if you played a joke on someone, you were open to have a joke played on you. One of the main rules was you could not bring harm or hurt to anyone with your practical joke. Besides, I liked a good practical joke too.

Back to the counselors!

At one point, the counselors got together and decided to protest this practical-joke rule. I, in turn, gathered my boys together and voted on "glue" in the chair as an answer to their protest.

The counselors met later that afternoon outside my office. I opened the office door and asked which counselor was the spokesperson. I led him to the chair in front of my desk and sat him down abruptly while the others waited outside. As he began the counselor's grievance, it took about a minute for him to realize he was sitting in something wet and very sticky. His rehearsed speech went by the wayside. For that matter, so did his composure.

I cleared the office so this particular counselor could remove his pants. The boys laughed their heads off as the counselor left my office with a towel from the office bathroom wrapped around his lower anatomy. Needless to say, I do believe that was the last time the counselors complained about the practical joke rule.

~ Chapter 14 ~

MUD DAY

Amarillo, Texas, early 2005

It was a bad day to go to the doctor's office in Amarillo. Doctors I have found do not read the Farmers' Almanac. It had been raining off and on for three days. Water covered every crevice and stood in deep, muddy ruts, creating havoc for both drivers and pedestrians. Evidently my mind today was elsewhere, lacking the focus to concentrate on my driving. Deep in my own thoughts, I almost missed my turn. As I swerved to catch the turn, I noticed a young man standing on the corner, dressed in a raincoat, tie, and suit. How did I know he had a suit on? His rain coat sadly to say was open. Too late, I saw the big muddy puddle by the curb directly in front of the young man. I caught it with my front tire; the watery mud flew into the air with the vengeance of a tsunami. He was drenched from head to toe: glasses, raincoat, suit, shoes. It was a direct hit! He looked like a drowned rat. I wanted to stop and apologize, but he, removing his muddy spectacles, was already walking across the street.

I drove in the parking lot, thinking to myself he looked like one of those young pup doctors. And since I had seen two young pups this year, I relaxed because today I specifically requested an older doctor, at least fifty-years old, who knew better than to make that silly statement "for your age." Two hours later, bored and still sitting in the waiting room, I began to look at the pictures on the wall of the doctors in the office. One face stood out with familiarity, but I could not place him.

Finally, the nurse called my name, and here I was, seeing the third doctor about this little friend of mine. Why, you ask, would I call this mass in my throat a friend? Simple—this little friend was moving and motivating me to get off my backside and start doing things. It was a great incentive to push me to complete things that truly were important to finish. Three years ago, I married a Texas man and moved to Texas. I became a devoted wife and put my career on hold just when it was taking off. The pay was lousy. I actually set down one time and figured, maid service and horizontal conversations and came out with (35) thirty-five cents per hour on an eight hour day. (Which most good house wives put in more than eight hour days.) He assured me at the time he would always take care of me. What an absolute pill of ca-ca! He basically used me for arm dressing until I became sick. How sick? I came down with food poisoning. (Read my book, "The Divorce" Subtitle; It could happen to you; coming out in November 2018 to find out who poisoned me. I have eliminated my two miniature Schnauzers. This book will open the eyes of many!

Now I am writing and updating my children's program, so others will benefit from them long after my Journey in life is completed.

Perhaps this older, more experienced doctor could give me some common sense approaches and we could discuss a more natural cure. I asked for this man because, in addition to being a doctor of medicine, he also advocated healing herbs.

The nurse escorted me to the little examining room to wait for the doctor.

As the door opened, in walked the doctor, but a very young-looking doctor. He was the same man I had soaked on the street earlier. He also recognized me. We both struggled to gain our composure. Finally I groped awkwardly for an apology and then asked where my doctor was—"the older one."

It was his turn to apologize. "Your 'older' doctor had an emergency call and had to leave. He requested that I take over his appointments."

I decided not to waste his time or mine. To our mutual relief, I excused my embarrassed self. I could still see him in my mind's eye, standing there on the street corner, dripping wet. He looked like one of my boys on Mud Day, with one exception: they were laughing, and he was not.

The house parents thoroughly dreaded Mud Day, yet due to their insistence they helped create Mud Day. But I rated it right up there next to most of the legal holidays like Memorial Day, or Fourth of July, a Jim dandy of a day—except for one occasion.

We naturally celebrated Mud Day in the winter and required lots of rain. Living in the Sierra foothills, we knew there would be lots of rain in the winter and early spring.

During my first year at the ranch, I discovered boys, especially the little ones, loved getting muddy. On several days in the winter and springtime, the house parents tromped into my office to complain about the boys tracking mud all over their clean floors.

"René, why can't you do something to make these boys listen to us about tracking up the floors?" they asked. I had to admit it was a challenging situation—boys who loved mud versus the house parents who were required to keep a clean house. I needed a creative solution, and soon, because the complaints were driving me up the wall.

One wintry day, caught up with reports and paperwork in the office, I went to the barn to see what my boys were doing. I periodically checked on them to see with my own eyes what they were accomplishing. On this day it was about sixty degrees. I looked around and could not find a boy outside and it wasn't that cold.

I called the house parents together, I asked, "Where are my little ones, the nine-and-ten year olds." I figured the older ones were out in the shop.

The house parents replied, "We put the younger boys on "in-house restriction." The boys had tracked the floors up with mud for the umpteenth time, and the house parents of all three houses were furious.

I went through the roof! "How do you expect them to be boys if they're on restriction all the time for doing boy things?" So rather than watch the house parents have a nervous breakdown, I reminded them of the old saying, "If you can't beat 'em, join 'em." Thus began Mud Day.

My boys all loved it when "Mom" cut them a deal. The deal went something like this: "You, boys take care not to track mud in the houses, and I will furnish you with one great Saturday called Mud Day."

My Marvellous Mud Day consisted of one very muddy riding arena and eighteen behavioral problem boys ready and willing to participate fully in the day's activities. The boys simply loved this day for they could get as muddy as they wanted without any restrictions.

I, being a kid at heart, sometimes helped things along. If the arena was not muddy enough the little ones would get concerned. They asked, "Mom, are we still going to have Mud Day, 'cause the arena isn't very muddy?"

I would simply say, "Yes, boys. God and I are pretty close and I've talked to him today, and he says it's going to rain tonight. Now, are you boys questioning God?"

They would look at me with those eyes larger than silver dollars and say flat out, "No ma'am, not us."

Around midnight when the entire ranch was sound asleep, I sneaked outside and literally flooded the whole arena with the water hose, leaving an obvious mud puddle or two to step in around the arena; I had to be extra careful to make sure no one saw me. The boys woke up the next morning and ran out to the arena, and sure enough, God (with a little help) made it rain during the night. No wonder those boys thought I had a kinship with God. Actually, the majority of people have the same kinship and understand God often works through human agents. I knew I was no Joseph or Moses, but He, God, kept giving me these crazy and fun ideas to solve the problems that occurred at the ranch.

All wearing old clothes, the boys lined up in the arena. One boy at a time made himself ready for the ride of his life. A horse, ridden by one of our cowboy counselors, took off in the mud at a gallop and ran to the other end of the arena. The horse pulled a sled made of blue plastic tarp with a boy lying flat on his stomach and holding on for dear life. We put goggles over the boy's eyes for protection. And every year, it just seemed to get better and better. We kept adding new events.

The sled event was the main event but we added the muddy pig contest; then there was the "goat ribbon contest." One of the older boys rode a horse from one end of the arena to the middle, dismounted the horse, and ran to a goat staked out with a long rope around its neck. While the older boy held the goat, one of the little ones' ran on foot in the boggy mud to the goat and pulled a ribbon off the goat's tail. This, in the mud, is not an easy task. And if we used calves for this event (instead of goats) that were fresh off grass, it could be real messy. Sometimes my young ones would fall face first in the mud entertaining the whole ranch. We borrowed wild goats from a neighbor's ranch. He was more than willing to bring the wild goats over and help us out. Usually, he came over to watch the events and laughed while the boys made fools of themselves. The ranch offered prize money just like a regular rodeo. We only paid three monies: first, second, and third. We also gave out prize ribbons with five places so everyone had a good chance of winning something.

The cowboy counselors enjoyed the day of fun as well. When the boys went flying off the sled, tumbling end over end and through the mud, the cowboys laughed so hard they nearly fell off their saddles. You just can't imagine my delight when I saw these precious abused boys—my family—just being boys, enjoying their growing years. I stood outside the arena in a dry safe spot, laughing and enjoying the entertainment.

Even the older boys went flying off the sled and ended up in the mud. I especially enjoyed watching the older boys who had called me "you f—— bitch" when they first came to the ranch, end up in the mud.

The cowboys knew the "little ones" were special and rode slower to allow them to have fun. Not one boy was hurt during Mud Day events. The cowboys participated in the contest also. They took their turns in the mud; at the ranch if you laughed at my boys, the boys had the opportunity to laugh back. The boys eagerly watched as their almighty counselors' drug one another to the other end of the arena. Most at the ranch considered Mud Day one of the best days of the year, except of course, Christmas.

The third year, we included steer riding in the mud. Steer riding was created for the older boys. The muddiest received a price. The loser, that is the cleanest boy at the end of the day, usually got the old "one, two, three" and was tossed into the muddiest part of the arena.

The house parents complained constantly: "The boys will catch cold," or "Washing these clothes is just awful." Sometimes I think the house parents were more trouble than the boys.

No matter how hard it was to get the boys or their clothes clean, it was worth the price. It was a day filled with the greatest psychological remedy for behavioral problem boys, just having fun.

However, I remember one Mud Day that didn't quite measure up although it became one of my most memorable. Mud Day usually started around eleven o'clock in the morning; that day I had committed to speak at a Rotary Luncheon. I dressed for the occasion in a conservative, but expensive Lilli Ann suit. The light beige tye-silk suit created the perfect image that I intended to project, conservative but not over the top. This suit was my favorite. A matching pill box hat finished the outfit.

I must take time here to explain something about the ranch. Remember, if a joke is played on you, good sportsmanship builds good character. This was something I personally reminded the boys of on a regular basis.

Unexpectedly, one of the juvenile court appointed Judges stopped by. He and I were good friends; he was very aware of my boys ranch and loved the program.

During our conversation, he became curious about Mud Day. I obliged him by guiding him to the arena, although I was already dressed for my luncheon engagement with my usual braided German buns, heels, hose, and everything coordinated. I felt relatively safe and led him to the safe area. Of course, safety depended on whether or not I paid attention. We became quite engaged in our conversation about the good and bad changes in California's children's programs. Lost in the conversation, I didn't hear the horse's hooves until they were right upon me. As I turned to look out into the arena, I caught the mud full force right along with the Judge, as the horse, rider, and boy went by at full gallop. Usually the riders rode straight down the middle of the arena, but every now and then, the horse shied away from the sled and headed toward the right side of the fence—my safe area—which all considered fair game. To this day I do not know if the cowboys planned it or if the horse truly did shy from the sled. What do you say following something like that?

There I stood in my light tan, beautifully tailored Lilli Ann suit that was now dark brown, thoroughly covered with mud from head to toe. I heard laughter all around the arena. The cowboys were laughing. The boys were laughing. Even the house parents were laughing. The Judge wasn't quite there yet, for he too was covered with mud from head to toe.

The boys started shouting, "It's your turn, Mom; it's your turn!" Since the entire purpose of Mud Day concerned good sportsmanship and naturally a solution for the house parents, I had little choice but to quash my anger over my ruined Lilli Ann. I kicked off my heels, opened the gate, and traipsed across the arena, ankle deep in mud. The moist sludge oozed through my pantyhose to nest in the crevices of my toes. Nevertheless, I lay face down on the blue tarp sled and through my clenched teeth, quietly said to Bob, the grinning cowboy sitting on his horse waiting to pull me, "If you go too fast, you will be riding fence in the high meadow on a donkey for the next week." One of the boys handed me the goggles, and I heard someone struggling to suppress his laughter as he wished me "Good luck." Bob took off at a slow gallop and I held on for dear life. When I arrived in one solid piece at the back of the arena, I swept my muddy fingers across my goggles only to look up and see the Judge leaning on the fence and holding his sides in laughter. In the middle of the muddy arena lay my poor pill box hat, what was left of it. Let me say, it was my very first experience with pantyhose and mud between my toes, and I can tell you firsthand—this is not something you want to experience.

Helen, hearing the news at the main house, laid out another suit for me and asked what to do with the Lilli Ann. "Send it to the cleaners and say a prayer the silk cleans up well." I knew in my heart the suit had just been sacrificed for Mud Day.

I hurriedly showered, dressed, and sped off to the luncheon. This luncheon consisted of Rotary Club members who were mostly ranchers in the area. After my speech, a kind-looking western type gentleman came up to me and said with a smile on his face, "The speech you made was heart-warming; however, the mud behind your left ear has us all wondering about what happened earlier in your day." He had a sparkle in his eyes and added, "It must have been pretty exciting."

Yes, folks, that was my "not-so-happy Mud Day," and yet, when I think back about the whole thing, it was pretty funny. In retrospect, my least favorite Mud Day turned into one of the most memorable. It's the only time I can ever remember having the honor of entertaining the whole ranch family and making everyone happy, including the Judge. Later, he wrote me a thank-you letter for his enjoyable tour and requested an invitation for the following year to Mud Day. Occasionally, I still have twinges of regret for my beautiful Lilli Ann.

~ Chapter 15 ~

THE REPORTERS

We posted a sign out in front by the gate that read: "Reporters Caught Past This Point May Die of Lead Poisoning." The boys painted small rocks with white paint creating a mound that resembled a small grave and placed a wooden tombstone at the head; it read: "Here lies the last news reporter that trespassed through these gates."

Reporters abide by one presumptuous goal: to sell papers at whatever the cost. Unless they sell papers, they lose their income. Unfortunately, they usually sell more papers by reporting disasters or by tearing someone's reputation to shreds. Obviously, readers need to be informed about disasters, but I draw the line when they tear innocent people's reputations and lives apart. When they destroy a reputation without knowing the facts or before the state has time to process the truth, it has a domino effect, they usually destroy not only the person, but also his or her children and family as well.

Reporters frequently called and asked if they could do a story on my ranch. I politely told them, "There is nothing to report." Some reporters have written negative things about other boys ranches or children's homes and never once considered the children they just destroyed. They, for the most part, look for negative things to write about. And some reporters get only half of the story before it's printed.

One such incident happened to a nice couple that operated a wonderful children's facility. Their program activities focused more on fishing and boating rather than ranching. One day, a reporter nosing around came by and talked to one of the children playing outside. The boy the reporter questioned was a new client on restriction for an infraction of some rule. The child told the reporter he was being abused, and of course, the reporter ran to his typewriter and printed the story.

The day after the article was published, state licensing learned of the story and immediately pulled their license and closed them down. The reporter, I'm sure, received all kinds of pats on the back.

This is what actually happened. The reporter failed to research the wonderful couple's twenty-year clean record and their numerous awards for helping abused children. The reporter also failed to investigate the young lad's history. He had history of being a pathological liar in reporting abusive behavior on directors of previous facilities. Naturally, with a record like this, no one would take him except this family who saw him as a child in need—this child that no one else wanted because of his history. There is a saying among good and devoted directors of facilities: "A child is just a child, who with kindness, love and guidance may someday become a productive adult."

The reporter's sensational story brought the state-licensing agency knocking on their door. They not only pulled this child out of the program, but they removed all the children, including the couple's biological and adopted children. In America, the law states that all people are considered innocent until proven guilty, except with children's facilities. The directors of children's homes are presumed guilty with accusations and must prove their innocence after the fact.

My heart ached deeply because for the life of me I had no magic plan and watched helplessly while they were destroyed. I believed I suffered right along with them and encouraged them to believe in our court system. I can tell you truthfully on issues of this nature our court system sucks. There was no hearing before trial. It took one hundred and twenty days to get into court and prove their innocence.

They had literally given their lives to children no one else wanted.

The seemingly secondary losses included the ranch, their income, and their life savings. The outrageous attorney fees drove them into bankruptcy. The reporter's unethical story ruined them financially and emotionally. And what do you know—the boy who caused all the problems admitted on the first day in court that he lied. The defence attorney asked, "Why have you not come forward before this?"

He replied, "Social Services give me all kinds of attention when I say I am abused." This child was ten.

Vindication sounds so benevolent. One of their adopted children had attempted suicide before being placed with this loving couple. The Christian couple promised him no one would ever take him away from their home and settled the child by adopting him. They loved him, and basking in their love, he focused on making his adopted parents proud of him with good grades in school. For the first time in his life, he loved and was loved. Then Social Services removed the boy from this wonderful family home. He and the other children in the home cried because they did not want to leave their home where they were never abused. Their cries fell to deaf ears in the system. Social Services placed their adopted son in yet another foster home, and before the case came to trial and before the court vindicated them, their precious new adopted son succeeded in taking his own life.

The couple received their birth and adopted children back, but financial and emotional damage had already occurred.

My friends buried their adopted son. Then, as they packed their belongings to move from their beloved ranch, the State licensing agency paid them a visit and informed them their license could be reinstated. They owned nothing with which to start again; more devastating, their hearts were shattered. I wonder how a reporter seeks absolution for the death of a child and the destruction of a family and their home.

I have protected my boys against anything and everything I felt might hurt or harm them, including rabid reporters seeking sensationalism to sell newspapers.

That same year a rumor circulated around town, claiming I roped a reporter snooping on the ranch and dragged him off the ranch. Did I really do this? I have never confirmed or denied this story.

On one occasion, I ran into a very persistent female reporter named Patti Russmaker. She served as special-feature editor for a local newspaper. Patti learned about the boy's ranch from the locals and was anxious to interview me. I simply told her what I told the other reporters, "There is nothing to report."

She replied, "I disagree with you. I think there are lots of good things to write about, and I want to be the one to write the story." I had very few people challenge me in those days, and the fact that she did impressed me. The way she said "good" was the keyword that caught my attention, but not enough to let her come to the ranch.

A week went by, and I received another phone call from Ms. Russmaker. This time, she used a different approach. She invited me to lunch. I replied that my busy schedule excluded two-hour lunches with a reporter. She was very patient with my rude behavior. She said, "I understand," and she hung up.

I expected that to be the end of this reporter. I was wrong. The next week, she phoned again. This time she used the "just call me by my first name, Patti, because I feel I already know you" ploy. I replied, "Patti, you do not know me, and I do not know you."

This lady had done her research. The next thing I knew, she was saying, "René, I have heard you are a fair person and you pride yourself in being fair with everyone. You do not know me, yet you refuse to give me a fair opportunity to prove myself." There was a brief pause. I said nothing. Then she added, "I'm not a bad person."

Well, she had me. I was known for my fairness with the boys and everyone else. She really had me and I knew it.

"Okay, here's the deal. You, Patti Russmaker, may come to my ranch. I will see you, and under certain and agreed-upon conditions, you can write your story. However, if these conditions are violated and your story hurts my boys or this ranch in any way, I will spend the rest of my life ruining your career. Do you fully understand these conditions?"

Without hesitating, she asked, "What time should I be there?"

She did not know it, but I liked her already. It was just her darn chosen profession that I found distasteful.

The next week, she showed up promptly at nine o'clock in the morning. Helen escorted her to my office. We began talking about the dos and don'ts of her upcoming editorial.

I explained with my normal straight forwardness, I had no time to sit around and answer her questions as I wore several different "hats" at the ranch. She would just have to follow me around and write her story as the day progressed.

Before she broke out of the roping box, Patti had already dropped her piggin' string by bringing a photographer with her. The hair stood straight up on the back of my neck when we were introduced. I think I took time to say, "How do you do," but I was not polite. As a matter of fact, when she told me he was a photographer, I do remember telling him he was not invited, and there would be no pictures taken of my boys without my written consent. Patti immediately interjected, "We will not publish any pictures without your approval." I presented them with a short and to the point contract and added this paragraph requesting a signature from both.

She was trying hard to take that extra step with me, although I knew that she didn't understand my belligerence, so I felt a need to explain, "You see, Patti, this ranch is the boys home, a place of security, a place they feel safe, and a place they feel loved and protected. If your photographer takes a picture of one of my boys and he goes to school and is teased for being in a group home or because he has no real parents, this will destroy everything we are trying to do."

"I would simply have to adopt the boy, and in his best interest as a parent, I would feel obligated to sue you." I have never sued anyone in my life, but I really needed to get my point across. "I will protect my boys from any kind of harmful publicity."

The young cameraman seemed nervous but appeared to understand fully the situation.

My day began by going to the neighbor's and presenting a final real-estate contract to buy them out. Patti and the photographer followed me around the ranch like two puppies, occasionally taking pictures and looking at everything. The photographer asked permission for every picture he took. Finally, I said, "Take your darn pictures, but be forewarned; I want to see everything before you print it in the paper. There will be NO close-ups of my boys."

About lunch time I told Patti I needed to change into a suit and speak at a luncheon in town. I would be gone for about two hours. She told me she also had an appointment for lunch and would see me back at the ranch around two o'clock. When I arrived at the luncheon, to my surprise, I found that Patti was also one of the speakers. Neither of us knew the other was on the program. It's the first time she saw me laugh.

We met back at the ranch afterward, and I changed into my Wranglers and boots and continued with my day. Patti followed my every step, taking notes as fast as she could flip a page. She sat quietly through face-to-face evaluations of the boys little discrepancies, to the arena where I gave riding and roping lessons to the boys, to the stables, barn, and shop. At the end of the day, we sat down in my office to give closure to her interview. She said, "René I would like permission to interview the children" I hesitated; the thought entered my mind can I trust her? Silently I prayed, Oh Lord I hope you're watching over this little matter. She interviewed my boys for about an hour before returning to the office. She graciously thanked me for my time and effort and left.

The next morning, she called and said it was urgent that she see me. She singled out a picture of one of my boys she wanted to use in the article but knew she needed my permission. Most of the pictures were taken from a distance, so the boys could not be identified. This picture was a close-up of one of my boys holding a puppy next to his face. It was a fantastic picture showing a boys love for his dog. I stared at the picture for a long time and realized the effect it would have on the newspaper readers; I indeed felt it would be a positive one for the ranch.

I said, "This is not up to me. The boy must be brought to the office and we explain what may happen if the picture is printed. It must be his decision." She agreed.

When he came into the office, I told him about the consequences, both good and bad, if he allowed the newspaper to print his picture. I wanted him to make an informed decision. He listened and said he understood people would recognize him and it was okay to print the picture.

Patti thanked us both and left. I still worried about the ramifications this newspaper article would have on the ranch.

The weekend came, and there for the world to read was Patti's article. It even had a title I liked: "Where Boys Can Be Boys." It was a full two-page spread with several pictures, but none of the boys could be identified, except for one. The picture of my boy and his puppy spoke volumes. It reached out and grabbed the reader's heart. Later I found out Patti was not just a reporter, but also the executive editor of the paper.

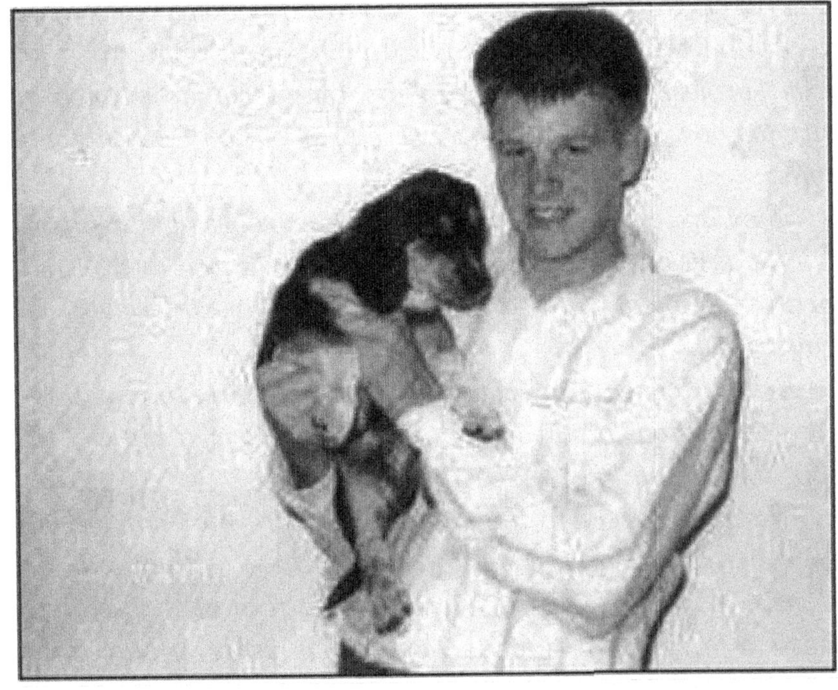

Boy and his puppy

I've included the article below. Patti was not quite accurate about some things, such as how many boys we had or the acreage of the ranch, but it came from the heart so I didn't quibble. This is what she wrote:

They're trying to find their way out of a world of illusions—a world where things are never quite what they seem and people rarely mean what they say. It's an incomprehensibly dark and frightening world of instability, of change and contradiction. For ten young boys living in Oakdale, the lighted Path out of such darkness is a sense of purpose and a solid code of conduct. Their guiding beacon is a ranch that was conceived a little over four years ago by René Monroe. The Cottonwood Ranch Youth Center is a non-profit project designed to provide long-term assistance and care for boys suffering from severe physical and psychological abuse.

They are children at the end of their ropes. Their future a grim succession of beatings, emotional trauma, and physical torture coupled with a deep sense of worthlessness and isolation.

René Monroe has committed her future to creating a different vision for these boys, to giving them a big chunk of hope to grab on to.

"We want them to have a place where they can be boys. To roll around in the mud and get dirty if they want to," Monroe says. "We want them to feel that it's possible for them to have a home for at least a few years, a place where they feel safe."

It's hard to imagine at first glance that any of these children have known anything but love. All ten have angelic faces with soft, clear eyes. They are well-scrubbed, well-mannered, and well-dressed. They laugh and joke and play. But ever so often, the pain oozes through. The arguing and the fighting may begin . . . the whining . . . the desperate need for attention. "They each take a piece of you," says Monroe. "It can be very exhausting."

Monroe is 43 and without children of her own. Counseling and caring for people has been a way of life for her for a very long time. Her mother operated a home for senior citizens in Sutter County for over 18 years. Monroe licensed her first facility in 1975. She is a born nurturer and must have inherited the "compassion" gene.

The reason her ranch is for boys is simple: "I know what to do with boys. I can teach them things . . . like riding and roping," She's been riding since the age of five, "plays" at roping and does a bit of barrel racing. "God has given me the talent to read these boys," she says. "I know what they need."

Best laid plans aside, the project was a nightmare to put together. According to Monroe, the paperwork packet alone was 123 pages of extensive documentation. The ranch was in a state of dilapidation. "I did most of the work alone," she says, referring to the constant battle with state and federal agencies and the extensive renovations the ranch needed before it was up to code and licensable by the government.

"I have to wear a lot of different hats," she says, "I'm willing to do whatever it takes to get the job done."

The day of this interview she changed "hats" literally three times. From a casual felt hat for a neighborly call next door to inquire about property plans, to a prim black pillbox hat, complete with veil for a Rotary luncheon speech, and then to a tall straw western hat and full cowboy regalia for afternoon lessons on riding.

René Monroe knows how to play the political game. Since receiving her M.S. in Psychology, she has initiated and managed three different types of counseling facilities over the last 10 years. Monroe realized the need for a different type of youth facility a long time ago. The type that concentrated on long-term care, rather than just keeping them six months, and trying to do a reunification with the family; a program that would be geared for the ten-and-twelve year old age groups.

"For some reason there is a real need for that particular age group," Monroe confides. "We have a long waiting list."

It was her involvement in the Women's Professional Rodeo Association and her introduction to Harlan Madison that prompted the need of a ranch style center for these children. Oakdale seemed the perfect setting. She is a licensed real estate agent and through her business dealing with Madison, Monroe discovered the land owned by a mutual friend was for sale at a reasonable price. She bought the ranch and formed Constructive Youth Assessments, a non-profit corporation under which the center operates.

"Without the non-profit label it would be practically impossible to receive government funds." But, Monroe added, the funds they do receive are totally inadequate to meet the needs of the children. The federal government allows a mere one hundred and thirty-five dollars per year per child for clothing and twenty-six dollars per month per child for recreation.

"By the time I buy boots and jeans, I've spent that money and then some," she says. "Have you tried to entertain yourself on twenty-six dollars a month lately?" Monroe depends heavily on donations. "That's how we survive."

Her accountant claims that at least half of Monroe's salary from the corporation goes back into the center for clothing and a money management program she has invented for "my boys."

In her office, Monroe has a large crayon board posted with each child's name and conduct report. It is here that a boy can sign up to do what Monroe calls "pay jobs . . . work of their own choosing for which they will be paid a monthly wage." The jobs vary; the boys are paid from five to ten dollars a job depending on that job's difficulty. The monthly wage fluctuates depending on how often the child performs his tasks. They each have their own checking accounts under Monroe's name and are encouraged to spend their money wisely.

"I think it's important," she emphasizes, "that they learn the responsibility of handling money. To learn what doing a

job well can do for them. It also teaches them how to handle a checking account at a very early age."

She encourages them to buy clothes. "I do not believe that a child can build self-esteem and not dress well," she says. Her trips to town with ten check-wielding young boys can be very hectic, but extremely entertaining.

"We're getting good response from the community now that they know what we are doing. This is also true of the school system. They've been very good to us," Monroe says, "especially Fair Oaks. They try not to overload the boys and try to understand their individual needs."

Some of the boys are on an independent study program called ACE (Accelerated Christian Education); they have not been able to adapt fully to the school environment. This program allows the child to study and achieve at his own pace building a tremendous self esteem until he is at his academic level.

"It's because of the trauma they've been through," Monroe claims. She may try to send some students out of the district. The small, un-crowded classroom where a child can receive more individual attention is what she is looking for.

*The staff at Cottonwood consists of René, four live-in counselors, and Shelly Browning who does a variety of ranch duties. [*We had two sets of house parents she did not include in this article, plus the ranch hands.*] There is a vocational instructor, and two on-call psychologists, both with PhD's. "But the facility is far from clinical. I play mom as well as counselor," Monroe says. And most of the boys in residence choose to call her "Mom."*

The center consists of a ranch house, stables, barns, shop, riding arena, built-in pool, BBQ area, and office. Most boys share a room with another. There are twenty horses on the ranch, and every child is assigned one horse to ride and care for. There are young calves to rope and cattle, steers to ride, chickens to feed, and a wild array of cats and dogs. Although it sounds like a boys dream come true, it is not all fun and games. Monroe is a strict mom.

"We stress manners," she says, "I feel that even if a child has nothing going for him, but he's polite and well-mannered, he will survive. Behavior at the center is defined and structured."

Each child is expected to perform certain duties as well as strive for and maintain a positive, respectful attitude. They are expected to concern themselves with their own personal hygiene, to keep their rooms clean and to wash and iron their own clothing. They are also expected to use their time constructively.

In a weekly counseling session the boys are graded individually in these areas of responsibility and given positive or negative points according to how they've performed. It is part of an incentive system devised by Monroe to encourage the children to grow and develop both physically and emotionally. Upon arrival at Cottonwood, each boy is placed at Level One. It is here that he first learns what behavior is expected and where most of the difficult socialization takes place.

When a child builds up enough positive points in his weekly sessions, he may request a change to Level Two. At this stage the boy has usually been at the Ranch three to six months, [boys could go to Level Two as early as three months, and most saw this to be an advantage] *according to Monroe, and most of his undesirable social behavior had been corrected. The child is somewhat accomplished in social situations both inside and outside of the facility, and because of his willingness to take responsibility for his actions, he is allowed many more privileges than he had at Level One.*

Level Three is something like a junior counselor position. The boy is assigned a child to sponsor, and it is his responsibility to see that the newcomer adjusts to what is expected and accepted.

For the young man who is long-term, but the government funding has run out for one reason or another, Monroe has devised Level Four. These boys may remain at the ranch and work for their room and board and hold some sort of outside job. They would usually be at least 16 or older.

"It's hard for them to leave," Monroe confides. "A child becomes very settled in this type of environment."

And settled they definitely are. Not one of the children interviewed expressed the desire to leave. In fact, the fear that they may one day have to leave pervades their thoughts. They don't mind the stern rules and obligations they must follow.

Surprisingly, it is the lack of rules and their regular enforcement that seems to be at the root of the deterioration of the parent/child relationship. These children equate strictness with love and caring. As one young man put it, "They care about you here.

They care what you do. It's like a real home." Another said, "Mom is strict but fair, and she loves us enough to be there for us. [Until this writing I did not know what response my boys would have, or what questions she would ask.]

Monroe has big plans for the future. She has recently purchased the land adjacent to Cottonwood and plans to expand the ranch to accommodate four more children. By June of 1987, she hopes to have acquired enough land and houses to have 18 boys. It is a big project and she will need help both with money and with labor and materials.

At present, the ranch is operating around $2,000 to $3,000 a month in the red. "We're a non-profit facility," Monroe explains.

And although the need for funds is there, Monroe prefers that the children participate in earning it. "We try not to hand them money," she says. "We want them to contribute and feel they have responsibilities."

Monroe is working on a horse trailer project where the ranch will purchase them wholesale and try to sell them locally at retail. She thinks the profit will be about four hundred dollars per trailer. If individuals or clubs would like to purchase the original wholesale trailers for the boys to sell, the profit for the project would be that much larger.

This article actually helped us a great deal. I swallowed hard and wrote Patti a thank-you letter on behalf of the ranch. But not all reporters are like Patti Russmaker.

By the late eighties the ranch was in full swing. I bought the properties next to mine, expanded, and increased the number of residents to eighteen boys. However, we were in dire need of a school, and we needed it now.

A neighbor, who drove by everyday and watched the boys ranch build and grow, stopped and introduced himself. Come to find out this gentleman was one of the top Teamster executives in California and said, "If you ever need my help for anything, just call."

A few months later I called and asked for a school for my little ones. Keeping the younger children in the public school system became an ongoing problem; they just had too many psychological problems.

The gentleman listened politely as I stressed the urgency of my situation. Within a couple days, he phoned, "You have your school. All you have to do is pay for the hauling of a twelve by sixty foot modular building from Walnut Creek to Oakdale, about one hundred miles."

For a brief moment there was silence between us. He was waiting for a wonderful thank you, and I, on the other hand, knew the ranch was on a very tight budget. I responded with courage, "I do not have the money." The gentleman spoke softly as though he knew and appreciated my circumstances and my honesty; "Give me a few hours and I will see what I can do."

The next morning, he called and told me they were going to foot the whole bill. In return they wanted some good publicity. This did not seem like too much to ask. I called the local news media, and they spread the word to the main newspapers. I invited reporters to the ranch for the opening of the school. The positive influence of Patti's article was still creating warm and fuzzy memories.

The article was printed, and a picture was taken with a couple of boys facing me, away from the camera. The headline read in big letters: "TEAMSTERS GIVE RANCH BIG GIFT." It wasn't until I read this article that I fully realized who had given this gift—one of the most powerful Teamsters Unions in the State of California—not one, but two Teamsters Unions. The article:

Cottonwood Boys Ranch in Oakdale received a very large Christmas gift from the California Teamsters Union Locals 857 and 748. The gift, now installed at the ranch, is a twelve by sixty foot mobile office, which will be used as an on-site school for the resident boys.

Ron Ashberry, Secretary-Treasurer Teamster Local 748 and a trustee of the Cannery Workers Medical Examination Trust Fund, said that the trailer had been used for a few years as one of three trailers utilized in providing cannery workers with health check-ups during the processing season.

Cottonwood Ranch, part of Constructive Youth Assessments, a non-profit corporation licensed as a group home facility, has reached the lives of many unfortunate youngsters. It has grown to include two other facilities located on the ranch, Pinewood and Cedarwood.

Conceived a little over six years ago by René Monroe, executive director of the facility, the youth center is designed to give long-term assistance and care for boys who are suffering from severe physical and psychological abuse.

The ranch provides a home, guidance, and security for the boys. It also gives them an opportunity to work with animals and work outdoors. But most importantly, it helps the boys regain their self-worth.

In addition to Monroe and Larry Appleby, administrator, there are at present eleven staff members including two psychologists and the vocational director. The facility contains three homes on 25 acres in rural Oakdale and has land leased for the cattle project. This ranch provides an outstanding ranch-type atmosphere in which sixteen children may develop. (This article was written before we expanded to include eighteen.)

According to Monroe, the new "school" building donated by the Teamsters Union, Local 857 and 748 will enable the ranch to work more closely with the children they serve.

This article sounded like a great article for the ranch. However, three days later, I received a call from my administrator, Larry Appleby. He was in a panic. It seemed there was a reporter, whom we refer to as a head-hunter, in his office, and she wanted to know all about me and my connection with the Teamsters Union.

He told her to call and make an appointment, but she refused to leave the ranch without seeing me. I laughed and told Larry to deliver this one to my house in person, and I most definitely would see her.

Before she rang the door bell, I was already past mad. To think this so-called pushy female reporter would have the nerve to come on my ranch and give orders. The whole thing just plain frosted me. I opened the door and immediately took charge of this space. "I understand you have demanded to see me. You are seeing me; now what do you want?"

She came right to the point: "How do you know the Teamsters, and who do you know in the Teamsters?"

"Neither of those questions are any of your business," I answered, "Next question."

She asked, "Do you mind if I come in?"

I replied through gritted teeth, "As a matter of fact, I do mind."

She asked, "Could I have a drink of water?" I knew she was stalling for time. I recognized this old trick, when I heard it.

"Yes," I answered, "We have water on the ranch—some of the finest. However, it is for our welcome guests, not for you. You are not welcome on this ranch."

This female reporter wore an ironclad expression that identified a head-hunter in the worst sense of the word. Before she turned to leave, she said, "You will be hearing from me again. I will be back!" She had that hard cast look from working in the profession she had chosen.

I think I said something to the effect: "Not in my lifetime." Neither of us handled the situation with poise. I sure could read her mind. This was not the way to handle reporters who wanted to write something negative about you. She definitely visualized my head on a platter in her mind's eye.

I immediately called the local sheriff and filed a restraining order on her. At least I would have the law on my side. Her visit initiated one of the hardest fought fights for the ranch and the lives of my boys.

Her first vindictive step started at licensing where all social service reports are open to the public. She researched the ranch, the boys, and me. I called the state licensing bureau and informed them company was coming in the form of a wily reporter. Licensing called a few days later to inform me that indeed the company had arrived in true form and definitely was making the attempt to find smut to smear my reputation. She went as far as to accuse Licensing of hiding records in regard to the teamster's connection, which licensing legally could not do. She wanted any illegal dirt she could find. She dug around for smut with all the locals, but found nothing as there was nothing to find.

I could handle her mudslinging gambits, but she drew a deep line in the dirt when she investigated my boys. For me to sit back and do nothing when my boys were involved simply was not going to continue.

The next day, I called a senator friend of mine and told him what was happening. Legally, she was within her rights to investigate anything and everything about the ranch or me. I resented her implications and the nasty aftertaste she left with her negative questions. Her questions implied some sort of guilt in the eyes of a few people, even if she provided not a shred of evidence. She had succeeded in forcing me to respond to ridiculous needling. The senator knew the editor and owner of the paper she worked for, so he made the call. The needling ceased.

This of course, was a different paper than the one that published the first article.

She finally wrote her article about the Teamsters giving the boys ranch a gift. The two little paragraphs were buried in the back of the newspaper; there was nothing negative. I called and left a thank-you message for her article on her answering machine.

There were other articles written, but they were written from a distance. One reporter asked me, "Don't you want the free publicity?" I said, "If publicity is what I wanted, I would have been a movie star." I never invited another reporter to the ranch.

~ Chapter 16 ~

THE THREE-MINUTE FIGHT

When boys first arrived at the ranch they operated mentally and physically with a built in survival mode from being on the street and/or from the many insecurities life had dealt them. I handled the mental part with counseling. Strictly enforced rules forbid negative physical activity such as fighting. However, they were in the age group when testosterone occasionally raised its ugly knuckles. I talked to state licensing about offering a boxing program. Licensing objected, saying that boxing could be seen as child abuse. Today there are group homes with boxing programs. So I tried to think of another way to solve the fighting problem.

Jacob and Joseph arrived at the ranch with multiple insecurities complicated by their small, undernourished bodies and by what many call "the little big-man syndrome." Joseph preceded Jacob at the ranch by about six months. Both boys touted sandy blond hair and blue eyes, similar enough to pass for brothers. Although Joseph was the taller of the two, both wished they were taller, bigger, and older, at least seventeen—right from the beginning both decided they hated each other.

Thus began a series of fights and arguments on a day-to-day basis. No amount of restrictions, group sessions, or counseling seemed to work. I had them on restriction so much that I felt guilty. Finally, I called a group session and warned all my boys the fighting would stop, or those involved would have to fight for three minutes.

Two days later, a fight ensued. The older boys had finished raking the shed row in the horse barn, a chore completed every afternoon usually after the five o'clock feeding of the horses.

When the boys finished their chores they came to the office and requested my inspection on behalf of their task. A counselor or I checked to see if they completed the job according to the ranch rules. I liked doing this little chore because it gave me a change of scenery. Anything to get me out of the office was, I thought, a good thing.

I sprinkled the shed row down to settle the dust and watched while the boys cleaned their saddles and gear. Normally I enjoyed the little pleasures of life that the ranch afforded me, except today. I sprinkled the inside and began sprinkling around the outside when the fight broke out between guess who, Jacob and Joseph, two boys supposedly blessed with biblical names. It had been such a nice day until now. How these two ended up with biblical names, I hadn't a clue.

I turned the water hose on the boys, which broke up the fight. Then I ordered them to fight for three minutes. This seems like a short period of time, but a three-minute round with angry fists evolved into an eternity.

Joe's wrestling lessons in school built his confidence and his ability, he made the first move, and down on the ground they went, rolling around like a couple of playful kids, except they weren't playing. After two minutes, they were tired and wanted to quit. I continued to sprinkle the ground around me and informed the two boys one minute remained to fight. I suspected they actually wanted to be friends, but pride was in the way. Pride or stubbornness blocked my good sense too. Although I felt indifference to their pleas, I knew a bad decision when I saw one. I also felt it in my stomach. At about two and a half minutes, Joseph's eye swelled up into a large, purplish knot while Jacob continued swinging. Then Joseph, the taller of the two, proceeded with a wrestling move and threw Jacob to the ground. While both boys wrestled, I inwardly cried, wondering if my tough love damaged us all. As Joseph threw Jacob over his shoulder to the ground, Jacob's head hit a two inch corral pipe and began to bleed. I called time. There is something I should say at this point—this was much harder on me than I figured. Not always do adults make the right decisions. If we were perfect, God would be bored.

Joseph ran past me, stopping momentarily to tell me—with tears in his eyes—how he hurt Jacob and he would never ever fight anyone again. He also told me I was the "f—— bitch of the county." Silently, I had to agree; I was not very proud of my decision at the moment.

Jacob ran around the barn, and I sprinted after him to see about the gash on his head. Although bleeding, the cut on the back of his head was smaller than I expected. With tears in his eyes, Jacob said, "I've hurt Joseph, and I'm never ever going to fight anyone again," and added as if he were quoting Joseph, "you f—— bitch."

Their previous fights had been mostly wrestling matches, and someone had been there to break it up before they had time to hurt each other. This time was different. I took both the boys to my office where I gave Jacob a wet washcloth for the back of his head and Joseph a piece of beefsteak for his black eye. I insisted they apologize to each other. They gave me dirty looks, which admittedly I deserved—much better for them to hate me than each other.

When my remorse had built up and finally peaked, I excused myself, went outside and threw up. "Thank you, God, for watching over us all." I guess this was some of that tough love I was supposed to handle.

Thus began a three-year-long close friendship, closer than any two brothers could be. The two actually ended up roommates. Needless to say, the problems with fighting on the ranch after this incident ceased, and thank goodness for that.

~ Chapter 17 ~

THE EDUCATIONAL FISHING TRIP

There is another story that involves Joseph and Jacob, and their favorite pastime—fishing. Their friendship encompassed a shared love for fishing and exploring in the High Country. Sometimes we took three or four boys on a privilege trip. The privilege trips were planned a month in advance, and boys earned the right to go on these trips. One particular mountain excursion included five saddle horses, five packhorses, three boys, Tom, and me.

The three boys were Jacob, Joseph, and Trevor. I still cannot fathom how Trevor earned the points to travel with us. All three of these boys had been up in the High Country before and were raring to go again. By this time Jacob and Joseph were superb trout fishermen, and then there was Trevor. I called him the mangler, underneath my breath, for he mangled every fishing rod, line, lure, hook, and nearby tree. I had watched him fish, doing most everything wrong and still managing to catch a trout once in a while. I really think the good Lord obviously felt sorry for him and put that darn trout on his hook. It sure had nothing to do with his fishing ability.

Jacob and Joseph

All of us wore Wranglers as we rode into the High Country. Once there, the boys could be one hundred percent boys and wear pretty much what they wanted, usually cut-offs and no shirt. The temperature dropped at night, and the Wranglers and heavy jackets were appreciated by all.

Joseph "dressed" in his personal clothing for the High Country; Tom's over shirt, Justin boots and spurs, and LOUD shorts

We traveled slow and easy for the horses' sake. We made camp and took the horses to the meadows where we hobbled and line tied them. The horses needed to acclimate themselves to the high altitude. It also gave us a short rest and gave the boys extra fishing time at Kibby. The boys loved this lake for its fantastic fishing and even better swimming. The lake below the timberline provided the warmest water in Yosemite National Park therefore—the water was not icy cold, just cold. It also allowed the boys special time with mom. We discussed their future goals in life and how to succeed in reaching those goals, and of course, how to better their fishing techniques.

There were two main camps at the lake. With our motley crew, we took the higher campsite next to the meadow, leaving the lower camp, next to the lake, for the weekend tourist.

As we walked down to the lake to gather water with the boys, I noticed two men camped at the lower-level campsite. Their brand new, expensive fishing gear leaned against the nearby trees. Later that evening, Tom, a personable western-type gentleman, invited the two men over for coffee. All their gear was brand-new, including their tents.

They were doctors, and brought with them some of the finest handmade fishing flies for trout fishing that any human could ever dream of owning. The boys asked to sit in on the adult gathering. The boys sat listening to every word. Their manners were pretty good by now, and they wanted to hear about the fishing gear. My suspicions were our visitors were brand-new to fishing and perhaps the mountains as well.

When the doctors left our camp, the boys began to ask questions. Their main question was "Can we still catch fish with our super-dupers?"

"Oh yes, boys," I said, "I'm guessing you are going to catch more fish than they do."

In the middle of the night we heard a raucous and sure enough the new comers to the mountains had a black bear in their camp. Tom and I hurried down to their campsite to find the bear in one tree and the two gentlemen up another tree. They had hung their meat up in a little tree, and the bear being a bear climbed up the tree and proceeded to play with the rope. We arrived just in time to stop one of the gentlemen from shooting his pistol at the bear. I had a pan in my hand and a big spoon which, when used properly, simply scared the poor bear away. We chased the bear out of their camp and helped straighten their campsite. I covered their food with a blue plastic tarp and sprayed it with an odor that bears hate. We had a short discussion about bringing a hand gun into the high country with everyone retreating off to bed for the night.

The next morning I told the boys not to bother the doctors when they went down to the lake to fish. The boys took their "fifty-cent super-dupers," silver metal fishing plugs, and sure enough before lunch came back with nine fish to their credit. The next day, the boys came back with another good catch of the day—if I remember right, they carried seven nice trout on their stringers.

Early that evening, the doctors paid us another visit. They didn't bring their fancy flies, nor did they have much to say about the fishing. Finally, I could not stand it any longer. I guess it just comes with the female territory to be curious. I asked, "Did you have any luck fishing?"

They grinned at each other and one of them said, "That's why we came to visit."

The doctors, in two days, came up empty handed with their expensive handmade flies. They wanted to know what kind of fishing flies the boys were using. I asked the doctors, "Did my boys disturb you?"

One of the gentlemen replied, "No, except to make sure we saw the rather big fish they were carrying." All Tom and I could do was smile at each other.

The doctors wanted to know what my boys were fishing with to catch so many fish. I hesitated for a moment before speaking, "The boys are the ones you should talk to as they caught the fish." With this statement I motioned for the boys to join us.

What a sight to see these very well-educated men talking to our young boys about fishing and getting pointers on the right and wrong way to fish. Joseph at twelve possessed a lot of common sense for his age. He provided most of the explanations and suggestions in between Trevor's interruptions. Trevor managed to catch one very small fish in the past two days. Joseph and Jacob caught the rest, yet there was Trevor, trying to cut in on the conversation.

Joseph spoke to them without being condescending, "The fish really don't know how much fishing flies cost. Mom taught us how to fish with the shiny little silver super-dupers. Fish feed on a variety of insects that hit the water and reflect from the morning or evening sun. The shiny super-dupers reflect just like the insects. One of your problems is you are fishing in the middle of the day." During this time of explanation Joseph's expression on his face was serious as though he were the adult.

The boys gave the doctors some of their plugs, and the doctors offered the boys some of their expensive flies. One of the doctors stopped on his way out of our camp and said, "I have been educated in some of the finest schools in the country, but tonight, I have been educated by some very young teachers with a lot of common sense." As the doctors were leaving one turned and looked at the boys and said, "I thank you."

The next morning as we rode by their camp, the doctors held up three good size trout. They again thanked the boys for their generosity. They remarked, "What great boys you and your husband are raising." You see I never, ever, when the boys were with me, introduced them in any way but "my boys." I thanked the gentlemen for the compliment, agreeing with them, and added, "Yes, they truly are good boys," and rode on up the mountain trail. I didn't have to look back over my shoulder to know the boys chests were sticking out more than usual.

~ Chapter 18 ~

THE LIVESTOCK PROGRAM

Oakdale, California, 2006

The clouds had come and gone and in my daydreaming underneath this friendly ol' tree, I must have dozed off. I was awakened by the sound of horses nickering in the old ranch corrals. I got up and walked over to the horses, which now occupied the ranch corrals where my horses once stood. They looked to be just saddle horses, maybe even pets of the people who now occupied the ranch.

We owned good using horses at the boys ranch; these good horses earned their keep by doing a lot of teaching in their own way. The pride of a rancher was measured by the quality of the using horse he or she owned. I still today like to set a little better looking horse than the average ranch would carry.

Early 80's

The livestock program, when first presented to the state of California, was only approved after much convincing on my part that it would work. The government's way of approving anything that works went something like this. "Yes, we will approve the livestock program; however if the state auditors disapprove, then you will have to repay the cost." In plain English, their approval meant that after six months when they came to audit our books, if the auditor had a bad day or did not like the idea, I was responsible for the purchasing and feeding of all the animals. I figured about fifty thousand dollars was the amount I could be stuck with personally.

Oh, well, I was known for my start-forward-full-speed-ahead female tenacity. I stuck out my hand to shake on the deal, smiled through gritted teeth and said, "Thank you gentlemen." The hand-shake surprised the state board; frankly they shook hands like wimps.

The ranch required a minimum of Twenty five hundred dollars per month per boy to accomplish everything outlined in the program, so the state promptly approved only two thousand dollars of my required rate. In their typical modus operandi, they approved this part of my program without fully funding it. I continued, "I will be back in six months with proof that the program works, and I expect you gentleman to complete the funding on my ranch program." Four months later, the program was working well and consequently attracted the support of another senator who loved the livestock program. It helps to know the right people. With the senator's support, I received a letter approving my program at the rate that I requested. Why in the world could they not do the complete funding in the first place! Bureaucracy—this wonderful country of ours is simply drowning in bureaucracy.

The bureaucrats and elected officials at the state and federal level who are writing these ridiculous rules and regulations should have to live in a facility with children before they write the rules. Officials make regulations based on budgets—not children's needs. They are not working for our children, who are the future of America. The current government's written programs are failures. They cost in the billions and accomplish nothing for the children.

Other programs such as boot camp programs are so restrictive and structured that even adults would have a hard time finishing the programs. A child must feel loved before he can learn, and just as importantly, a child must have fun. I visited facilities where children looked so sad because they had NO fun and NO opportunities to be children, but these government-funded failures paid homage to government's false deity. Hello America, our children are the future; the government should be serving our lost children, the street children.

Livestock, such as horses, dogs, cats, and practically every other animal, are a form of therapy that is sometimes overlooked by other institutions, mainly because the institutions are just that—institutions. The ranch settings provide therapeutic solutions for our troubled youth today.

Working ranches with cattle, horses, and other livestock do work to help these children overcome their challenges. Yet on the other side of the fence, the problem I've found through the years is that people use the term "boys ranch" very loosely to get a higher rate per child from the state. I have visited so-called boys ranches in different states that are not ranches but a bunch of houses on a few acres of land, with no pets or animals of any kind. My ranches were all working ranches that included cattle, horses, a rodeo program and vocational training for their future.

My ranch program was a structured program but allowed the boys time to grow, and the program nourished their growth and their ideas. I accepted and succeeded with some of the toughest boys in the country from varied backgrounds, and I didn't use boot-camp tactics on my children. The livestock program was not only therapy for the boys, but it was a teaching tool that built self-esteem and taught them financial responsibility. When a boy arrived at the ranch, I assigned him certain activities and chores along with a horse to take care of, but he could not ride until he was on Level Two. Occasionally, I deviated from the rule. If we had a boy who was pretty stubborn, we would go together to the sale and let him pick a "colt" to break himself. It was a contest to watch a boy who thought he knew it all, break the colt that thought he knew it all. Finally, after so many bumps and bruises, the boy would get a cowboy to help him, but only after the boy had learned the lesson.

The boys who were on Level One worked without pay and watched the other boys ride horses, rope, and participate in the pay job program. I made Level One the most miserable place to be. A boy on Level One had to clean his horse's stall and watch while a boy on Level Two was paid for doing the same thing. It was a psychological incentive to progress.

When a boy worked hard enough and made good grades in school, he had the opportunity to buy his own livestock and pay for it out of what we referred to as "pay jobs." There is nothing that gets a boys attention like money. Once on Level Three, he could earn twice the amount as on Level Two and buy things such as cows and calves. They had to keep a record of everything, including the feed bill. A note was drawn between the ranch and the boy.

The boy went to the sale and purchased his cows. He could only buy four on Level Three. In the spring of the following year when the calves were yearlings, they were cut from the herd and sold. The boy put fifty percent of what the sale brought against his note with the ranch, and the rest went into his checking and savings accounts. And yes, even my behavioral-problem kids had checking accounts.

When I first started the banking part of the program with kids who had failed sixteen placements or more, they had everything from forgery to theft in their backgrounds. Everybody, and I do mean everybody, became upset. Allowing juveniles to manage their own bank accounts had never been done before.

Probation officers called on the phone and told me I had lost my mind. The state licensing department threatened me within an inch of my life. The probation officers let me know they would not be responsible for any action regarding this matter. State licensing told me I could lose my license if something went wrong. Oh well, what did they know? They really didn't know who my silent partner was, so I continued to teach my boys banking and finances. And what do you know? It not only worked, but the boys learned how to balance their check books, make their own deposits and keep good records. These financial transactions taught loyalty and trust in its highest form. Either a boy readjusted to this concept, or he did not belong on the ranch. It took a little longer with some than others, but all the boys soon learned that developing loyalty and trust were mandatory.

Regardless of the number of livestock purchased, the ranch was willing to pay the feed bill; if the boy kept his feeding records properly, the ranch then reimbursed him for the feed. If proper records were not kept, the boy paid for the feed out of his own money. Boys who could not add two and two became experts at figuring the feed bill, so they would not have to pay for their own feed. They say children with psychological problems are not as intelligent as the "normal" child. Put this over-labeled psychological problem child in a situation where the child must think or lose his money, and what do you know? He becomes a very normal child.

The boys on Level Four could buy two or three horses to break and sell at the ranch-horse sale in the spring. They had to be very good hands. Usually, this did not happen with all the boys, as most were not good enough until they reached the age of sixteen to seventeen.

By the time the boy was on Level Three, he could balance a checking account. He had enough experience at the ranch to be making up to three hundred and fifty dollars per month with the pay jobs, and he was doing most of his own clothes shopping, with my supervision, of course.

Another important rule was good manners, which were introduced from day one. It took them very little time to figure out the good manner code. The smart boys, and even the little ones, knew the more positive points they receive the more positive things they could do.

You would think that everyone appreciated good manners, but I remember one afternoon, one of my boys came through the door and asked for a private session. He had gotten into trouble with one of the teachers for calling her "ma'am."

I asked, "What kind of trouble?"

The boy answered this teacher with the response I taught him (that is, saying "yes, ma'am," when she spoke to him), but filled with false humility, she insisted that he not call her 'ma`am" again. Naturally the boy became confused.

The very next morning, I entered her classroom before class started and proceeded to educate her on life itself. "I understand you scolded one of my boys yesterday because he called you 'ma'am.'"

She looked at me condescendingly, kind of smiled and said, "Well, yes."

For the next ten minutes, she heard about the real world we live in, or rather, that my boys live in. "Ma'am, my boys are being taught how to survive, and that includes good manners. Do you have children of your own?"

"Why, yes," she said.

"Do you plan on your children going to college when they graduate from high school?" I asked.

"Why, yes," she replied, "my husband and I have a college fund for our children."

"Well, ma'am, my kids, most of whom do not know who their parents are, don't have a college fund waiting for them. What they do have is me, and I am here to see that they make it when they leave the ranch. They will not have the same opportunities that your darlings will have. It's a very good chance they will never go to college. But they will have the tools to make a good life for themselves and make it honestly. One of the tools that they will have is good manners."

"You see, ma'am," I continued, "When my boys go for an interview, they will be up against your educated children. My boys know that over half of the employers interviewing them will be between the ages of forty-five to fifty-five. These professionals will appreciate the fact my boys have manners and yours do not, even though yours may have a college education. My money will be on my boys getting the job."

"Another thing, ma'am," taking a quick breath I continued, "My boy in your class deserves an apology for you're over zealousness. And if, in fact, you do not apologize to my boy, you will apologize in front of the school board. Am I totally clear on this subject?"

Other teachers had challenged me before and lost each time. I guess you could say I had somewhat of a reputation for protecting my boys. Don't get me wrong; most teachers understood my program; and I backed them if they were right and my boys were wrong. I admire what they stand for and totally respect what they do. But they do not always see the true picture and the ultimate goal that the program strives to achieve.

That afternoon, my boy came home with the biggest smile on his face and told me how the teacher had apologized and said he had the best manners in the classroom. We did the hug thing, which always followed with the little ones, and he was off to do his list of chores for the rest of the day.

I can only think of one time the animal program ran into a little trouble. One of my ten-year-olds whom we shall call Sam liked animals, but he had been badly mistreated by the adults in his life and had many problems. He had been abandoned as a young child of four and placed in some bad foster homes, including not one but two different foster homes found guilty of molestation. Can you imagine the extent of mistrust he felt for adults? Children who have been molested have a tendency to molest, so they must be constantly watched.

When Sam finally got to Level Two, he could ask for an animal of his choosing. He asked for a goat. I couldn't see anything wrong with his choice and gave him permission to purchase a goat of his choice at the next sale. He played with the dogs and cats well and was excited about getting the goat. I was still rather naïve about certain things and totally missed this one.

The day of the goat sale arrived. Sam and I along with some of the other boys were off to the livestock sale. Before the sale we went out back and looked at the livestock. I watched Sam going through the goats and looking at each one very carefully. I thought how wonderful it was to see this child so involved with the purchase of his baby goat.

Finally, it was time for the sale. Sam was so excited. I asked, "Have you found that special one?" He replied, "I have and she is so beautiful." We sat for what seemed like an eternity before that special little goat came through the sale ring. We could not leave until Sam's goat came through the ring. I remember thinking to myself, *I should have used the bathroom earlier*, but I still could not leave until this darn goat was purchased. Finally, there was Sam's goat.

Sam said with excitement in his voice, "there she is mom." She was a yearling female, and she was so cute. What surprised me was the goat Sam had picked was a half-grown goat, rather than a baby goat. Oh well, after all, it was his choice.

When I told him to raise his hand, he did, and he did, and he did. Then the auctioneer said, "Sold to that young man in the corner." Sam had his goat, and I ran to the bathroom arriving just in the nick of time. We took Sam's goat home, and the goat seemed to do wonders for Sam's personality.

I remember Tom coming into my office before the goat was purchased and asking me if I thought this was a good idea. I had been busy doing something and did not pick up on his true meaning. I just said, "Yes, I think it's a very good idea," and continued working on my paperwork.

Sam called her Katie. Katie and Sam were together every time we turned around. He constantly brushed her and led her all around the ranch.

Meanwhile, I'm thinking what wonderful therapy Katie is for this little boy. And in most ways, it was. However, I had forgotten a very important factor. With molestation in his background, I should have been more aware.

A few weeks went by, and everything seemed to be going okay with Sam and the goat. The only problem was, Sam seemed awfully tired. I asked Tom to watch and see what was going on that was making Sam so tired.

Well, Sam was getting up in the middle of the night to play with his female goat, that is, play with her behind, for he was trying very hard to have sex with Katie. She did not like the idea and refused to stand still. Thank goodness for that! The mystery of Sam's exhaustion was solved. Needless to say, Sam was brought into the office, and we had a very long talk about his goat, and the do's and the don'ts with a goat.

Katie was sold and we never purchased goats at the ranch again. We leased them once in a while for the goat tying events with a nearby neighbor bringing them to the ranch and leaving with them the same day. Sam, by the way, handled it pretty well. We replaced the goat with a horse, a very big grown-up horse, and a gelding to boot. Things got back to normal. That is, our kind of Normal!

All the boys at the ranch had to abide by all the ranch rules before they could take advantage of the privileges. The rules stated they must have good grades in school. Most who came to the ranch were not straight A students but rather straight F students. I remember the first time one of the new boys came to the ranch and started the program with a D. I think I bragged on that kid for a week. Eventually, all the boys made good grades, not great grades, just good grades.

I found the animal-incentive programs worked wonders for changing negative attitudes into positive attitudes with my boys. If I ever do another ranch program, it will definitely have an animal-incentive program with one exception—NO goats.

~ Chapter 19 ~

THE BASEBALL GAMES

Oakdale, California 2006

The children of the old ranch house handed me a glass of ice water to drink. They were carrying a baseball and catcher's mitt. The boys headed out to the old baseball field, and I followed along at a safe distance just to watch. Baseball was one of my favorite sports and one I thoroughly enjoyed with my boys. I watched as the three boys played catch with the imagination of innocence: The boys played as though the weeds were not there.

I am still fascinated by the way a child can have fun and not allow a lot of things to interfere. Before adults can go out and play baseball, we have to elect a committee of some sort, have a fund-raiser to redo the field and buy uniforms. Yet children—they just play ball. Could there not be a lesson in this? As I watched the boys playing, I could almost hear my boys shouting, as we played, "No batter! Slide, Mom, slide!"

In the late spring, the boy's ranch hummed like a bee hive with anticipation for the summer. The horses were shedding their heavy winter coats. The boys brushed and exercised them for the many rodeos and high country mountain trips we planned in the late spring and summer.

The boys had no time for school sports, so I decided we needed a sport at the ranch, something other than the regular physical work and rodeo activities. I settled on baseball because it would not interfere with our other activities. During group session that week, I suggested we vote on whether baseball would be a good idea. One of the boys answered, "But we don't have a baseball diamond."

I replied, "That presents a little bit of a problem. What if we build one next week?"

I liked to play baseball and actually played in a women's league. The boys attended some of my games. I always felt so loved as I crossed home plate. The boys yelled at the top of their lungs, "Slide, Mom, slide" or "Hit it out of the park, Mom." When the women's league played hometown games, everybody knew the situation with my boys at the home games, but out of town games, with all different nationalities created a different environment.

I decided not to wait until the next week. The next day, I began building a baseball diamond, right out in the middle of the pasture. The cowboys came unraveled. Even Tom, who rarely voiced his opinion said, "You are going to ruin the pasture." He knew when I decide to do something, nothing stood in my way. Tom figured he was wasting valuable nap time arguing with me.

I took the tractor and disk and began tearing up the pasture. By nightfall—in the dark—the field looked pretty good. At the morning's light, it didn't look quite that good. I needed a quick plan of action. I needed Tom's help. Unfortunately, his irritation at my destroying good pastureland needed some serious soothing. Sacrifices on my side of the fence were needed. I hate breakfast! What is it with men; they all seem to like breakfast. So, I invited Tom to breakfast at his favorite restaurant. Over eggs and a rasher of bacon, the two of us talked about everything except the baseball diamond. Eventually, Tom asked, "How are you doing on the baseball diamond?"

I thought to myself, "*Oh, Tom, if you only knew how you are literally being set up.*" I hoped the good Lord wouldn't judge me too harshly for playing the devious female. I replied, "Well, it's a lot harder than I thought. I sure could use your help. It needs a man's expertise." Most men and women like to hear you need them to help you. The more helpless you sound, the more help you get.

"Have you staked out the corners?" he asked.

I remarked, "I hadn't thought of that!"

I actually had, but this ego thing men have was sure working in my favor.

Tom sighed as if I could read his mind, he was thinking, *I have been had.* But she does need my help, "If you stake it out, some of the hands and I will help build the baseball field." I excused myself near the end of our meal and made a quick call to Helen at the ranch. I needed her to pull up all the corner stakes before we made it back home.

In about three days, the boys and I played our first game on a great baseball diamond. Thus began some really fun times. During our games, I always played on the side of the little ones, and we played against the older boys. To make the games more interesting, we usually played for a trip to town for pizza. The losers bought the pizza.

Unfortunately, right in the middle of an epic ballgame, the staff usually interrupted our game with something that the counselors could easily handle. These interruptions continued until in frustration, I sat down and wrote one of my fiery memorandums. I passed it out to everyone on the ranch. It stated simply, "The next counselor or staff member who interrupts a baseball game in play will be FIRED!" That brief memo turned out to be one of my better ideas. For the next three weeks, the boys and I enjoyed playing our baseball games without interruption.

One afternoon, some very special visitors came to the ranch. A state representative and a state assemblyman decided to stop by and visit. I met these fine gentlemen on one of my many trips to the state capitol and left a standing invitation to visit the ranch.

Politicians were always good for the ranch, and the boy's ranch was always good for the politicians, especially around election time. I told them if they wanted to see a real boy's ranch, they needed to visit mine. But after meeting the politicians, I promptly forgot what they looked like.

A staff person met the two gentlemen at the door, invited them in, and gave them something cool to drink. They remarked to my staff person they had an open invitation and asked to see the director. The counselor hesitated for a moment and then replied, "She is busy at the moment and cannot be disturbed."

The gentlemen said they understood—they had no appointment and realized they probably caught me in a meeting.

"Oh, she's not in a meeting; however, I see no harm in showing you where she is. But you cannot interrupt the game until the game is over. If you interfere with the game, it will mean my job."

The two gentlemen followed my counselor out through the back door, down by the barn, and out to the middle of the pasture, where we were engaged in the top of the ninth inning in a crucial tie.

At the state capitol, I always dressed in a suit, perfectly groomed. I always topped off the ensemble with a hat, my personal trade mark. The men failed to recognize me in my T-shirt, jeans, tennis shoes, and baseball cap. Neither did I recognize them. In fact, I was so busy at my shortstop position yelling, "No batter; no hitter!" that at first I didn't notice them. When at last I saw them out of the corner of my eye, I continued playing because they looked like state licensing evaluators. They could just wait until the game was over.

The state representative asked, "Which one is she?"

The counselor said, "Oh, she's the shortstop that has her cap turned around backward and is yelling, 'no batter' at the top of her lungs." He reminded them again as a word of caution, "This is a time we are not allowed to disturb her and the boys, and they are playing for who has to buy the pizza."

The counselor offered chairs to the gentlemen, and when the inning was over, I managed a wave. One of the boys asked who they were, and I said, "They look familiar, but they can wait, because this game is just too important."

The gentlemen said, "We would like to stay and watch the game." And stay they did. In the bottom of the ninth inning, with two of my young ones on first and on second, I was up to bat and managed to hit a home run. As I was headed toward home plate, I simply forgot we had company watching and slid into home plate, face down hands stretched out reaching for home plate. In the process, Tony, who was catching when the ball was thrown a little high, jumped up to catch the ball and accidentally came down on my hand. I yelled as the dirt exploded into a foggy cloud around me and then settled.

This injury caused a bit of a disturbance, and before I knew it, my younger boys were yelling obscenities at Tony and threatening to tear him a new "you know what." Tony felt pretty safe through all of the commotion, since he was sixteen years old and a tall five nine. The much younger boys, some hardly reached his waist, weren't big enough to hurt him. I asked the umpire if I was safe, and he said, "Yes."

I was covered in dust and dirt along with a little horse manure from one end to the other, and my hand was hurting. We won the game, and the older boys had to cough up their money for my young ones and pay for the pizza.

The state representatives laughed at the contrast when I walked up. There they stood in dress suits, ties and what once had been polished dress shoes, while I stood there drenched in sweat with my face, hair, and clothing covered in dirt, and my poor hand dripping blood. One of the gentlemen said, "We thoroughly enjoyed watching this baseball game." They introduced themselves, and I swallowed hard and welcomed them to the ranch.

We visited a little as I showed them around. Every once in a while, I thought I saw them grinning about something. I have always said if someone sees you without makeup, running in and putting the darn stuff on after the fact, never made any sense to me. We went into my office and talked about various problems the other children's facilities were having with state licensing. The state licensing office regularly sent out clueless, uninformed people. True, they had passed the test for their position, but failed on a continuing basis to understand fully what directors in the field had to do to accomplish their tasks. I was heading up a committee to take our grievances to the state capitol. I then asked the politicians for their support in the matter.

They said, with big smiles on their faces, "Anyone who is this good of a baseball player and this involved with the boys, you can count on our support."

During my conversation with the politicians, my little ones were playing doctor. They followed us into the office with a pan of warm water and Epsom salts. Just as these gentlemen and I were in the middle of our conversation, the boys took my hand out of the warm water and dabbed it dry. I focused on the two visitors, and hardly heard David whisper, "Mom, this is going to hurt a lot, but we need to 'disinflash' your hand," as he poured alcohol over the bleeding scratches on the back of my hand; I screamed, the boys jumped, and of course, they spilled the alcohol all over the office floor. As I was trying to recover my composure, the boys wrapped my hand with a bandage.

How could I stop my little ones from doing something that made them feel needed? I couldn't! My poor hand looked like it had enough bandages to wrap my entire arm.

Meanwhile, word spread like wild fire over the ranch that I was hurt, and some of the other boys started busting through the door: "Mom, what happened?" and "Who did it?"

I continued our conversation, as if these interruptions were the norm. Mass confusion happened at the ranch at least once or twice a day, and in a way that was normal for the ranch.

After the gentleman left, I went into the bathroom to wash up. What a mess I was; my hair, full of dirt, was braided into two pigtails. The front of my shirt had changed colors, from bright white when I started playing to drab brown. Dirt powdered my forehead and cheeks. I looked like the tomboy from h——. I thought I even heard the good Lord laughing.

The next week, at the state capitol, while I was running around with my committee, we ran right into the same state representative. He was with a pretty powerful senator, and as he introduced me, he smiled and said to the senator, "If you ever want to see a good baseball game, you should visit René's boys ranch."

We were invited to play a baseball game with another boys ranch that summer, and so we had to come up with some kind of name. The boys suggested Cottonwood Lions, and I answered Cottonwood Kittens. We laughed, and the boys went out and tried again. Finally, the day arrived, and we still didn't have a name. On our way to their ranch, we came up with Cottonwood Boys Ranch. Was that original or what?

Keep in mind, my boys worked more with horses than most boys ranches and the ranch we were going to play, we were to find out, was serious about their baseball. They did not have horses or livestock, so they played lots of baseball.

It was a disaster. They beat us something like twenty-three to two. When the game ended, I yelled something to the effect, "Come on, girls, let's go back to the ranch."

On the way home, one of the boys asked "Are we still looking for a name?"

I said, "No, not unless it is the Cottonwood Hussies."

After that experience, we decided to play baseball only on the ranch and avoid further embarrassment.

~ Chapter 20 ~

THE WEDDING

Sometimes we look at things around us, but look past what we are supposed to see. Then something happens in our lives to turn things around, and suddenly for the first time in our lives, we really start seeing things—the color of the birds, not just the bird; the elderly couple walking in the park holding hands; we see the happiness in their eyes that tell us they are still in love. We notice the wrinkles for the first time, instead of just the faces, and feel an admiration for this couple who has shared many years together.

Romance, oh yes, we did have romance at the ranch. We even had a wedding of sorts. And now, sitting under the old walnut tree, I can still see the minister up there in this old walnut tree hanging on for dear life.

My life at the ranch was anything but normal. For instance, I never wore shorts or low cut blouses or jewelry in front of my boys. I stressed over and over high-moral standards and felt a strong sense of responsibility to set the example for the ranch. Most of these children had no one that was stable in their lives. I tried very hard to give the boys someone they could look up to and trust.

Before Tom and I committed to each other, we were just co-workers, and the boys accepted our working relationship; however, on the ranch, everything moved along at a pretty good pace, including our relationship. The attraction between us continued to grow until finally he moved from the bunkhouse to my house on the hill. We never foresaw any problems with the move because the boys saw us dating for two years. They considered Tom somewhat of a father figure.

Tom and I went to the attorney's office and signed a prenuptial agreement, and that was good enough for me. I did not use his name, and did not want the wedding ceremony. Tom, on the other hand, thought we needed to do the "whole nine yards," even if we were not going to finalize it. I felt a legal marriage would interfere with my devotion to the boys. I wanted to be sure the ranch and the boys would not be in jeopardy if our relationship did not work out. The older boys handled our living together pretty well, but the little ones did not. California law, under the community property law, as long as you break the continued chain of consistently living together. You keep the marriage from being legal. So every year to be on the safe side and to protect my boys, I paid for Tom's Rodeo performance tour. He had to be gone for 30 days. This worked for me and he was simply delighted.

One afternoon I heard two of my younger nine and ten-year olds arguing outside my window. I was knee-deep working on one of the many individual reports required by the state. As the boys arguing intensified, I called one of my counselors to check on the ruckus outside my office window.

The boys were arguing over whether I was doing something. David said, "Mom would never ever do something like that."

The other one argued, "She does so do it; I heard the older boys talking about it."

"Does not," David said.

Sam, equally convinced, replied, "Does too, does too!" By the time the counselor arrived on the scene the boys were exchanging punches and the language was flying. The counselor brought them to my office, and sure enough, their argument concerned my virtue.

The boys had been arguing over whether Tom and I were "doing it" (meaning sex). David, the white knight in defence of my honor, already sported a swollen red eye. He glared at me as he asked, "You're not doing it, Mom, are you?"

I answered his question with a question. "Do you think your parents ever had sex?"

David answered, "No, they never ever did anything like that!"

"Well, son," I said, "according to your records, you have three brothers and two sisters. That means your parents had sex at least six times."

"Tom and I have a contract agreement," I continued, "which means, we share a bed together, and yes, we now have a loving and caring sexual relationship. We live together as husband and wife just as your parents did." But for your protection we are not legally married.

"My mom and dad didn't do that stuff," little David insisted, 'cause I asked them, and they said they didn't."

This conversation turned somewhat awkward corners, not at all as I planned, so I scheduled an open group session for that evening. Before the meeting I analyzed the situation. I knew a full-blown question-and-answer session would swing into action.

My summary of the discussion was that, (1) I did not get married to Tom in a regular ceremony and we could not ever have a legal marriage; (2) yet I told my boys sex before marriage was wrong; (3) and most importantly the bottom line, which was a legal marriage to Tom might end in a divorce. At which time he, Tom, could claim half of our possessions even with the prenuptial. I would then be forced to sell the boys ranch, thus putting all my children in harm's way.

My younger ones immediately began bombarding me with questions. This was an "open" session, which meant any question could be asked. Willie, a ten-year-old, with drug addicts for parents saw them do "everything" with everybody in front of the children. His raised brows revealed his concern when he asked, "Do you and Tom do everything?"

"Everything" to this little boy included a pretty big range, so I knew I needed to provide specifics. "Willie," I said, "Tom and I only make love to each other. It's a feeling of caring, touching, and sometimes lovemaking. To show feelings for someone in a caring way comes from the heart, and giving of oneself is part of that caring. The sex is a small part of marriage."

This group session lasted about an hour, but it seemed more like three hours to me. David spoke up; "Then, Mom, you are 'doing it' with Tom?" By this time David's eye was black from defending my honor earlier in the day

Sensing his hurt that I had betrayed him, I asked David, "What do I have to do for your approval to 'do it' with Tom?"

David never hesitated, "You have to have a real wedding, and we know you didn't 'cause you didn't invite us; and we're your kids!"

This whole thing was getting more and more out of hand. Tom wanted some kind of wedding ceremony, and I did not see how I could possibly fit it into my busy schedule, and there was the legal side of the marriage, putting the boys at risk. Tom leaned against the wall at the back of the room with a grin on his face a mile wide, wondering how I planned to get out of this one.

"Okay, boys," I said. "What if Tom and I have a 'real wedding' right here on the ranch, and what if we invited all of you boys to the wedding?"

By this time, they were all talking at once. Willie and David came around the desk and began hugging me. Willie wanted to know, "Are you and Tom going to have any more kids like us."

I replied, "No, we don't need any more children—we already have all eighteen of you!"

Tom finally quit grinning long enough to ask when the date would be so he could go tell the cowboys to shine their boots. Oh how he was enjoying every minute watching me squirm. The meeting was over and as Tom headed toward the office door, I said very loudly, "Tom and I will not sleep together again until we have the official wedding." This meant Tom would be moving back to the bunkhouse. The big grin left his face and the door slammed rather loudly as he left the room.

What had I just done? This group session had not gone as I intended. Oh well, it was going to be interesting to try and fit this darn wedding into my schedule.

Two days later, my little three musketeers Willie, David, and Conway entered my office and sat down in front of me. David wasted no time in getting right to the subject matter.

"Mom, what's so great about sex? Is it bad or is it good?" It seems the older boys' main source of chatter the last two days revolved around sex, and the little ones wanted to know the real truth. David continued, "Mom we know you're busy, so could you keep it simple."

I looked upon the wall at my degrees and could not remember anything that would answer this nine-year old's question in an educational sense. So I followed David's request and kept it simple.

"David, sex is better than going to the doctor or dentist, but not as great as Christmas!"

They all sat there with their elbows on my desk looking at me. Finally, David said, "Thanks Mom, for keeping it simple," and left just as abruptly as he, Willie, and Conway, had entered. They seemed totally satisfied with the answer I gave them.

The next couple of weeks turned into a living nightmare. The boys were all excited about the wedding. I, on the other hand, created a list of a million things to accomplish. First, each boy needed to be properly fitted for a tuxedo, and my motherly intuition demanded that I remind them all of the teachings on the ranch program regarding respectable etiquette. The clerk at the tuxedo-rental store commented on their manners and politeness. My teaching techniques succeeded until the boys tried on the funny black shoes and weird baggy pants. They all informed the tailor that their dress boots were polished and ready for Mom's wedding and that they did not intend to wear "those funny-looking shoes." Toni, one of the older boys spoke up saying, "Tom said we could wear our Wranglers to the wedding, especially since we were all going to be horse-back."

That's the first I had heard there were going to be horses at the wedding.

If this scene wasn't confusing enough, with eighteen boys of all nationalities and ages, the clerks could not help themselves but ask that darn question: "You are just now getting married? Are these children his and some are yours, maybe?"

I simply said, "No, they are all mine. I have just been rather worldly and too busy having children to marry."

The date was set, and the ranch was abuzz with wedding plans. Tom and I set the date. I ordered the flowers and the ranch was decorated. We kept the guest list private, just the ranch hands, house parents, and the boys. Since Tom's plans included horses, naturally we arranged for the wedding to take place in the roping arena, where else! The local minister required some heavy persuasion when he heard about horses in the wedding ceremony. Regardless of the problems this so called wedding was creating, I kept reminding myself of the main reason. After all, it was just a wedding for the boys.

Two days prior to the wedding, we decided to rehearse the ceremony. All the boys decided that David should be the one to walk or should I say, ride with me down the aisle. David enjoyed the idea until he heard the words "give her away." He rejected the idea of giving his mom to anyone, even Tom, so he threw a royal fit. Tom, wounded and frustrated, demanded, "Is a nine year-old going to control the whole wedding?" Then he literally stomped off like one of the little boys. Personally when someone would ask me how many children I had at the ranch, I would always include him by answering NINETEEN, instead of the eighteen.

The boys wore their western hats, their cowboy boots, and yes, they wore their Wranglers. I picked out a wedding dress but wore my Wranglers underneath with my cowboy boots. I was not about to set my horse without boots. I surely was not going to ride side saddle either.

I sat David down, who by this time was red faced from all his crying, and gave him a big hug and the two of us had a long talk. I explained he was not losing a mother, but gaining a father. "David," I said, "you will always have me as your mom until the state says different." I knew in my heart he really liked Tom, but his little face showed a lot of confusion. I asked him, "Why don't you want to give me away to Tom? Tom will take very good care of me."

It never dawned on me that little David watched his father and again his stepfather beat his mother. A third relationship fared no better. The physical abuse led to an emotional and mental breakdown. Distraught and overcome with mental illness, one day, she drove little eight-year-old David downtown in the city and dropped him off. One mother abandoned him; he feared losing another—me. David and I talked for a long time and then finally agreed to the wedding ceremony. He walked off into the night toward the ranch house.

Meanwhile, Tom, apologetic for getting upset, said he really understood and we said our good nights. I went home, and Tom reluctantly retired to the bunkhouse. He was having a hard time with this situation, but my boys always had to come first, plus I felt a responsibility to David's sense of virtue when he wanted to protect me so desperately.

Two days later, we had an outdoor wedding. The boys, mounted horseback, faced their horses toward each other, creating an aisle for David to lead me down. He rode his pint-sized seven-hundred-pound horse, and I sat astride my big roan, my roping horse—Gentle Ben, who weighed almost fifteen hundred pounds. We were kind of a mutt and Jeff look alike. Since David could not offer me his arm, we each held onto one end of a blue ribbon. Tom, with a silly cowboy grin on his face, watched the procession from his horse. When David handed his end of the ribbon over to Tom, he asked with a serious expression on his face, "Are you really going to take good care of Mom? 'Cause if you aren't I am not going to give her away." He was so serious that it was hard not to laugh.

Tom replied, "I will take very good care of your mom."

It was quite a wedding ceremony! Before the minister finished with all the pretty words, a wind came up and blew my white veil off my head and tossed it in the air. It finally landed on the head of a colt one of the boys was riding. The colt began to buck and spooked two more horses, and the "wedding rodeo" was on.

As the colt began to buck, I turned my horse around, wedding dress and all, going off into a gallop and started giving out orders. "Get his head up," I yelled. Meanwhile, two of the ranch hands rode along side and tried to pull the colt's head up to keep him from bucking. Two more three-year-old colts spooked and were running around the arena.

I chased them, my wedding dress billowing behind me like the sails flapping on a sailboat in a windstorm. The skirt of my wedding dress somehow caught on the arena fence, which ripped a rather unsightly streamer in my lovely dress. The streamer hung almost to the ground. By this time, G.B. became incensed with the situation. He flared his nostrils and pinned back his ears in protest, crow hopping a little. Even a gentle horse would have spooked at a white sail whipping around his feet. While I kept his head up, saying sweet words to keep G.B.'s mind in a good nature, one of the cowboys dismounted and cut off the dragging skirt of the weddings dress. G.B. settled down, and I grieved for just a moment, for I knew this wedding dress was not salvageable for future foster daughters. Tom yelled at the top of his voice, "René, get back over here and let the ranch hands handle this."

About this time, John, the boy riding the colt, bucked off his horse and hit the ground. The ranch hands finally caught the horse, and everything began to calm down.

We looked around for the kind minister; until that moment, we were unaware he was afraid of horses. When all the commotion started, he climbed onto the arena fence and into the big walnut tree next to the arena to avoid being trampled. It took an awful lot of conversation to convince him to come down out of that darn tree and finish the ceremony. The minister concluded the ceremony by saying, "You may kiss the bride." By this time, we were off our horses and standing beside each other. Tom, in a quiet voice, whispered, "Gotcha!" even if it's not legal. He kissed me with such love and tenderness that I wondered why I waited so long to bring him closer to me.

My little ones were happy, especially David. I stood with Tom as the ranch hands and the boys filed past offering their congratulations. When little David came by, I knelt down and gave him a big hug. He whispered in my ear, "Don't worry, Mom, I called a meeting like you do, and me and Willie and some of the other boys are going to watch and make sure Tom is good to you, cause if he's not I'm tak'n you back!"

The marriage was never recorded, but as far as my little ones were concerned, it was now legal; and they had a dad as well as a mom. And most importantly, they had saved Mom's honor.

It might be noted the only casualties were one torn wedding dress and a very frightened minister who, to my knowledge, never performed another horseback wedding. John, the boy who was bucked off, was not hurt except for his dignity. The boys teased John for a week or so. Soon the ranch was back to normal with my little ones happy again; they had saved mom's reputation, and to them it was official.

~ Chapter 21 ~

SMOKING OF THE WEED

I walked back to the house and thanked the lady for the ice water and hospitality. As I was leaving, she said, "We all have a special place in our hearts. You are more than welcome to come and visit the ranch again."

"Yes, I would like to visit the ranch one more time before I leave town, if I am not imposing." As I was leaving I replied, "Thank you for the invitation."

I really wanted to see some of the people who had made this Journey of mine just a little bit easier. I drove back into town and passed the police station. The police chief of Oakdale had been a good and loyal friend, and I wondered if he was still around. Not to my surprise, the man I knew retired. I drove out to his ranch, and we sat on the porch having a good old-fashioned conversation. The retired gentleman asked me, "How in the world did you keep those boys off of drugs? None of them were ever arrested for drugs, and for that matter, I never had any problem with them speeding. Why, I can't remember ever giving your boys a ticket."

I developed an easy solution to the problem of speeding tickets. I paid for the boys insurance until they received their first ticket. The boys could not drive if they could not afford insurance. The cost of a vehicle and its insurance for a sixteen-year old is almost insurmountable without parental assistance. Every month, when I wrote the check for the insurance, I brought each boy into my office, showed him the bill, and asked him, "When do you plan on getting your first ticket because I am getting tired of paying your insurance." The boys examination of the monthly bill became a regular, reminding the boy that driving a vehicle and the cost of that privilege was a big responsibility.

Like the speeding ticket dilemma, the good Lord constantly sent me ways to solve other problems, some of which turned out to be quite enjoyable.

One of the many things that caused me to wonder about the sanity, or rather insanity, of young people is how in the world, when they only have one body, do they justify destroying themselves with drugs?

Some of the boys who came to the ranch had experienced drugs. I asked them how they got started. Surprise, surprise, their parents were the main source for their drugs. Let us understand my boys had the worst of the lot for parents. This is not true of all parents, of course. Most concerned parents want the very best for their children.

In the many trips to the High Country, there were some I remember more than others. At the ranch, we developed many rules to avoid problems. One of the main rules concerned the absolute ban on drugs and alcohol at the ranch. We even included a "no smoking" rule, one of the few ranches with such a restriction. Some boys smoked when they came to the ranch, but I refused to waste my time if they refused to quit. I wanted only the boys who strived to better themselves, beginning with good health habits.

I allowed the boys to bring up for discussion some of the ranch rules. The no-smoking and no-alcohol rules were not included. Everyone knew if a boy became intoxicated or was found with drugs, I was the only one to hand out the punishment or restriction rather than a counselor. It was also known that if "Mom" restricted a boy, he forfeited any chance of an appeal when alcohol or drugs were involved. Depending on the situation it could mean immediate dismissal from the ranch. If the boy was allowed to stay on the ranch, he must take the restriction like a "man." Anything less was unacceptable. Oddly enough this issue never occurred at the ranch. The good Lord just gave me a solution before it became a problem.

Three particular boys attempted to test the rules—Joe (aged twelve), Harry (aged thirteen), and one of the favorites of my heart, Trevor (aged fifteen). Trevor possessed a lot of talent; however, it just had not arrived to the brain yet. Trevor pictured himself as the fearless leader; he managed to find things that came with a capital "T" for trouble. As a matter of fact, he stayed on restriction for nearly the entire first six months at the ranch. Trevor gave me some of the best memories and lots of free entertainment.

With Trevor I could always expect a visit to the office when he was on restriction, with a story that resembled Clinger's stories on Mash. I listened politely and then admired his tale, "Trevor, that's the best story yet." Then I dismissed him. On one occasion, he came limping into the office with his arms slung over two boys' shoulders. His ankle, wrapped in ice and a double layer of Ace bandages, certainly looked swollen. With a tremble in his voice, he said, "Mom, I'm so sorry, but I hurt my ankle and can't clean the stalls in the barn."

"I replied, "That's too bad because if you cannot clean the stalls assigned you by the end of the day, you will surely be unable to attend the skating party tonight. I'm so sorry you're hurt." Amazingly Trevor had a miraculous recovery. Not only did he clean the stalls but also won the limbo game at the skating party that evening.

On the second day of one of our many trips to the High Country, Trevor spotted a weed that looks remarkably like marijuana growing on the mountainside. He believed and convinced the other two boys that he found the real "Mary Jane." He persuaded the boys they could hide it from me on the long trip. He claimed, "She'll never suspect us."

Unfortunately for them, Tom developed a habit of finding a high spot and sitting down for a spell where he watched the boys make fools out of themselves. After everybody settled in for the night, Tom told me about the conversation he overheard. Tom never let the boys know they were being watched, so as far as the boys knew, they had successfully sneaked this "marijuana weed" back into camp, right under my nose. Tom asked, "What are you going to do?" I simply smiled I'm sure with a twinkle in my eye and said, "Let the games began." This is my favorite saying; it simply meant I would oblige and meet a challenge with a challenge.

The next morning, I secretly watched as the boys, ever so skillfully, hid the weed from me. After breakfast, we packed our lunches and prepared for the Journey ahead. The boys mounted their horses and watched as I handed lunch sacks to Joe and Harry. I walked around to Trevor's saddlebag, the hiding place of the so called "marijuana," and lifted the top flap putting Trevor's lunch inside.

Trevor quickly leaned back to assist and stammered, "I'll do it, Mom." Trevor turned a rather pale white in color at the thought of my discovering what was there.

"It's Okay," I smiled. "I've got it," and pushed the lunch sack in the saddle bag.

That day, we planned to ride twelve miles to Lord's Meadow. It sits in a beautiful canyon, traversed by meandering streams of fresh water, lush grasses for the horses, and a great campsite. We stopped periodically during the morning to let the horses catch their wind, a cowboy term for letting a horse breathe slower or catch his breath.

We stopped for lunch at the springs, the halfway point. I told the boys when we stopped for lunch to pull the light gear, which consisted of removing the bridles and saddlebags to give the horses a rest. The horses wear halters underneath the bridles. The halters for some, carried looped around the saddle horn, are standard riding gear in the mountains. The horses were tied with lead ropes to trees that were now hitching posts.

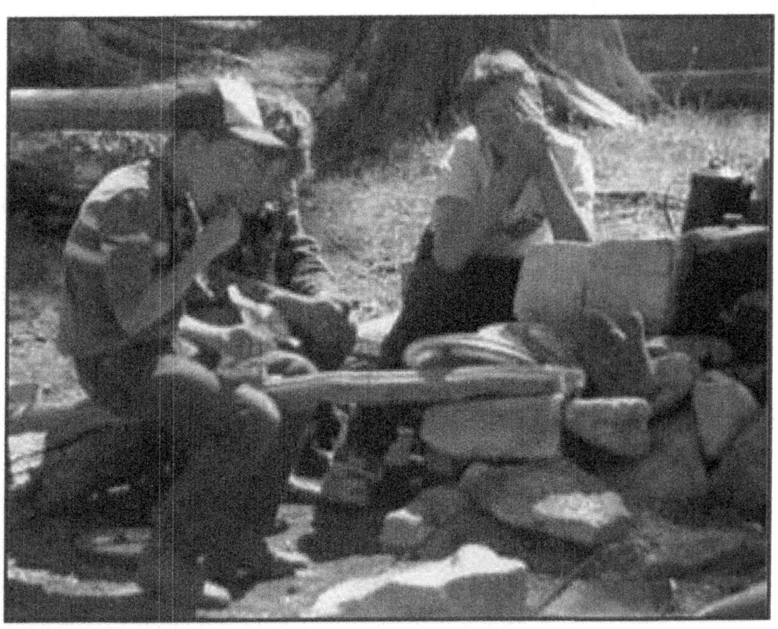

Joe, Trevor, and Harry at Lord's Meadow

Trevor protected his lunch that day. Tom asked if he needed some help carrying his saddlebags. Of course, Trevor said, "I can handle my gear just fine."

When lunch was over, Tom went over to Trevor and reached down for Trevor's saddlebags. Tom said, "Trevor I think your horse is kind of sore over his back." Before Trevor realized it, Tom had those saddlebags draped over his saddle horn and rode off. Trevor and the boys rode the next six miles wondering if Tom was going to find their stash.

I wanted to get in on the fun and started talking about some of the new restrictions at the ranch. Harry was behind me on his horse listening to every word, when he spoke up, "What new restrictions?"

I answered rather loudly, "The new restrictions are all about drugs. I sure wish someone would mess up so I can see how well these new restrictions work."

When Tom and the boys unsaddled that evening, Tom finally handed the saddlebags back to Trevor. I suggested Tom and I go to the meadow and check on the horses. This ploy gave the boys ample time to check on the so-called weed and see if it was still there. Of course, we did not go to the meadow. Instead, we walked around a cliff of high rocks over looking the camp and climbed up into our balcony seats to sit and listen. The mountains provided surround-sound acoustics for the boy's campfire amphitheater. By this time, the free entertainment was in full swing, and all Tom and I lacked were a pair of theater binoculars and a box of buttered popcorn. We heard the boys' laughter when they discovered that good old Tom overlooked their stash.

Trevor laughed the loudest as he said, "Man, did you see how close Mom and Tom came to the marijuana? They are so dumb." After the laughter subsided, Trevor continued, "Harry, it's your turn to hide the stuff for tomorrow."

"No, Trevor." Harry replied, "I'm not sure I want to go through what you went through today. Dumb or not, they scared me. And Mom has new restrictions for anyone caught with drugs."

Trevor insisted, "Harry, you got to take your turn. We're in this together."

Harry said, "Oh, okay, but I'm going to put it in my sleeping bag." The problem with that idea was this particular weed makes you itch, although Harry was unaware of this little detail.

Tom and I couldn't help enjoying the humor. It was better than Shakespeare's "Fools and Jester" in his second scenes. Hereafter, Tom and I plotted to enter into the scenes and toy with the boys and their hiding places.

So the next morning, Harry was itching. I asked him several times what the problem was. "Is there anything I can do for you to stop that itching?" I asked.

"Oh no ma'am, I'm fine, just fine," he said, as he continued to scratch.

Tom suggested some old-fashioned liniment might just do the trick. All this liniment accomplished was a stinging sensation, which required a bath in a very cold mountain stream.

After breakfast and his bath, Harry continued itching. I walked over and looked closely at the rash and said, "Yep, looks like poison oak to me. Guess you had better put some Calamine lotion on that itch." So for the rest of the day, I noticed Harry dabbing more Calamine lotion on his arms, face, neck, and stomach. Our Harry was a young-looking pink cowboy. It did stop the itching, even if it wasn't poison oak.

That afternoon I made a suggestion to Harry, "Harry lets go to the river and wash your sleeping bag. Instead, Joe immediately jumped up to help his partner in crime stating; "Ah, Mom, I'll help Harry wash the sleeping bag, why don't you rest."

Down by the stream, they carefully took the weed out of Harry's sleeping bag. To keep their secret, the boys had to hide it first one place and then another.

Tom and I continued to sit near the spot or fish near the spot where the stuff was buried. The next day, the boys buried it behind a large rock just out of camp. Tom told the boys he had to go to the rest room. In the High Country, you bury your waste by digging a hole in the ground and then covering it up. The boys watched nervously as Tom took the camp shovel and headed straight for that rock. He walked around behind the big rock, right about where the boys had buried their stash the night before. In a few minutes, Tom shouted that he had found something. "Come on up here and see what I found."

I looked at the boys and insisted they come along. The day before, Tom found an Indian arrowhead and stuck it in his pocket. When we rounded the rock where Tom was standing, he held the arrowhead up and said to the boys, "Look what I found!" When Tom held up the arrowhead, the boys nervously breathed a sigh of relief.

The night before we broke camp to go home, we roasted marshmallows, and I talked about how the country was going to ruination in a hurry with all the drugs our young people were experiencing. "Why, it's a wonder kids today have any brain cells left," I remarked.

Joe asked, "Why?"

I told him the truth. "Brain cells are the only part of the body that is not replaceable, and drugs and alcohol destroy brain cells."

The next morning while breaking camp, the boys put their heads together in a pretty serious discussion about their contraband. They argued back and forth about taking this weed to the ranch to smoke. Trevor, being older, was the fearless leader again, "Look you sissies, we have come this far and they haven't caught us yet, and they won't catch us if we take it back to the ranch. Are you two in or out?"

Joe spoke up, "We're in."

By this time, Tom was bored with the whole thing and wanted to know what I was going to do. I told him, "The punishment for this deed is forthcoming. If they smoke it, the results are punishment enough."

Back at the ranch, the boys made a deal between themselves not to trust any of the other boys at the ranch. I, hearing this, was pleased; otherwise, I would have the whole darn bunch sick.

Back at the ranch a few nights later, I climbed on to the barn roof and waited for some time. If the boys were planning something, they met behind the barn. Sure enough, a couple of hours after bedtime, the three met at the usual place, where they proceeded to grind and roll this mountain weed into cigarettes. Joe purchased cigarette paper at the corner grocery store. We knew about this because the grocer, a friend of the ranch, called me immediately. That's how we knew this was the special night.

You just had to be up on that barn roof to experience these young pups smoking the so called "Mary Jane." As the three began smoking, each one seemed to wait for the others to quit. Finally, all three were pretty sick; they started rolling their eyes all around, making moaning sounds and holding their stomachs. Joe said to Harry, "If we survive this, we're going to draw straws to see which one gets to choke Trevor to death."

I waited until those pups left for their rooms before I got down off the barn roof. As I was getting down, my foot slipped, and I went end over end off the roof. I tried to get up but couldn't. My ankle throbbed, and it was painful enough I could not walk on it. I waited, and sure enough, Tom came searching. Finding me on the ground, he picked me up and carried me to the main house, which was some distance. He helped me undress and get into bed and wrapped my ankle in an ice pack. As I told him the story, his concerned look gave way to his sense of humor. Grinning, but showing his intelligence by silence, he kissed me and held me in his arms until I drifted off to sleep.

The next morning, I woke the boys a little earlier than usual. After breakfast, I could barely walk to the barn where we proceeded to castrate calves and doctor some old cows that needed medication for worms on their backs. One of the boys asked me why I was limping. I just said, "I had a fall late in the night and hurt it a little." Actually, it hurt a lot. All of the staff knew what happened. I had to keep busy so as not to laugh at the boys. Actually in my heart I felt sorry for them; they were so sick. Tom and the cowboys were laughing at me. They bumped into me and called me "Granny." Anyone who survived the ranch had to be a good sport. Sometimes my teaching came back to haunt me.

The three boys were pale. I must have asked them a dozen times that day if they were feeling all right. "Oh, yes, ma'am," they assured me they were all right, but every once in a while, one excused himself, ran around the barn, and threw up. They really learned a hard lesson smoking this "real" weed. I finally told all three of them they probably were coming down with the stomach flu and took them all to the medicine cabinet for some Pepto-Bismol.

Thank goodness, none of the three boys had experienced smoking pot before and were fully convinced they never wanted to smoke pot again.

Group session the next week was all about drugs and the harmful effects it had on the smoker. I reinforced what the boys had just experienced, how most people did not get a good feeling from the experience. Those three boys just nodded their heads. They stood up and told how they had tried it once, naturally before they came to the ranch—it was THE worst stuff they'd ever tasted—they explained how deathly ill they became.

About a year later, after one of these group sessions, I heard Trevor talking to Joe about that memorable trip. Trevor said to Joe, "Do you think Mom knew about that darn "Mary Jane" we smoked?" Joe was younger in age, but so much smarter. Joe just looked at Trevor and said, "Of course, she knew, you moron."

Trevor said, "But she didn't punish us."

Joe looked at Trevor and said, "Trevor, she had more fun watching us make fools of ourselves."

When Trevor left the ranch, he asked me flat out if I knew about the weed they smoked. I looked right back and said, "It was one of my most memorable mountain trips and the most entertaining. And, yes, Trevor, I knew from the very first day, and so did Tom. If I remember correctly, you, boys, were pretty sick. I considered that punishment enough."

~ Chapter 22 ~

TREVOR'S FIRST OUTSIDE JOB

Oakdale, California—visiting an old retired police chief friend

As I sat on this kind gentleman's porch, he told me of his illness, and well, it was better if I just listened, for he was not handling it too well. The doctor told him he really did not have long to live, maybe two years. I said, "We're all getting older and dying; it's something we all have to do." I knew immediately that he regarded my statement as hopeless and insensitive. This was not what he wanted to hear. He wanted another kind of response. I gave him some gentle conversation and my theory on the matter. Death, I believe does not happen until a higher power says so. I didn't burden him with my little medical problem. It wasn't necessary or helpful. Besides, I wasn't sure if my little problem compared with his death sentence.

A friend of mine had called right after my diagnoses and asked, "René are you going to die?" I thought the question an ironic one and answered her with, "Aren't you!" We both had a laugh and discussed our positive tomorrows.

On the way back to town, I passed an old tractor sitting out in the middle of a hay field. The grass and weeds were mowed around the tractor; the tractor looked like it had been there for many years. How in the world could some of these farmers go off and just leave expensive equipment in the field? Oh how I yearned for a reliable tractor when I had the boys ranch. The tractor reminded me of an incident on the ranch with Trevor. I never met so talented a boy. He required all the patience of Job and the genius of DaVinci to direct his talents away from getting into trouble to staying out of trouble.

At almost sixteen years of age and at Level Four in the ranch program, Trevor earned the privilege of working off the ranch. Trevor came to me one day and asked to use this privilege. My heart lodged in my throat. After regaining my composer, I discussed the leap of faith at some length. We left the discussion of this subject matter until the next day. I had to gather my thoughts as to who and what kind of job Trevor's talents could accomplish. The next morning Trevor showed up on time, an accomplishment in itself. I suggested that he consider working for one of the local farmers, perhaps in their almond orchards.

Trevor surely couldn't get into any trouble in an orchard. His slightly cocked head and sweet smile bewitched me. Trevor certainly used some kind of an incantation with his charmed personality; it caused a mental lapse that overlooked previous experiences with Trevor. What could possibly happen with dirt, irrigation and almond trees? I should have been worried—seriously worried.

Trevor (on the right) and a friend; Trevor was nearly sixteen in this picture.

A few weeks earlier, a retired lady who lived not too far from the ranch, asked if I had a boy who could help her with irrigation. In the local area, there were two ways to irrigate almonds. One was flood irrigation and the other for our hilly terrain was a straight line sprinkler system. The system required moving every few hours. This task seemed like a simple-enough job for Trevor. So I met with this very sweet elderly lady and introduced Trevor. They hit it off, and she hired Trevor for his first outside job.

Trevor was close to losing his privileges on Level Four because he neglected the community service volunteer requirement. The boys were expected to volunteer to help the elderly as well as work for paying jobs. I called him into my office and extended the time period for five days. This sweet elderly lady presented him with an ideal opportunity to solve his volunteer requirement.

Trevor won the sweet elderly lady's heart the first day by cleaning her flower beds without charging her. She was totally unaware he was required to volunteer for points to stay on his privilege level.

Into the second week, I began to wonder just how well Trevor's outside job was working out. You see, Trevor could create mass confusion standing still. He was about six feet tall and had elephant-sized feet. He wore size thirteen boots. Thin and clumsy, he was at that "I-don't know-where-to-put-my-feet" stage; rarely missing a meal through those growing years. One particular time he was unloading my groceries and began by throwing a sack of fifty pound potatoes over his shoulder. As the heavy sack of potatoes landed on his shoulder he began to stumble with his feet. The potato sack opened and potatoes went everywhere. When he finally gained his composer, he blurted out, "Don't worry Mom, I've got them under control." I believe there were eight or ten potatoes left in the sack. You never had to tell him to go back for seconds at meal time. He simply loved eating. I can't recall Trevor ever being late for a meal, except one particular time shortly after going to work for Mrs Simpson.

Trevor normally arrived home around five-thirty in the afternoon, but at six o'clock our usual dinnertime, Trevor was missing. I stood at the head of the table as we said the blessing and then told the boys and counselors to go ahead and eat while I checked on Trevor.

When I drove up into the yard and looked out across the almond orchard, I spotted the sprinklers going at full force while Trevor stood nearby getting soaked every time the Sprinklers circled by. I yelled at the top of my voice, "Son, what are you doing over here this late? Did you forget your watch?"

Trevor stood about six almond trees down the row and yelled back, "I can't move; my boots are stuck in the mud!" Every time the sprinklers went around, the water hit him and the clay mud acted like quicksand mixture.

I sized up the situation and shouted, "Leave your boots there and walk out of the mud."

He shouted back, "What about my boots?"

I replied, "Just step out of your boots. They won't catch pneumonia, but you will." He thought about that statement for a moment and walked out of the old clay mud, leaving his boots behind.

On the way back to the ranch, he looked at me and said, "Mom, are you mad at me because I really think my boots are probably ruined?"

"Why should I be mad at you because your boots are ruined? After all, they are your boots. Just remember," I continued, "the rule of the ranch has always been if you ruin it, you replace it— with your own money. I figure you are going to make just about enough money to replace your boots out of this next pay check."

It was pretty quiet the rest of the way home.

Mrs Simpson liked Trevor. She made him cookies and sometimes paid him a little extra. I have to admit that Trevor was one of my favorite boys. He was just one of those kids you couldn't help but like. That boy was always entertaining. At fifteen, Trevor, like any other kid, thought that horses were okay, but he preferred driving anything with a motor and wheels.

Late one morning Trevor, pale as a White Mountain goat's coat, came through the office door and immediately asked for a "private session." Private Sessions required that I drop everything and listen to the boys problems, whether night or day. I dismissed the two lads already in the office and gave my full attention to Trevor. These sessions required the boys to speak with complete honesty and that I commit to solving whatever problems they faced. The private session's "safe zone" meant they could tell me anything and I lessened the restrictions because of their honesty.

"Okay, Trevor," I said, "What major disaster have you created?"

Trevor nervously began to tell me what happened; pacing back and forth in my office waving his long arms nervously and twirling his hat in his hand with his fingers. It was early summer and Mrs Simpson was on vacation, but was due back the next evening. This little elderly lady stored a tractor in her barn, but her tractor was not any tractor; it was an antique! Mr Simpson died some years ago and considered this antique his favorite tractor, so Mrs Simpson religiously cared for the tractor with the devotion of a widow's love. Trevor had washed it for her in the barn and then carefully covered it with a tarp. Trevor explained, "I moved the sprinklers like I always do in the morning, but had some time on my hands and decided to take the tractor for a little spin up and down the rows in the almond orchard." He stopped pacing and turned to me with a seriousness that befitted a summit meeting. "Mom, it hot-wired real easy." I suddenly recalled the reason Trevor was at the ranch on my program; prior to Trevor's arrival at the ranch the police caught Trevor stealing a neighbor's car. When the car ran out of gas three miles down the freeway, he refused to leave it for fear that someone might strip it. Trevor's crazy logic crafted this unusual ethical code.

After hot wiring the tractor, Trevor proceeded to drive it straight down the nearest orchard row—the same row where he had just moved the sprinklers. These sprinklers had been running most of the night; it was now mid morning.

It did not take much of an imagination to figure out what happened. One very heavy tractor plus one very wet and muddy almond row definitely equaled a very stuck tractor. Getting the picture, I asked, "Okay, how bad is the tractor stuck?"

"Well, Mom, I think it's stuck pretty deep."

"Okay, Son," I said, "let's just get through this and solve the problem, and then we will discuss whether you are going to make it to your next birthday. I'll go get my truck." My truck was a one-ton diesel heavy duty Ford, which usually pulled out most stuck vehicles around the ranch. When we drove in the driveway and looked closely down the almond rows, I could see where Mrs Simpson's tractor was stuck; I knew my truck would not do the job. The poor little old lady's tractor was buried clear above the back axle.

Trevor remained remarkably quiet, which at this moment was probably the healthiest thing he could do. I simply could not believe my eyes. I looked at this antique tractor and knew God's helping hand would be needed. Unconsciously I began my pleading with the good Lord; "Trevor needs a miracle, and he needs it now!"

In the same breath, I turned to Trevor and said "Trevor, it's not stuck. It's buried." My voice became louder; **"All we need to do is put a white lily on the hood and hold a eulogy."**

I went back to the ranch and told two of my ranch hands to go over and keep Trevor out of trouble until I got back from town. I walked into the heavy equipment rental shop. Voicing my request as I entered the building, "I need to rent the biggest tractor you have; I need it right now," I reported. "Have it delivered to this address!"

The ranch hands made good use of their time by comforting Trevor: "Ms René went to purchase some flowers, and if they could not dig the tractor out, she left instructions to dig the hole wider so we can bury you right alongside the tractor."

I returned to the almond orchard, grabbed a shovel and began working alongside the ranch hands. We were all knee-deep in the mud trying to find enough of the tractor to hook the chain around. Shortly thereafter the large tractor from the rental firm was delivered.

During this time, I noticed Trevor avoided making any kind of eye contact with me. Finally, we were able to attach a chain around the axle of Mrs Simpson's tractor and, very slowly and ever so gently, began to pull the antique tractor out.

What had once been a very shiny, beloved tractor was now a very muddy mess. The two cowboys and I were covered with repulsive, smelly grey clay; the orchard had recently been fertilized with a mixture of different unsavory smells such as cow manure.

"Trevor," I said as I tried to get some of the mud from my boots, "It's up to you to wash this tractor and put it back exactly as you found it. Do I make myself clear? And yes, if you can get these two cowboys to take pity on you and they agree to help you, that's okay with me. When Mrs Simpson gets back home, her tractor MUST be exactly the way it was when she left. Good luck, Son."

The cowboys stayed behind to help Trevor clean the tractor and fill the hole created by the tractor. I still, to this day, do not know all Trevor promised to do for them. I do know those two cowboys had the cleanest horse stalls and the shiniest boots in the country for the next couple weeks.

The next day I paid Mrs Simpson a visit, accompanied by Trevor. Trevor and I sat side by side on her couch. I asked about her trip, her health, and a few other socially polite things. Finally, I inquired about her antique tractor, stating I heard it was a beautiful thing to see. She, of course, volunteered to show me her late husband's pride and joy. Trevor was a might bit nervous as we approached the barn. I could see where Trevor and the cowboys had washed the old tractor. Mrs Simpson asked if it had rained some, and I said, "Oh yes, ma'am, it rained late last night." I hated myself for that little white lie which was not totally a lie. It had rained "some," but not enough to create a mud puddle of this size. When we reached the barn, and removed the canvas cover, her eyes became larger than life and said, "Oh my goodness, you wonderful boy, you have washed my late husband's antique tractor. It's so shinny!"

We came out of the barn, and the three of us walked back to the house. I told her what a wonderful antique treasure she had and complimented her on the preservation of such an antique.

On the way back to the ranch, Trevor asked, "Am I going to see my sixteenth birthday? I answered, "Yes, Trevor, you will make it to another "birthday," mainly because your birthday is just around the corner. However, you are still going to be on restriction for ten days."

"But, Mom, the tractor was super clean," he remarked.

"Well, that's why you only have a ten-day restriction instead of a thirty-day restriction," I answered.

"Ah, did I blow my level?" Trevor asked.

"No, you are still at the same level, because I know how hard it was to tell me the truth about what happened," I replied. I could see he was thinking, and by this time, even Trevor had figured out ten days would be horrible, because it meant he would not be allowed to leave the ranch, except for school which was due out for the summer in one week.

You see, Trevor had a girlfriend, and the school dance was only five days away. Before the tractor incident, Trevor asked if he could take Beth to the dance, and I gave my permission. It always amazes me how adults say these boys have no brains. Most adults provide the solutions and miss the chance to let the boys use and develop their brain capacities. "If you don't use it, you lose it." I need not discuss as a lady what that refers to, but the same principal applies. They need plenty of opportunities to use their brains in beneficial development.

When we handed out restrictions, we allowed the boys twenty-four hours to ask for a discussion on the matter. During the discussion, they needed to prove a justifiable and valid objection to the restriction and replace the restriction with something equivalent. The reputation of "no runaways" existed in part, because the boys recognized the fairness of the restriction system.

The valid objection required the boy bring a staff member with them to vote for or against the point they presented. I thought this system was fair. If they provided a good and reasonable cause for the change in the restriction, we voted on it; however, if they lost the vote, the original restriction could double. Most of my boys took the original restriction. I wanted Trevor to use his brain on this one, and figured this created the right spark-plug—the anticipation of dancing with the lovely Beth. The question being, could Trevor activate his brain enough to find a solution to this problem?

Sure enough, within twenty-four hours, Trevor and a staff member came to the office.

"Mom?" he said.

"Yes, Trevor," I answered, "what can I do for you?"

"Mom," he continued, "I would like to object to this ten day restriction."

"Yes, son," I answered, "I kind of figured you might. And what do you think is a reasonable substitute for the current restriction?"

Through my many years of trial and error, I discovered that nothing gets the brain of a teenage boy working faster than the opposite sex. Trevor was infatuated with the enchanting Beth. He looked at me, and in a nervous but steady voice began reading from his yellow legal pad. I could hardly believe how hard he worked on proving his justifiable objections, especially since he loathed writing.

I put on my best "judicial expression." It might be noted, for these hearings I had a black robe I wore to create a judicial courtroom atmosphere. Sitting down at my desk, I listened as Trevor read from his proposal: It went something like this: (1) I will read every night for a month to the little ones; (2) I will clean your personal horses' stalls and groom the horses for a month; (3) I will mop the kitchen floor and do the dishes for one month; and (4) I will help saddle the little ones' horses for one month. He paused for a moment.

"Is that all? I asked with one eyebrow arched and managed a judicial pose, trying to play my dramatic role to the hilt.

I got up from my chair and walked around the "courtroom," extending the judicial moment, and then sat back down. "Do you understand the privilege of being at Level Four? You must set an example for the other boys to follow. Do you fully realize the responsibility of showing the younger ones how productive this ranch can be?"

"Oh, yes, Ma'am," he replied for the umpteenth time. I figured that I had dragged this so-called court session out long enough, so I asked the cowboy attending this presentation to vote. He voted in favor of Trevor and then whispered something to Trevor.

"Trevor," I asked, "Do you have anything to add to your objection?" He looked at me and then the cowboy attending this presentation and took a deep breath.

"Yes, ma'am," he replied, "I realize I had no permission to use the tractor. I realize I was wrong and could have made the other boys look bad at the ranch. I am willing to apologize to the other boys in a group session and take the punishment assigned me by them. I am requesting this because I really want to take Beth to the dance, and I do realize my mistakes."

This was the hardest I had ever seen Trevor work. Yes, this is great, I thought to myself, "I knew this boy had a brain." I was elated.

I made my decision. "Son, the original ten-day restriction is lifted. These are the terms: undoubtedly you worked very hard on your petition. I will waive two of your penalties, but the boys here at the ranch will vote as to which two. Yes, you can take Beth to the dance." I put my metaphorical gavel down on the desk, and when I opened the office door, half of the boys and staff, who had their ears pressed against the door, nearly fell on top of me. They were all pulling for Trevor to go to the dance. He was such a likeable kid.

Anytime a boy made the other boys look bad while working outside the ranch or by doing something negative, the other boys discussed putting a restriction on that particular boy for his negative actions. This additional restriction could be anything from cleaning the entire barn, worse yet, performing personal services for the other boys, such as laundry or making their beds. This group decision reinforced the value of one boys reflection on the entire ranch—another fair way of doing things. The boys voted on Trevor's suggested punishments: he did not have to take care of my horses or do the dishes. They voted yes, however, concerning the duties with the little ones. He certainly would read to the younger boys and saddle their horses. My little ones loved Trevor.

Trevor went to the year-end school dance looking ever so good with pretty Beth by his side.

~ Chapter 23 ~

TOM AND THE BEAR

We made many trips into the mountains, which created a storehouse of fond memories to feed my soul constantly. Visitors to the ranch often told me what a wonderful thing I was doing for these needy children. They could not imagine their faulty assumptions, for it was I who received joy and fulfillment for multiple lifetimes. The experiences, both the good and the bad, offered loads of spiritual sustenance for years to come.

To give of oneself openly with God's blessings and guidance provides the most rewarding life one can receive on this side of heaven. God gifted me with the ability to read the boys troubled personalities and guide them, but when the boys and I played a splendid practical joke on one of the counselors, during my bedtime conversations with God I asked, "Am I supposed to be having this much fun?"

The northern back wilderness area of Yosemite's high country is right up there with chocolate ice cream, home cooking, and horizontal conversations.

When I rode horseback above the timberline, I slowly took in all the spectacular scenery. As I reached the plateau of the high mountains going into the area that's referred to as above timberline, I found myself against a backdrop with dark blue lakes and clear running mountain streams that painted a tapestry only God could create. The white fluffy clouds floated so closely over my head I felt like I could reach out and touch them. Looking down in the canyons and along the horse path at deer and wildlife grazing in the meadows below, I realized that it just doesn't get any better than this.

The bears in the High Country contributed to some of my best memories. The black bear is pretty much like most other mountain creatures—misunderstood. When you say bear, people immediately think "killer bear." The fear, through wrong information or lack thereof, creates many problems for the gentle, non-aggressive black bear. The black bear has been confused with the aggressive Grizzly bear. They have very different natures, not that the black bear, if spoiled by enough people through their ignorance, can't become unruly. This is why in all the national parks they have signs that read "DON'T FEED THE BEARS."

Forest rangers use the back wilderness area of Yosemite National Forest as a dumping ground for bears people have spoiled. The back wilderness areas of Yosemite require long, arduous hikes or long horseback rides over some treacherous mountain trails. Few tourists venture into this area; it is not a trip for the average tourist.

On one of our trips to the High Country, the bear had the last laugh, and the laugh was on Tom. You remember Tom—

six feet two inches and 220 pounds of very tough rodeo cowboy. On this particular trip, we had two new boys, one of whom was Jake you met in chapter one, eight other boys, and two fairly new cowboy counselors. Tom and I rounded the trip out. It was a full house as mountain trips go.

We set up camp at the lake and settled in, with the boys pitching their tents around the campfire. Things went along pretty well for the first two days, until Jake decided to throw one of his fits and begin the name-calling. According to his records, Jake had run away some twenty times from social services facility placement. I planned to take Jake to the High Country where his inclination for flight could be handled in a different way.

He was new to the ranch and I understood Jake's main problem. He feared caring or showing any positive emotion. Jake acted out by name-calling, throwing tantrums, and threatening to run away. I needed to take him into my territory, the mountains, or face losing him at the ranch. I wasn't about to give up on this one; I was already attached. Usually, I required the boy throwing the fit to gather wood for the night or bring water to camp. Jake refused to do anything I asked of him.

By the third night, after dinner, I had had enough. He continued to call me the usual names. Verbal creativity was not one of my boys talents. They all called me "f—bitch" for the first few weeks. Jake followed the usual protocol. As this situation unfolded the other boys were whispering to each other; "Boy is Jake burying himself" and "He won't make it out of the mountains." I continued to ignore his behavior for a time, believing that the other boys boisterous fun would soon rub off on him. Their joy failed to penetrate his toughness. Finally, he responded, "I'm running away from this stinking camp." I had waited patiently for him to say these words.

I stood up enhancing my authority and spoke; "I think that's a great idea; you will make the bears in this neighborhood a great meal. Get out of my camp." I threw his jacket to him and pointed to the trail. This psychological strategy completely caught him off guard.

As he started toward the trail, he said, "I've changed my mind."

I replied, "I haven't changed mine," and picked up some rocks and started throwing them close to his feet. I shouted, "Go on, get out of my camp, and don't come back." Was this strategy easy to do? NOT!!!

Dusk shadowed the quickly approaching darkness. At night, the mountains can be a very scary place for a young boy.

Even though at six years old, Jake hitchhiked from Florida to California "and made it." The High Country was different, there really was no place to run and offered no sheltered hideaways.

Darkness set in. Sounds carry in the High Country, and I could hear Jake crying and knew he was close. I sent one of the cowboys to see just exactly where Jake was sitting. He returned saying Jake was just over the big rock that shadowed the camp. My little ones could also hear Jake crying and asked, "Are you really going to let the bears eat Jake?" Their concern broke my heart, but at least I had his attention (or he had mine). I needed to halter the boy, and if this bit worked out like I expected, this boy would be coming back into camp with a different attitude.

Meanwhile, my motherhood instincts struggled with my mind, and worry was sitting in rather rapidly. Tom sensed this, and offered his thoughts on the matter. "Why don't I go around and up on the mountain behind Jake and growl like a bear?" He thought that would scare the boy back into camp.

As the darkness quickly draped the entire mountain, my mental anguish offered no better plan. So, Tom, in the dark of the night with only a cantalope slice of a moon, proceeded forward with his plan, going up and around and behind where the boy was sitting.

About twenty minutes passed when I heard something coming down the hill in back of the camp. There was the most god-awful sounds, bushes breaking, sounds of limbs breaking off, and then, there in the light of the campfire stood Tom, white as a ghost standing in front of me. Tom spent a lot of time tanning in the tanning booths, so it was pretty hard for him to be real white. But tonight, Tom was not only white as a sheet, but when he came into the brighter light of the campfire; I could see he had scratches all over him. Without taking a breath he said, "Jake can sit out there until you know what freezes over."

"Did you find the boy?" I inquired.

"Yes, I found the boy and much more than I intended." It seems Tom found Jake and sat down behind the bushes to make some bear calls. He grunted out a snorting sound, as a bear would do for mating, and right behind him in the dark, a real bear snorted back. Tom literally ran through the bushes in the dark or maybe "fell" down the steep hill getting back to camp. He had scratches on his arms and face; what a mess he was standing there in the light.

In all the commotion, Jake was scared so badly, he too decided to come to camp. So in a roundabout way, Tom's plan did work. I had retired to my big tent to doctor Tom's cuts. I heard a boy crying so I opened my tent flap and there stood Jake.

Jake asked, "Can I please come in your tent `cause someone took my tent." Tears streamed down his cheeks. He was starting to cry harder. He continued, "They took my sleeping bag and I have no place to sleep."

I replied, "I took your tent and sleeping bag because I did not want to leave it outside." Actually, I didn't want him sneaking back into camp in the middle of the night and going to bed like nothing happened. I needed the boy to confront me, or my efforts would be wasted. My tough love approach hurt me more than the child.

It was the first time Jake had cried since coming to the ranch. He apologized, and all was forgiven as I held out my arms and told him, "Hugs are free." He fell into my arms and hugged me back for a long time as though he was afraid to let go. He slept that night in his sleeping bag in our very large tent.

The next morning as the camp began to rise and shine, Jake sat up and looked at me as if to question, "Am I O.K?" I spoke with some softness but firmness in my voice, "Jake, this is a new day and the beginning of the rest of your life." I gave him another hug, and this time he hugged me back with meaning.

We doctored Tom for a few days. The cowboys and I were the only ones that knew what really happened that night. But with the cowboys knowing, the jokes on Tom were just beginning. Every time one of the cowboys walked past Tom, they teased, "Have you seen any bears lately?" Or, "Tom, we hear its breeding season and you have a great mating call."

When we arrived back at the ranch, those cowboys told everybody in town that Tom had the best mating call for bears they had ever heard. It continued; one night after dinner Tom was sitting in his big recliner reading when one of the cowboys dressed up in a big black bear suit came up behind the chair, leaned over and growled loudly. Tom jumped across the living room, all in one movement. I can't ever remember a cowboy looking whiter than Tom that night in the High Country. I would say the bear definitely won this one hands down. But more importantly, Jake won the ability to trust an adult. That's what this trip was all about.

~ Chapter 24 ~

SHAWN'S SYMPHONY

Children and teens need special times in their lives to grow in their direction—not their parents' directions, not their teachers' directions, not any other person's direction. Many times at the ranch, I caught myself, like other parents, in a teaching mode. I became so busy teaching and correcting and correcting and teaching that I forgot the most important part of teaching—the time to care, the time to listen, and the time to explain my responses. I hear parents telling their children, "You're not wearing that outfit," or "I forbid you to run with that person." These statements come from the heart of a parent, but often the heart of a child needs what should follow—the explanation. I have labeled this simple strategy, "The No Cost approach. A parent might say, "When I was young, I wore that same kind of outfit and couldn't get the respect I needed from employers to get a job." Sometimes all the motivations the parents need to convey is a simple, "Because I love you." Children still need to hear this; it works great with teens too.

In group sessions, on occasion the title of my session might be, "When I Was a Kid." The boys became aware of the fact that I too experienced mischievous behavior as a teenager.

From time to time, I asked the boys to give me a list of things they truly wanted to do just for fun. The list helped me stay in touch with their growing minds and develop their special areas of interest, provided of course, they weren't criminal. I added this statement for clarification to this type of a child.

Little Shawn, for instance, wanted to attend an opera or a real live symphony. I had him tested, as I did with all my boys, and found his IQ to be very high, so I began to buy things he alone would be interested in and found a totally different child. By developing his ideas, I found the child more willing to listen and to learn.

I enrolled little Shawn in a private music class for piano; he wanted to be a conductor of music. Naturally his teacher disagreed from the start. Shawn lacked social skills. After several conversations with his music teacher, who in turn lacked experience handling children such as Shawn, I decided to pursue other alternatives.

Shawn and I went to the music store once a month and looked at everything in the classical music section. Shawn mulled through the CD's of classical music until he found that special one. Concerned the other boys would steal his CDs, Shawn needed my reassurance not to worry. No one but Shawn and I wanted to listen to his choice of music. Sometimes he brought his tapes to my office and played them, mainly because the other boys ran him out of the ranch house.

I watched out of the corner of my eye as Shawn stood behind my podium and conducted as though he were the only person in the room. He escaped into his own little world. Others in most respects considered Shawn a troubled child. To me, he was an absolute joy to watch. He possessed such a beautiful mind. This child was confused and perhaps dangerous at times, but controllable especially with this simple tool called classical music.

Encouraging his individuality and letting him grow in an area of his interest solved other problems. Some parents confuse negative behavior with letting their children grow, when actually they need to know radical behavior leads to adult problems later in life. Franklin Roosevelt defined radical behavior as "A child or persons with both feet in the air." Radical behavior such as orange hair or baggy clothing should have parent intervention. When children are allowed to grow with guidance followed by explanation in a positive way, learning does not become a negative issue. As Shawn became more open and began to trust, my job became easier than I ever expected.

One day I discovered several boys in a heated discussion about the program on the television. Watching TV was a privilege at the ranch, so only a handful of boys were involved in the argument. Shawn lined up against the rest of the boys. The older boys hurried to finish their homework so they could watch the football game. Shawn completed his home work at school, which allowed him the privilege to listen to and watch a symphony program. As usual, he pretended to conduct the orchestra. The other boys were busy calling Shawn inappropriate names. Shawn, on the other hand, was crying and shouting back other inappropriate names when I entered the confrontation. The older boys pleaded, "Mom, tell him its football night and we're not watching that stuff!"

I understood the anguish of the little sports fans in the room, but losing what I had gained with Shawn simply was not an option.

So with a little spontaneous thinking on my part, I came up with a grand idea. "Shawn, I made reservations for the both of us to see the Sacramento Symphony in concert at the Performing Arts Theater."

This statement made him feel very special. Shawn's mouth fell open. In his excitement, he offered no objection to the other boys watching the football game. I agreed to a meeting with him the following afternoon when he came home from school to discuss the matter further. Best of all, I invited him to watch the rest of the symphony and continue his conducting in my personal living room in my house on the hill.

I hurried the next morning into the office informing my secretary of the situation at hand. And, yes, I told a little white lie to Shawn the day before. I intended to take him, and the confrontation had just speeded up the process. I planned our night out to be as memorable for me as it was for little Shawn.

Shawn had been at the ranch about a year and was due a change to a higher level. I decided the two of us would make an evening of it, and at the same time, he would be graded on his manners pertaining to his level change.

My secretary informed me the reservations at John Q's, a very exclusive restaurant, and the symphony were confirmed. The restaurant sat on the very top of the new Holiday Inn with a 360-degree view of Sacramento and our state capitol.

I accompanied Shawn to be fitted for his tux. I could not imagine most of my other boys being this excited.

Shawn, however, was in his own special time and place and loved the idea of dressing like the conductor of a symphony. Over the next two weeks, he asked me over and over, "Are you sure you and I are going to the symphony, just us, Mom?"

I continued to reassure him. "Yes, son, this symphony is your special time."

On the day of the symphony, Tom helped Shawn get dressed. It took the better part of the afternoon for me to decide on the proper gown. I wanted to look graceful, yet motherly. Comfortable cowboy boots for this occasion would simply not do. I owned several gowns but had not worn anything formal since my real-estate days. Finally, I settled on a conservative black gown topped by a three-quarter-length white fur coat. The night arrived with the usual happenings around the ranch until Shawn and I entered the main ranch house for everyone to see. Actually, we made a very handsome mother and son, dressed for a formal evening out on the town. We arrived at the restaurant early, and Shawn with sparkling manners opened the door for me. On the elevator going up to the top floor, a rather stately looking couple watched as Shawn offered his arm to escort me into the restaurant.

One of the many things taught to all the boys at the ranch, a lady does not talk to the waiter—she simply tells her escort what she would like, and the escort tells the waiter. At the ranch, manners were taught from the book *Amy Vanderbilt's Etiquette*; assuredly it is still appreciated today. It was so delightful to watch this eleven-year old boy sit there and just handle everything, including asking for the cocktail waitress. This request startled me!

Shawn dressed in his tuxedo

Tom and the rest of the counselors practiced schooling Shawn the entire previous week about his social obligations when he was with a lady. To my surprise, when the cocktail waiter arrived at our table, the waiter asked me what I wanted to drink. Shawn informed the waiter he would order for both of us. Before I could answer, Shawn ordered two Shirley Temples. I am sure my mouth dropped open. This order had to be Tom's idea of fun.

When it came time to order dinner, Shawn asked me what I wanted and signaled for the dinner waiter. The waiter stopped in front of me and asked if we were ready to order. Shawn informed the waiter, "Sir, it is totally improper for you to talk to my Mother; I will order our dinner." And he did without a mistake.

When it came time to pay the check, he asked the waiter to please figure his tip in the bill, which the waiter did with a smile. The ranch provided Shawn with money to cover our expenses for our evening. The waiter crowned our meal when he complimented Shawn for his manners. He said, "Young man, the entire staff has noticed your good manners. You and your mother are welcome back anytime." The waiter undoubtedly wanted more conversation. He added, "It is so nice to see a young man take his mother to dinner. "Is this a special occasion?" Shawn in his tux looked directly at the gentleman and said, "Yes, it is always a special occasion, when I am with my mother, and it is not just dinner, we are attending the symphony this evening."

Shawn acted graciously the rest of the evening including during the symphony. The lady seated next to me mentioned how wonderful it was to see such a well-mannered young boy accompanying his mother to the symphony.

For the entire following week, Shawn told everybody about the symphony until the older boys asked me to do something to shut him up. The end of the week came, and Shawn received his Level Three certificate with a job well done.

Teaching with respect and responding to the children's interest proved to be one of the greatest teaching tools I developed in working with the boys to correct their behaviors. There were other special times with other boys, but this one was one of my favorites.

Making positive, lasting memories with a child is one of the greatest things we can do. Memories I hoped, would carry into adulthood as a future role model for their children.

~ Chapter 25 ~

THEFT AND THE SOLUTION

David, did you give Tom the note?" I had reached my proverbial wit's end concerning the continual thefts occurring on the ranch and needed Tom's perspective. Normally he provided a simple solution to my problems. Often my solutions to similar situations I had simply made too complicated. The note I was referring to was a note I handed David when he was in my office earlier to deliver to Tom out in the vocational shop. Evidently Tom took the darn phone off the hook to catch a nap. I needed his undivided attention in this matter. My irascible impatience demanded instant action. "David, answer my question!"

David, sitting in front of my desk and quite adept at interpreting the tone of my question, immediately sat up a little taller and answered cautiously: "I went into his office Mom, and I did deliver the note, but he had a sign on his chest that read 'if you wake me,' and something else about 'death,' so I just left the note on top of his desk."

Apparently, I needed to handle this matter myself. I'd wake Tom and we'd see about death threats. Politeness was getting me nowhere. I walked into his office, and sure enough, there pinned on his chest was a sign that read in bold letters, "If you wake me, harmful slow death may occur to your body."

I spotted a glass of water sitting on his desk. Great opportunities simply shouldn't be passed up. I was polite about the whole matter. I picked up his Resistol hat that lay across his face. No sense in ruining a perfectly good cowboy hat, although no one could argue the point about it being well used. I then poured the full glass of water right over his head. It is amazing how fast a two-hundred and twenty-pound man can move. He leapt from his office reclining chair faster than a cougar on a rabbit. He regained his composure, and a silly grin came over his very wet face. The chase was on. I read men almost as quickly as I read boys. I took off in a sprint. He caught me before the chase began, picked me up and dropped me, clothes and all, into the nearest horse trough.

The days of summer heat were just around the corner, so the chase and the water trough quickly cooled my irritable mood. After a quick change of clothes, Tom and I sat down in my office to discuss solutions to outright thievery. We discussed the problem at length. Did I have rules against this behavior? Of course I did, but rules, regulations and restrictions were not enough to solve this situation. I needed this stopped. Tom assured me he would go to work on the problem right away.

Two days later he entered my office and handed me a fruit jar, which contained two mountain oysters also known as calf testicles. The lid was sealed tight and the mountain oysters were in formaldehyde. There was a sign on the jar that read, "This jar contains two testicles from the last thief that stole from this ranch." Tom looked at me and said, "It's up to you what the rest of the story is."

I sat there thinking, "This is so simple; it just might work with the right introduction." I needed some cowboy stories to back it up, so I put the jar in the bottom desk drawer.

I was planning a trip to the High Country, just as one of the counselors submitted his two weeks' notice. He planned to go back to South Dakota to finish his education but asked to go back to the High Country with me one more time, and I agreed. I realized this was the perfect opportunity for the right cowboy story to back up Tom's mountain oyster story. When I told the young cowboy my plan, he laughed and consented to leave from the mountains instead of returning to the ranch. He, two other cowboys, and I went up to the mountains on one of our annual pilgrimages to check the trails before we began the summer trips with the boys.

When I arrived back at the ranch short one young cowboy counselor, the boys were full of questions. The two cowboys spread the story around the ranch like wildfire over dried sagebrush. The next morning at the ranch, I retrieved the jar with the mountain oysters from the bottom drawer and set it right on the corner of my desk for all to see. The boys, one by one, started trickling into my office with a pretense of casualness to check out the jar. They heard that the young counselor turned out to be a lowdown thief and that Mom castrated him and brought back his below-the-belt anatomy.

Normally when I returned from an early trip, the boys pelted me with questions about the trails, mountain streams, and trout fishing. These were important questions, but today their focus was on the jar. I said nothing until they brought up the subject.

This day, questions veered off in other directions, specifically toward the jar and its contents. "Ah, Mom, what's in the jar?" I did not lie to my boys, I answered with two words, allowing them to come to their own conclusion; "Testicles, two," and I continued working.

Group meetings to educate everyone about riding for the brand and its meaning were discussed at length. This simply meant if you were working or living on a ranch, you respected the ranch brand by holding its reputation in your hand. Stealing was unacceptable behavior on any ranch.

I had prayed about the stealing that was going on at the ranch and asked the good Lord for his help in this matter, thinking he had forgotten me.

The cowboys told the story over and over, embellishing it a little bit each time. I once overheard one of my younger boys telling a newcomer to the ranch, "Another thing you should know about Mom, she does not like a thief. The last thief she castrated him and he never came back." This "cowboy rumor" grew until one day about a year later one of the little nine-year-olds basically said the same thing but added, "Yep, they say Mom buried him up there in the High Country." This rumor had grown enough, so I told the cowboys to quit making the story bigger.

The jar caused quite a commotion with the state evaluators, and when they inquired about its purpose, I smiled and said, "It's a demonstration in ethical standards." I received a call from the Director a few weeks later. He asked. "Do you have a jar containing male human remains on your desk?"

I asked him to repeat the question and then calmly replied, "I do not have any *human* remains in a jar on my desk."

"I have your word on this matter?" He asked.

I replied, "Yes," stopping short of giving him more information.

Every new boy who entered the ranch thereafter took one look at that jar and declared, "I am not a thief," or, "I fully intend, Ma'am, to respect this ranch and improve my history record on thievery."

Were my prayers answered? God sometimes answers prayers in bizarre ways. Just like he used a wet sheepskin to speak to Gideon and a burning bush to speak to Moses, He used a jar of calf testicles soaking in formaldehyde to speak to a group of street-wise and wide-eyed boys. We never had a problem with stealing again, and on the plus side, we serendipitously added a cowboy story to the growing list of modern-day western myths.

~ Chapter 26 ~

BLACK MOUNTAIN SPIDER AND BEARS

I hired a couple as house parents for one of my three houses on the ranch. Jerry and Kay turned out to be the ideal couple. They wanted to work on a ranch with children and perhaps gather enough experience in a couple of years to open a facility of their own. The couple, in their early thirties, I hired on the spot; they loved the ranch and the boys. Once in a while, the good Lord looks down and smiles on one of his flock and gives a very special blessing; this couple was mine.

When early summer came, I started making plans for the mountain trips. House parents normally used this time to earn continuing education credits, visit their families, and take a breather from the boys. Our absence was counted as blessings by most house parents. One morning Jerry and Kay came into my office armed with a battery of arguments in favor of their accompanying us on the next mountain trip. Usually, house parents did not go on the mountain trips. Each speaking in turn proclaimed, "We'll miss the boys too much. We've never been on a mountain adventure before. We can work hard to help make your job easier."

Of course, they convinced me with their first statement. This couple really had a great sense of humor, and most of the boys from their house were going. I saw only one drawback. They were from the city, but I gave in allowing them to accompany us. What would it hurt if they experienced a mountain trip or two?

I asked as they were leaving my office, "Can either of you ride a horse?"

They answered, "We have to ride a horse?" We all had a good laugh, and I suggested that they visit with one of the cowboys and take a few lessons before we left.

On this trip, we had eight boys, four of my little ones and four teenage boys, the couple, and me. By this time, the older boys were pretty experienced and could be a lot of help. The boys voted, and sure enough, we were going to Kibby Lake, one of their favorite fishing and swimming lakes.

The older boys were assigned the pack horses and gear. By this time they could tie down a pack as good as the hands at the ranch. Besides, it made them feel like they were young men growing into manhood; and they were, right before my eyes, truly a grand thing to witness.

As we headed up the trail, we ran into Joe Gordon, a forest ranger friend of mine. When we stopped to visit, he said, "René, I spotted two yearling black bear cubs in the Kibby Lake area. You warn those boys to be alert." I thanked Joe for the warning, and we continued up the trail, arriving at Kibby Lake late in the evening.

Kibby Lake swimming hole

Both Jerry and Kay knew of my practical jokes. I placed a big pan out on a rather large rock with a spoon in it, thereby getting curious looks from both. I figured they needed an explanation, "Jerry the large stainless-steel pan and spoon were not used for cooking but for scaring the bears away. Bears' ears are sensitive to certain sounds, and this creates a sound they cannot tolerate." Jerry replied, "Yeah, sure, René."

Some of the hands warned them not to believe everything I said. That night, after the evening meal, I repeated Ranger Gordon's concern about the two yearling bears in the area. Jerry just laughed and said, "René, we've already been warned about you." We all laughed and retired to bed.

For this trip, we packed two of the medium size tents. All our mountain tents included attached floor coverings for the boys. The four older boys planned to share one tent, and the younger ones slept in the other. The next night one of the older boys piqued my curiosity when I saw him circling the younger boys' tent. I noticed he deliberately tried to keep out of sight. After he disappeared into the tent assigned to the older boys and I heard snickering, it raised my suspicions. I snuck over to investigate. Sure enough, my suspicions were on target. The new boy planted pieces of candy on the ground surrounding the younger one's tent. Informed of the rules before leaving the ranch, he knew that candy was not allowed in bear country. His practical joke could create a dangerous situation for all of us. I knew the older boys needed me to recap some strong safety lessons. The idea of a lecture never crossed my mind. They needed a little visualization training—something they wouldn't forget quickly, so I mumbled to myself, "Let the games begin . . . ."

I always packed several items to counteract this kind of behavior. I waited until the boys made their nightly run down by the lake to water the forest and proceeded to pick up every piece of candy around my little one's tent.

We settled in around the campfire roasting marshmallows and began telling stories. I always packed the marshmallows carefully, avoiding the temptation of the black bears, which can smell a dead carcass more than three miles away. The saddlebags which contained snacks, along with the rest of the groceries including anything sweet, were packed and stored underneath a tarp. The tarp was then sprayed with a liniment odor, which covered the smell of anything sweet or intriguing underneath the tarp.

I took the older boys aside and told them not to give me away because I planned to scare the younger lads. They loved the idea and felt great being included in the practical joke. After a few stories, I asked Jerry and Kay to tell a mountain ghost story. Kay spun spine-chilling tales that arched the little one's eyebrows. Kay and her husband sat on the west side of the campfire, and my little nine-and-ten-year olds and I sat huddled together on the east side. Two older boys sat on the north side, and the other two sat on the south side. While Kay described the eerie mountain ghost story, I managed to slip away while everyone was engrossed listening to Kay's story. Behind a tree, I slipped on my costume—a white sheet with two holes cut for peepholes. I sneaked behind the younger boys and leaned over them and said, "BOOOO!"

Little David ran and jumped on Kay's lap, and Willie, my loveable little four by four, moved so fast he cleared the campfire and landed next to Jerry.

We all had our laugh on the little ones. My older boys were unaware I had discovered the candy around the little ones' tent.

They would soon learn what was in store for them. We settled back down around the campfire, and I sat with my younger boys and we laughed and hugged a lot. My David said, with his eyes much larger than normal, "Mom, you really did look like a ghost," as though he had seen several. I smiled a knowing smile at the older boys who were still snickering.

It was my turn to tell a story. I told a short story and then added a bit more information. I said, "Boys, make sure you check your sleeping bags tonight before you go to bed. This is the time of year when the big giant black mountain spiders come out of hibernation. These particular spiders are known to crawl into sleeping bags searching for a warm place to spend the night. Why, sometimes, a snake looks for a warm place to spend the night, and the sleeping bags are an ideal place for them to sleep."

"Yeah, sure, Mom," one of the boys said. I was sure getting a lot of sure Moms on this trip. They were not buying the tall tale, and everyone had a good laugh as I announced it was bedtime. The boys retired to bed in their designated tents.

Kay asked if I too was retiring to bed, and I told her, "Not just yet. I still have a few things to do before this night ends." With her curiosity stirred, she volunteered to stay up for a while and keep me company. Two hours later the boys soft murmurs and laughter finally faded into some slight snores. In our conversation I informed her of the situation at hand. They had baited the younger boys tent, and this could not go without retaliation of some kind.

I enjoyed her company, and by twelve thirty, the older boys were sound asleep. If you have ever stayed in a tent you know the front is like a small window and unzips from both the inside and out. The outside is a screen that looks like a window screen, and it too unzips. In the High Country at night, you always close both the screen and the canvas window to keep in the warmth.

Fishing line works remarkably well to create a spider web of sorts. I placed a big black rubber spider in the middle and then tied it to the outside screen window of the older boy's tent.

I knew from their habits in the past, one or more of the boys would have to go water the trees before morning. With a full moon that night, the shadow of the rubber spider on the tent resembled the real thing, and the movement of the tent when a boy stirred out of his sleeping bag would add to the reality.

By this time, Kay stifled her laughter as I returned from my mischievous deed. She asked, "Are you going to bed now?"

I replied, "Absolutely not. I wouldn't miss out on this for the world; besides the night is still young and the games are just beginning." This was just the start of tonight's visualization training games.

She continued to sit up with me, enjoying the conversation while we waited. Sure enough, within an hour, Tony unzipped the canvas inner window, which made the spider attached to the outer screen window start to move. He started to unzip the screen window, half asleep when he spotted the spider and began yelling. At the same time, in the crowded tent that was wall-to-wall sleeping bags, he stepped back in the middle of one of the other boys, whose scream woke the other two boys. It might be noted these tents were not very big. Four teenage boys had to lay their sleeping bags next to each other, which left little floor space on the tents covered floor.

By this time, the tent was doing a jitterbug in the moonlight. That poor old rubber spider was really boogying. The more the boys moved the more the spider moved. The boys were screaming at the top of their lungs, and no one was trying to unzip the screen window. Kay and I laughed so hard my eyes begin to water. Finally, I regained my composure and strolled over and asked, "What's all the noise about?" After very excited explanations from the boys, I showed them the rubber spider, putting it in my pocket. "Someone has played a joke on you boys. I really want to get some sleep, and I do not want to be disturbed again." Of course my voice was very firm.

To my knowledge there are no black mountain spiders as I described to the boys earlier, harmless brown and black tarantulas, yes.

I insisted all four older boys go "water the forest," so they would not wake me again. While they were gone, I slipped an old rubber snake into Manuel's sleeping bag. He baited my little ones' tent with candy, so I thought it only fitting he be the one that ended up with the rubber snake in his sleeping bag. I knew that I had the advantage because this was also Manuel's first trip to the High Country.

Kay asked me again if I was going to bed now, and I said, "The fun is not over." She retired to bed. A few minutes went by, and I heard Manuel say he thought he had something in his sleeping bag. The boys got out their flashlights, and from the screams, I knew the fun had started all over again. They yelled, "Snake! Snake!" and that darn tent was doing another dance, and this time the poor little tent collapsed and came down on all four boys.

I again composed myself as best I could and went over to the tent. With a rather loud and gruff voice I asked, "What in the world is going on?" By this time, they found the snake, threw it up in the air and discovered it was just rubber.

I said in a very unhappy voice, "I would like to get some sleep if you boys don't mind" and had them hand me that poor old rubber snake. This was the rubber snake's second trip, except this time one of the boys in the excitement mangled him rather badly. I doubted he would make another trip.

They went back to bed, and everybody in camp went to sleep, except me. There was still one more thing that needed my special attention. I stayed up until about four thirty and threw a few candy wrappers around the older boys tent. I also made a few fake bear tracks.

About five o'clock, right next to their tent I started banging on the stainless-steel pan and making all kinds of noise. I yelled as if yelling at a bear, "Get out of here, go on, get out of here!" The teenage boys tent was dancing again. I heard one of them say, "That's a bear Mom's chasing out of camp." Another one said, "Gosh, I think it's close to our tent!" Finally, they got the tent screen window open, and crawled out. I told them, "There had been a bear in camp, and they were really lucky I knew what to do. That darn bear was close to their tent eating something. Did you, boys, bring any candy with you?" I asked.

"No, ma'am," they simultaneously replied.

"Well, the bear sure seemed to like your tent," I said as I turned and walked away. The boys, when they thought I was not watching, picked up the candy wrappers and saw the so-called bear tracks.

I did not get much sleep that night, but I sure had a lot of fun.

A few days later, I picked one of the more experienced boys, and we started pulling horses out of the meadow. The meadows at that time of the year had just begun to grow, and the grass was still pretty short. With the meadows short of feed we needed to go off the mountain for hay. This was not an easy task! We saddled two riding horses and four packhorses. We placed empty panniers on each of the packhorses. We had to ride the five miles back down to the horse trailers where extra hay lay covered inside. It's important for us to supplement the feed not only for the horses, but for the meadows as well.

As we were leaving camp, I stopped my horse and said to Jerry, "There really are two young yearling bear cubs in this area. If they get close to camp, you're in charge. See the big metal pan sitting in camp with the spoon in it—just take the spoon and run it in a circle inside the pan, and the bear will run away."

Jerry started laughing again and said, "Yeah right, René; that's just what we're going to do."

"Jerry, I'm serious," I replied.

Jerry looked up and said, "You two handle the hay; I will handle everything in camp."

I said, "Okay," and tipped my western hat, nodded my head and guided Tony and the packhorses down the mountain.

Tony, following me off the mountain, remarked, "The boys figured out you probably put the rubber snake in Manuel's sleeping bag, but they weren't real sure who sabotaged them with all the other stuff." I never admitted to any of it. I just kept riding down the mountain, dog tired, smiling to myself.

When we arrived back in camp, the older boys came over to take care of the packhorses and unsaddle my horse. They unloaded the hay, taking the horses to the meadow and to water.

As I walked into camp, the wonderful smell of dinner cooking was a welcome relief from the cold sandwich earlier in the day on the trail. Kay handed me a drink of cold water. I asked how everything had gone for the day, and Kay started laughing. Jerry and the boys all started talking at once.

I caught something about a bear being in camp, Jerry's shaving cream, and Jerry running naked in hot pursuit. Finally, I went over and rang the cowbell, which was standard equipment on all of our mountain trips. Everybody knew when I rang the bell that it meant I wanted everyone's undivided attention—or it was dinnertime.

I asked Kay to recap the day in camp for me. She smiled and proceeded to tell me their experience with an uninvited guest in camp that morning. The couple had fixed breakfast. After breakfast was over, Jerry decided to take a mountain bath and then shave. The boys, having a jump start on fishing, were down by the lake.

The mountain shower consisted of a makeshift blue canvas tarp, with four sides strapped to four poles stuck in the ground. The added ingredients consisted of a rather large pan of hot water mixed with two pans of cold mountain stream water. The bather removes his or her clothes, rinses off with a small pan of heated water, soaps the entire body, and then pulls a string to release the warm rinse water. Every bather needs a trusted friend to avoid the temptation created by this particular situation. The trusted friend mixes the hot and cold water and hoists the bigger bucket up and over the makeshift bath. Normally three buckets handled the bathing process. The most popular joke was to receive the cold mountain water with no hot water. I need not count the times the third bucket for my mountain shower was just cold mountain stream water.

Jerry finished his shower with Kay's steady hand. Kay began cleaning up the breakfast dishes and putting camp in order.

After drying off, Jerry took the towel and wrapped it around his lower body, stepped out of the blue plastic canvas, and started to shave. To shave, Jerry hung his mirror on a tree and slanted it upward, at the outer part of main camp. About fifteen feet directly behind him was a big rock that stood about ten feet in the air. Standing on this rock and looking down, it was possible for one to see Jerry in the mirror and vice versa. Jerry put the shaving cream on his face and started to shave when he noticed a movement on top of the rock. He turned for a closer look and there, standing on top of the rock, looking down at him was one of those yearling black bear cubs.

Jerry, being a city boy, threw up his hands and yelled at the cub, which only made the cub "mirror" what Jerry had just done. The cub stood straight up on the rock and gave out a big growl.

By this time, Kay handed him the pan, and Jerry grabbed for the spoon. He began using it the way I had mentioned.

The young bear's ears began to hurt, and he turned running toward the lake with Jerry in hot pursuit. Puffs of shaving cream flew off in all directions; needless to say, the towel wrapped around his lower anatomy was lost along the way. The only thing remaining was his camp slippers.

"René," Kay said, "I want you to know I have not laughed this hard in a long time."

The boys said, "It was pretty funny, Mom, to see Jerry running after that bear cub with no clothes on and his face white with shaving cream." I can just imagine what the poor bear cub was thinking.

This wonderful couple finally purchased their own place and opened a foster home for children. But for a year and a half, I had some of God's best helpers with me, which made my job so much easier.

~ Chapter 27 ~

SHELLY

Female counselors did not last at the ranch. They came with good intentions, but the boys couldn't help themselves. The female counselors provided good manipulation practice, which most of my streetwise boys mastered at a very early age. Female counselors lasted approximately 45 days, and the majority left crying.

I managed to hire one female counselor who proved to be the exception. I don't know why I hired her, woman's intuition perhaps. From an educational standpoint, she did not meet the requirements of state licensing regulations for our counselors, so I gave her a different title and hired her. After putting her on staff, I went through all kinds of red tape just to keep her. Shelly related in a special way with the boys. According to her personal background, she had lived through some tough times in her childhood.

She made deals with them. If you do so-and-so, I will do so-and-so for you. Shelly knew where to draw the line between demanding respect and having fun. Shelly, was similar to someone else on the ranch when it came to giving out restrictions; she was fair, a God-given talent of mine.

I remember visiting with her about some of the unpleasant experiences she could encounter at the boys ranch. She looked at me and replied, "René, I can handle your boys, give me a chance and I'll prove it."

Shelly's opportunity to prove herself came unexpectedly after dinner one evening. She went out to the barn to feed the livestock and rounded the corner only to catch Tony in a compromising position that only a teen in puberty appreciates. She stopped short, hands on her hips, and said, "Tony, stop milking your mule; put it away and come help me feed the horses."

After they finished the chores, Shelly came into my office and told me about the incident with Tony and her response. I stood up, walked around from behind my desk, grasped Shelly on her shoulders and said, "Welcome to the ranch." I knew then Shelly was a keeper, there to stay, after only thirty days into her sixty-day probation period. Naturally the other thirty days were removed. Over the next two and a half years, she proved herself to be one of my better counselors. Her country ways begin to show a loyalty to the brand and the ranch. In my way of thinking there are only two kinds of people in this world, the ones who try to do better for themselves, by showing strong morals and standards; I refer to as "registered stock." The ones that don't; I refer to as "common stock". Shelly was definitely "registered stock". Shelly was a good hand with a horse and began taking some of the load off of me by teaching horsemanship, which I accepted and appreciated.

Shelly experienced one tragedy during her tenure at the ranch. Her tragedy affected us all. The tragedy followed placement of a new resident; a lad the probation officer said needed "one last chance." In retrospect, I realized the officer needed to drop his count base at the end of the month and dumped him on the ranch. As I opened his case file the history and evaluation documentation of this resident was missing.

The boy created problems his first day. I still blame myself for not recognizing his mental instability right from the start. He could not adjust to the program, and Shelly and he experienced confrontation after confrontation over minor issues. He resented any and all communication with Shelly. For that matter he seemed in general to resent everyone. Naturally, she was responsible for the home and its residents she was assigned to, and he, was one of her residents. Shelly played no favorites. He threatened to hurt her one way or another. For that threat, he ended up in my office, and we had a long, serious talk.

Shelly and boys on San Francisco privilege trip

I called two and three times every day and reported the missing documentation in his files and requested an immediate update for the history background. I received no response. My instinct told me that the omission was no oversight.

Shelly owned the cutest Welsh Corgi dog; the little dog looked like a fox except with very short legs. Sophie, the Corgi had the sweetest, most loving disposition and big brown eyes that melted the hearts of everyone at the ranch. Sophie became attached to the boys and immediately became a member of the ranch family.

None of the dogs, including my own, were allowed to eat dinner with us or be around the table. However, Sophie became an expert at crawling on her belly and sneaking under the dinner table without being noticed. Sophie and the boys, especially the little ones, played catch in the yard until they were all exhausted. It became apparent Sophie knew she was family. I would call group session with the boys and Sophie would attend.

Like most Welsh Corgis, Sophie ran close to the ground. We forbade dogs in the roping arena, so the boys built a special platform with steps next to the arena fence so Sophie had a good view to watch the boys work their horses. It took Shelly only two days to teach Sophie this was her place, not the arena. Sophie shadowed Shelly with every step. When Shelly entered the arena area, Sophie climbed the steps and lay there watching every move. As an animal lover, I always had a special little companion of my own. We just did not see what was coming until it was too late.

Three days after this particular boy paid a visit to my office, Shelly came running into the office, hysterically crying saying she thought someone had poisoned Sophie. We drove that very sweet little dog to the vet, only to find there was nothing that could be done to save her life.

I stayed with Shelly until she made the decision to euthanize her. We sat there and cried together. It was just so very sad. Shelly said she wanted to bury Sophie at the ranch at the other end of the arena, where we had our pet cemetery. One of the cowboys stayed up late that night making a little casket. If one of the animals died at the ranch, all the horses were saddled the next morning and everyone attended a regular western funeral service. Everyone at the ranch felt the loss of Sophie.

After a short interrogation with this boy, he admitted rather proudly he poisoned the little dog. I immediately put a 31 (24-7) watch into effect. I called his probation officer and made arrangements to have him picked up the next afternoon and reminded him not to be late. I personally felt this child had a Psychopathic personality, requiring Psychiatric care.

The morning of the funeral, everyone circled the horses around the gravesite and watched while the new boy dug the hole to bury Sophie. Usually, the graves were dug two and a half feet deep, but today Shelly's dog Sophie would have a much deeper grave. It would be four feet deep, and we all sat there on the horses until the boy finished. The ground was a sandy loom and not that hard to dig. Shelly laid her little dog Sophie ever so gently in the casket.

Tom lowered Sophie's little casket in the grave and then led us in prayer. On a homemade cross someone had painted her name with a little verse. It was simple and read: *"Sophie, the best little four-legged hand on the ranch."*

There wasn't a dry eye in the crowd, except for the boy who committed the horrid act of killing her. Shelly put the first shovel of dirt in the grave, and one by one, we dismounted our horses, throwing a shovel of dirt into the grave.

When we lost an animal at the ranch, especially one we considered part of the family, it was important to show feelings of caring. It was a healing the boys could understand. With this little dog, even I had a hard time understanding and blamed myself for not seeing the danger ahead of time.

When the probation officer came to pick up the boy, I informed him I would definitely be in court for the hearing. I could not blame a boy of this nature since this child needed my professional help in placing him with people who were more specialized in helping the mentally disturbed. My facility dealt with psychological behavioral modification; this child had been placed in the wrong facility. I called Shelly to the office to explain the professional side of this matter. Shelly needed to know a normal boy would not have committed this horrid act.

In court my psychological report revealed a more deep-seated problem than placing this boy in another psychological behavioral program for counseling. I pointed out to the court, "Placing a child in a placement facility without a thorough evaluation of previous placement history hurt not only the child but the placement facility as well. In researching his file upon arrival I found no updated placement evaluation history." "Your honor," I continued, "I am requesting that this court require the state to provide a complete updated medical history as well as an updated psychiatric evaluation before placement can occur." I declined any request to join in this evaluation because of my recent involvement. "Your honor, due to his violent tendencies which may be psychopathic in nature, Napa state hospital, a wonderful psychiatric hospital for children and adults, should be considered." The court agreed.

Further research uncovered a brain malfunction that created more of the same behavior. And yes, he revealed tendencies in psychopathic behavior. This behavior was controllable by medication, and he was placed in the proper lock-up psychiatric hospital facility with court evaluations every three-to-six months until he reached age eighteen.

What was God's plan for this horrid happening? There was good that came from this matter. Because of this misplacement, the policy of placement changed, and updated psychological evaluations were required before a child with a violent background could qualify for a placement.

The ranch was quiet that week, more so than normal. I noticed something I had not realized before. Was it my professional teaching or God's helping hand? I preferred to think it was a little of both. We had a lot of caring boys at this ranch—boys who had no feelings for anyone or anything now were able to show love and concern for others, including animals and people.

Some wrote Shelly sympathy letters; some gave her handpicked wildflowers, and some of the boys painted sympathy cards. Yes, these were my boys, and I would claim them any day of the week. Most had been on the program for some time and were maturing.

I gave Shelly a week off, but she wouldn't leave the ranch, for by this time we were her family too. The boys came to me wanting to know if we could get Shelly a puppy. I thought it a good idea, but Shelly had Sophie as her little friend for five years, so I told the boys we would have to figure out some way that the idea be Shelly's and not ours.

The boys went right to work, and I was so proud of them. They got the newspaper and found Corgi puppies advertised in the classified section. They came running into the office to tell me their idea.

Finally, after three weeks had passed, I called Shelly into my office and told her about the boys and what they were trying to do. She thought it was still too soon. I suggested she go and look at the puppies "for the boys sake." The boys were really trying to help her in her grief.

Shelly, this wonderful, warm-hearted counselor, agreed to go look "just for the boys' sake." Three days later, Shelly had her new puppy; I asked the boys to come to my office. I praised them for their thoughtfulness and caring. It wasn't a long meeting, but I felt a strong need to tell them how very proud and honored I was to be their mom.

God and I carried on quite a conversation later that night. If ever I questioned the "why," I would not question it again, because in this sadness came an understanding of what I was about and why I was here.

In our Journey God has chosen for us, if it is a teaching Journey for others as mine has been, then we are truly blessed. The true feeling of giving rewards us so much more than we can ever imagine.

~ Chapter 28 ~

TOM GETS FIRED

Romance for me came second to my boys. Nothing and nobody came before the boys and the ranch. On one of my not-so-infrequent parent-principal visits to one of the local schools, the principal commented, "You are worse than having four angry mothers in my office all at once." I understood the undue propensity of finger pointing toward my boys when any unexplained infraction of the rules occurred. I was extremely protective, and the people of the little town understood my devotion. Most people that is, not all.

One day, a state licensing evaluator paid an unexpected visit to the ranch. She asked to see my files, which were allowed and normally I did not mind this loss of time. Their visit meant they were probably looking for something they could not find in *their* files. Sure enough, she wanted to know where my copies were on the monthly reports from the vocational school. I shifted instinctively into the "buying time" mode. I personally knew there were NO reports in this area. Tom hated paperwork and avoided the necessary documentation due to his priorities, and all things with Tom took priority over paperwork. Of course, I omitted this tiny detail to the license evaluator. Instead, I responded, "My administrator recently rearranged the filing system on our new computer. May I call you in a few days?" I swore I would never use the new-fangled computers. Today, writing my books, I can't ever imagine doing without "Darrell." Yes, I not only own a computer, but he has a name, and Darrell takes priority over everything else in my office.

After they left, I called Tom into the office and said, "You have got to write the monthly reports and bring them up to date, or I'm going to be in trouble."

Congenial Tom agreed, "I'll get them to you before the end of the week." Well, the week passed, and pretty soon a month slipped away, and still no reports.

Tom excelled in procrastination. One day I asked him to fill a mud hole on the ranch drive way. This particular mud hole cost me several re-alignment's on my truck. He looked at me with such a serious expression on his face and replied, "I would fix that ol' mud hole, but I don't want to disturb it," and walked away.

I headed back to my office mumbling to myself, "Does he expect me to buy this ridiculous excuse?"

The license evaluator showed up with a trainee. License evaluators with a trainee meant no matter how much you were in compliance, they were going to find something wrong to impress the trainee. They found nothing, until she looked on her backdated sheet and asked if I had the reports from the vocational program.

I said, "No, I could not find them." I had just made her day, month, and year, in front of the trainee.

She began to write and gave me a fine of five hundred dollars, along with the normal thirty-day grace period. She could remove my license in another sixty days unless we produced those reports.

They left, and I called Tom to the office. I asked in a rather irritated voice "Where are the vocational monthly reports?" I glared and continued, "You promised me these reports more than a month ago."

Tom said he had just forgotten. A building project in the barn with the boys had distracted him, and he would be writing them within the week.

"Tom," I said, "If, in fact, you do not have these reports written and on my desk by the end of the week, I will fire you. Your negligence on these reports has cost me five hundred dollars. I have thirty days to bring my facility into compliance or they will issue another warning which includes threatening to close me down, which would endanger my boys."

Early in our relationship, I told Tom of my devotion to my boys; he needed to know the boys trusted me with their future. Nothing could interfere with my responsibility toward my boys.

A week passed, and then another week. No report, not one single page, was turned into the office. On Monday morning, I called Tom to the office, and asked for the reports. Again, he went through the "Oh, I forgot' routine," and I sat and listened. When he finished, I said, "Tom, you are fired."

He laughed and said, "Look, I know you are mad, but really, you can't fire me! Remember we're have a partnership in life."

I said, "Tom, this is not personal. It has nothing to do with our relationship. It has everything to do with your job and your lack of doing your job properly."

He was definitely unhappy with this decision. "You aren't really serious about firing me, are you?"

I said, "Yes, you are fired. And I will have the accounting department write you a check."

He left the office only to return in a couple of hours with his clothes in the back of *his* old pickup and informed me he was leaving and would not be coming back.

I said, "Good-bye."

Tom had a very good job with the ranch. He walked away from a good job, which provided a very good salary plus all expenses, a line of credit at the local western store, and a new truck to drive. Basically Tom had no overhead.

I was hoping he could not find anything to compare to this arrangement, and I was right. About ten days went by before I heard from Tom. He came to the office and said he wanted to talk.

I replied, "Make an appointment."

He said, "Don't push it."

I didn't. Frankly, I really missed him and had told the boys Tom was off to a rodeo.

The conversation remained short and to the point; He said, "You know I can do those silly reports you want."

I replied, "Yes I know you are capable of doing the reports, but this time NO Procrastination, just do the darn reports, you have one week."

The word spread like wildfire among the townspeople and local ranchers that I had fired Tom. Although none of them knew the circumstances, all chose sides. Some understood my devotion to my boys and the ranch. Others deemed me as some kind of spitfire lynx.

Tom left my office after our meeting and agreed he would write the darn reports. Late that night when I walked into the main ranch house, we shared a cup of coffee as if nothing happened. It took him just two full days to complete all the reports, which I discovered were two years behind—that is twenty-four reports!

The deep understanding and feelings for each other was as strong as ever. Neither of us discussed the matter again. Tom is one of two people in eight years that I had to fire. No one ever questioned my loyalty to my boys after the firing of Tom.

~ Chapter 29 ~

CREATIVITY IN DEMONSTRATION

Visual demonstration takes on a new meaning when you are dealing with children, especially if those children are between the ages of nine and ten. My nine and ten year olds could humble me with one sentence. So I was forced by my younger, more challenging audience, to create situations in teaching that children could respond to openly.

For visual demonstrations I needed props as a teaching tool. Props could add emphasis to the psychological demonstrations. Sometimes my ingenuous creativity surprised even myself. In one such demonstration I was creating a psychological example, hoping to instill the bad side of alcohol, cigarettes smoking, and drugs.

I spoke to one of the counselors, "Jim, could you please dig me some night crawlers for the group session class taking place this evening with my boys?"

Jim started to leave my office and turned toward me replying with a funny expression on his face, "Ma'am, let me get this straight. You want me to dig up some fishing worms for you? Are you taking the boys fishing in the middle of winter?"

"Yes Jim," I replied. "It's going to be a great demonstration, on alcohol, smoking and drugs." Knowing full well that this cowboy dipped Copenhagen on occasion, I added, "You might want to attend."

Jim's curiosity was in full swing. "What do the worms have to do with...." He hesitated for just a moment. "Oh never mind." Cowboys for the most part are not by nature a curious lot. They mind their own business. Conversation sometimes with a cowboy is hard to come by. I think his cowboy personality kicked in about this time.

I answered his second question, "No, we are not going fishing." I paused, "You should really consider coming tonight."

Will you please have them in my office at least an hour or so before my session?" "And Jim, thank you," I dismissed him verbally and looked down at some papers on my desk.

He turned to leave and then stopping for just a moment, he asked, "How many shall I dig for you?"

"Five or six will do just fine." I replied.

He started to ask something else, but changed his mind closing the door behind him. I thought I heard him mumbling.

By the time the evening rolled around I had my props in place. It consisted of four clear one gallon glass jars. I covered each jar with paper and wrote "Alcohol" on one and "Cigarette Smoking" on the second and "Drugs" on the third. The fourth I wrote "Clean Living." I drew a little worm on each jar. Underneath this drawing, I put the word "Worms."

I thought to myself, *"Oh this is going to be a great demonstration on positive flow for a better way of living healthier."*

When the evening session began, naturally the boys were curious about the jars on my desk. I could hardly wait to begin the session. I had poured the first jar full of alcohol, the second was covered with water and held very soggy tobacco, the third I had filled with water and a mixture of over-the-counter drugs to simulate drugs. The fourth I filled with good clean looking soil. In each of the first three jars I placed one worm. Jim had brought me six worms, so there were three left over. I put all three in the jar that was marked clean living.

That evening two of the house parents showed up along with a few curious cowboys. At these sessions all the boys were required to attend. So I had a great attendance to show off my educational background. Ah, I thought to myself, it's wonderful to have a full classroom for my great demonstration.

When everyone was settled in; I began by pointing out the various jars sitting on my desk. "We have a crisis growing in this country. We are not paying attention to our human God-given bodies. See these jars; there are four jars different in origin, meaning the point at which something comes into existence or from which it derives or is derived." At this point Willie who is ten raises his hand, "Yes Willie, please stand."

"Mom, what is what you just said?" he asked as he stood there fidgeting.

I replied, "Willie, you may sit down. Will you please hold your questions, all of you, until I am finished; then I will be happy to answer all your questions."

I began again, "Three jars symbolize negative behavior while the other symbolizes positive behavior. In jar one is alcohol." I turned picking up the jar as I called on one of the teenage boys to walk it around the room showing it to everyone as I continued explaining, with my great educational knowledge, and was simply carried away by the moment. The first jar filled with alcohol showed the worm was very dead. Since he was floating on top, his demise was obvious. The second filled with water and cigarette tobacco produced another dead worm. The third, well, it was the same results, another dead worm, which made three who had met their demise.

"The things we decide to put in our bodies tell us by this demonstration we could very well be killing ourselves by putting the wrong elements in our systems." I paused for just a moment to see if my class was following this demonstration. I was getting some very curious looks from my younger ones. Then I asked, "Were the worms dead or alive?" The class shouted, "DEAD."

When it came to the fourth jar, I asked for a volunteer to dig down in the dirt and see what he could find.

Keep in mind the first three jars were all the bad things we use and abuse, alcohol, tobacco, drugs, and the fourth was the live worms. Conway, another one of my ten year olds raised his hand and I asked him, "Conway, could you see if you can find any worms in this jar?" I lowered the jar, and what do you know? He found a real live worm. When he pulled the live worm out I said, "Great, Conway you have found the live worm. You may sit down now."

Addressing the class, I said, "What have we learned from this simple demonstration?

David raised his hand first. "I know this one, Mom. Can I please, can I please answer this one, I know this Mom, honest."

It was not my first choice to have David answer this question, because I never knew what was going to come rolling out of his mouth. After looking around the room, saying, "Anybody, want to volunteer anybody? I was left with the fact that no one else raised their hand and gave me very little choice but to call on David.

"Yes, David," I responded to his excitement, for by now he, David, was jumping up and down. "Go ahead, son, tell us what this demonstration means and what we learned from it."

Of course, the lesson to this demonstration was clean living resulted in clean health.

David spoke up, "Mom, it means as long as you drink, smoke and do drugs, you won't get worms."

My mouth dropped open leaving me speechless.

After David's comment I dismissed the class knowing full well I had failed miserably in this demonstration. I did not want to discourage David from responding in class. As he was leaving, I heard him tell the other young ones, "It sure feels good when you can answer a question of Mom's and get it right." I would straighten this out with David later.

Joe, on the other hand, came up to the desk and having the depth of an adult spoke, "Mom, we older boys, well, we got the message about clean health and stuff, but I still feel you drowned perfectly good fishing worms." As he turned to walk to the door, he hesitated, "Where did you say you dug for those night crawlers?"

Still being in shock over David's answer, I mumbled, "Ask Jim."

As the rest left the room, smiles and sounds of laugher filled the room and as they were leaving, comments flowed abundantly. Tom remarked as he past my desk, "Highly educational, one of your best." Grinning from ear to ear as though he knew who won this round. I was humbled by a nine-year old.

Joe had a point in the matter; I had drowned three of God's creatures to prove a point in psychological theory only to come up short.

~ Chapter 30 ~

SCRAPPY

Amarillo, Texas

Sitting in this doctor's waiting room was not my idea of an enjoyable day. What was worse, the sun was shining outside, and there was no wind, a rare occurrence in the Texas panhandle. I could be riding my horse and really making use of a great day. I looked around the room and my eyes came to an abrupt stop when I saw a young boy about the age of eleven, with dark brown hair and pretty blue eyes. Goodness gracious, what a lady-killer he is going to be when he grows up.

My eyes locked with his and the young boy gave me a smile that just melted my heart—clear to my soul. Then it hit me; this boy favored a boy I had at the ranch. We called him Scrappy. Sometimes at the ranch I took a special case with special circumstances.

One day I answered the phone to hear a familiar voice on the other end; it was John, a probation officer that I had known for quite sometime. He placed a couple of boys with me in the past and was aware that occasionally I took special cases. We talked a little, and finally, I came out and asked, "John what's this phone call really about?" He knew one thing about me—don't waste my time; just get to the point.

John had a mother sitting in his office, and her eleven-year old boy in lockup. The mother, a single parent, was trying to cope with this child. She admitted the child was uncontrollable, remarking, he hated her.

John remarked, "She works as a nurse and is in dire need of help. She truly loves her son and requested help from me and I recommended your ranch facility."

The boy was not a bad boy, but the devastating divorce from the father was a bitter one. If I interviewed the boy and agreed to take him as a placement for "reunification" (there is that darn word again), the county would drop the charges against the boy upon reunification back with the mother. This reunification could actually work. John continued, "René, if you decide to help this mother, we will okay payment for the entire one and a half year stay."

I thought to myself, "*Sure you will, because the county has no proper place to put this eleven-year old boy.*" I agreed to meet with them the following day. In this situation, I needed to meet with both the mother and the boy.

Upon meeting with the mother, it didn't take a whole lot of common sense to figure this one out. She sat in front of me with big tears streaming down her face. She was small in stature, five feet and three inches tall and maybe one hundred ten pounds, and looked older than her thirty-five years. She began by telling me about her childhood and the abuse she suffered growing up; then came marriage and abuse from her husband. The son, even at his young age, had learned and saw enough from his abusive father that the boy was becoming abusive.

When I asked the boy about his mother, he said, "I hate her." It was obvious; he blamed his mother for the loss of his father. Although not all cases are fixable, I felt hope for this boy and his mother. As I continued the interview with the boy I caught a confused sadness in his bitterness towards his mother. Through her love and her desire to do whatever was necessary to earn her son's respect again, she assured me I would have her full cooperation. This mother truly loved her son.

I explained to the mother she would be required to undergo counseling at the ranch herself. We would arrange her counseling, which was once a week when the boy was in school or on an outing. The first few months would be the toughest. She could neither see, nor telephone her son, until he leveled out at the ranch. I agreed to keep in contact with her and receive all telephone calls from her at any time. Updates on his behavior during her counseling sessions would be short on her son's progress, as these sessions were about her and working through her problems.

She shook her head in agreement and said, "I'm a nurse and can't lose my job, but whatever it takes I will do."

I assured her, "I will work with you around your schedule; we are here for you and your son."

When I accepted Scrappy to the ranch, he created havoc from the beginning, testing my patience and strength. This eleven-year old mafia-want-to-be Italian boy was into something every day. Fighting was an everyday occurrence; he never considered the size, the age, or possible outcome when he took on any opponent, thus earning him the nickname—Scrappy.

One day after one of his fighting escapades, we sat staring at each other, neither one speaking. Finally I stood up, said nothing, just motioned him outside to the arena, and introduced him to an old-looking steer in the corral. I said, with a very serious look, "Scrappy, if you can ride that old steer the full eight seconds, I will buy you that battery-operated race car for your birthday you spotted in the store, provided you make an attempt to stay out of trouble."

This was bribery in its truest form; if bribery works, then go for it. Sometimes a boy's negative energy needs a bit of redirection. Replacing physical aggression with a physical challenge works as a valid therapy; I turned and walked away from the boy, without speaking of the mayhem he created earlier.

Tom headed up the rodeo program on the ranch. After a honeymoon period of two fights or so, he nicknamed the boy Scrappy and took an instant liking to the boy. For the next few weeks, Tom conditioned and trained Scrappy to ride that old steer that was a pro at bucking boys off his backside. No boy managed to stay atop thus far, but I neglected to mention this little detail to the troubled boy. Was this fair? If this therapy worked and handled his aggressive behavior, then yes, it was fair.

The next week, Scrappy came to my office and told me he was ready to ride Samson, the steer. "I'll be collecting my race car right after this ride!" My goodness, this boy was so cocky. I was assured in my mind's eye that this was going to make my day.

I followed him out to the arena and watched as they opened the chute gate, and Samson, the steer performed his usual feat—bucking Scrappy off over his head and then looking back as if he were laughing at the boy, who was now lying facedown in the dirt. Yep, this did make my day! As I was leaving the arena, I stopped long enough to remark, "Oh by the way, we have great food in the kitchen son, there isn't any reason for you to eat the arena dirt, but it's which ever you prefer."

For the next few weeks, I watched over and over as Scrappy tried to ride Samson. The one thing that impressed me was that Scrappy never showed a sign of "spitting the bits out" (a western term for quitting). Every afternoon when he came home from school, Scrappy and Tom talked about how to ride Samson. By this time he had forgotten all about fighting, and was so into riding this darn steer that other things started to happen in a more positive way.

Scrappy earned his Level Two; which meant he qualified for the rodeo program, provided the other boys voted for him. They did. Being voted into the rodeo program was a major step; the other boys approval initiated a string of changes in Scrappy. The ranch rodeo team began to help him with his riding. He forgot some of his problems; he wanted to be a better person. We continued the counseling sessions concerning his mother.

Scrappy continued to challenge me as he did his mother. I did not give an inch. Naturally, he began to show the respect required to grow into a productive adult. When this respect began to take form, he was able to show respect for others—but not for his mother—however, I felt he was moving in that direction. Tom suggested I not watch him try to ride that darn steer, as he felt it interfered with Scrappy's concentration, and I agreed.

Four months went by, and one day, the door to my office swung open; there stood Scrappy with a grin a mile wide.

"Do I owe you a race car?" I asked.

Scrappy at the finals

He said, "Yes, ma'am."

On his birthday, I bought Scrappy the one hundred and sixty-nine dollar battery-operated race car he wanted so badly. I still have a picture of that moment. It was the best money I ever spent. Six months passed and he was becoming good at this sport. So good, in fact, that he rode his fourth steer to the eight second whistle and placed third in the go around. The eight second whistle means the rider must stay on the bucking steer for eight seconds to accomplish a qualifying ride.

At the ranch, the boys had to ride eight seconds in competition to earn their chaps, which I made for them. Now that Scrappy did his part, I would do my part. Scrappy won his chaps at his fourth junior rodeo. I was sitting in the grandstand when he finished the ride. He came over to the fence and told me, "You owe me a pair of chaps, get to sewing!"

Scrappy wearing his chaps

Meanwhile, Tom and Scrappy become inseparable. I'd never seen Tom take such an interest in any of the boys. Scrappy placed his boot print in every boot print Tom made. Tom worked with Scrappy, teaching him everything about roping and riding, to woodcrafts and mechanics. I loved watching them from the window, heads bowed with their Stetson brims touching, working some intricate rope knot. Scrappy loved living at the ranch, and we loved him as our own, as I did with all my boys.

His grades in school started improving, and for the first time in his life he was doing so many things he had little time to think about his problem and his mother. Scrappy was becoming settled and had moved up to Level Three. It was time now for him to start facing his problem with his mother and move forward with his life.

I invited his mother to a local Rodeo in the area, asking her,

"Would you like to come and see your son ride?"

She came to the rodeo and sat by herself away from the boys at the ranch until Scrappy rode his steer. She then moved next to me, informing me of her concern for her son riding a steer. she showed an uneasiness regarding their relationship. Responding to her uneasiness; "Look I understand this is not going to be an easy walk in the park." I tried to reassure her by saying, "Scrappy will probably see you and a part of him may resent your intrusion; but with each meeting, there will be improvement." And then added, "He really is a good little steer rider."

To love a child, watch him grow, see him succeed in life and still remember what my responsibilities were—to reunify Scrappy with his mother, who also loves him—sometimes became a very heavy burden to carry. As parents, just imagine loving your child and having to give him up. This was always an emotional roller coaster for me.

Scrappy came into the office one day and asked, "May I call you 'Mom' like the rest of the boys?" Oh, how I wanted to hug him and say, "Yes, oh yes!"

"Scrappy," I said, "It's time for a little educational session. You, my boy, are one of the lucky ones here at the ranch. You actually have a birth mother, one who loves you with all her heart. She is taking counseling to better understand your needs, so consider yourself one of the lucky ones. She truly wants you back home." I continued to explain, "I will always love you, but how very lucky you are to have a mom, as most of my boys have no mother, at least none we can find. I am their mom because I am the only mom they know, and that's why they call me Mom.

What was so special about Scrappy? Why was he different? Today, in reflection, I know why Scrappy was so special and so different. His mother truly cared for him.

As we progressed along on the program, the state sent out a social worker to interview Scrappy. Scrappy's mother Sherrill, the social worker, and I sat down in my office. I told Scrappy ahead of time this interview was just a simple periodic routine visit. He need not worry.

Meanwhile, the older boys caught wind of what was going on, and told Scrappy if he agreed too much, he would be sent home in the middle of rodeo season. The interview was a disaster. The questions went something like this:

Talking to Scrappy, the social worker asked: "How old are you?"

Scrappy: "I'm old enough to know what I want."

Social Worker: "And what do you think you want?"

Scrappy: "To stay at the ranch."

Social Worker: "If you went home, would you mind your mother?"

Scrappy: "No."

Social Worker: "But you have been minding René."

Scrappy: "Yes, ma'am. She is my second mom, and she is tough; but she loves me."

Social Worker: "Do you love your mother?"

Scrappy: "Yes, ma'am, but I don't want to go home right now."

The boy had come a long way. We dismissed Scrappy and his mother, at which time the social worker reminded me what my job was—to reunify the boy back home to his real mother. Reluctantly I agreed, knowing the social worker was right. Perhaps my involvement was standing in the way of my judgment.

After that, Sherril began coming to the ranch every two weeks, then every week. She went on skating parties with us and sometimes stayed the weekend at the ranch. It wasn't easy, but Scrappy began to let go of his bitterness. They began to have fun together. Then the time came for Scrappy to take the next step—a weekend visit at home. Eventually, we extended the visits until Scrappy stayed at home an entire week with his mother.

Tom and I stifled our inner feelings when the time came for Scrappy to leave the ranch. He climbed so many tall mountains in his emotional world: his grades improved, he made friends easily, and he won our district's state championship in steer riding. No matter how proud Tom and I were of him, we were no more proud than his very own mother when she took her respectful, happy son back home.

For a while, Tom and I did not talk about Scrappy—it was just too painful. Tom refused to get that close to any of the boys again.

To be successful with the boys as a ranch mother, I faced the pain of real motherhood. I needed to let the boys go forever. There must be realization of the pain you go through to get the results you are seeking for the sake of the child. The reward, of course, was knowing that Scrappy was settled back with his mother and would probably continue to grow in a positive direction, due in part to the contribution of the people at the ranch. But, oh, how it hurt to see my little steer-rider leave.

~ Chapter 31 ~

OTHER RANCH ROMANCES

The teenage girls at school went crazy over Tony, one of my fifteen-year olds. In fact, we transferred Tony five times to different schools; he was one of those boys, girls simply loved to be with, and oh how he loved the attention. Tony was half Indian and half Mexican and had natural dark skin and dark brown eyes, plus the prettiest black wavy hair, which made him drop-dead good looking. Tall for his age, he was already developing upper body strength and muscle tone.

One of many memorable incidents happened at the ranch involved Tony and a very special young lady; this infraction could have been a disaster of the worst kind for the boy's ranch.

I caught Tony with a girl in his room. The female visitor rode her bike eight miles out to the ranch. I put her bike in my pickup and gave her a pretty good scolding about what was proper and what was not during the ride back to town. I did not know she was the mayor's daughter until we turned up the driveway of her parents' home; I recognized him as he walked towards the pick-up. This was not good. She pleaded with me not to tell her parents. Somehow the mayor already knew about the situation. Oh the wonders of living in a small country town. Everyone in the county knew what kind of ranch I had, including the mayor. The mayor and I on occasion conversed in a positive way on several matters concerning the community. Volunteer work and helping the elderly was one such program.

This program, helping elderly folks paint their houses, and mow their yards, had the respect of the whole community. We were not strangers to each other, nor were we friends.

The daughter ran past her father and into the house, and by this time tears flowed like a fire hose under full pressure. She was only fourteen. We visited for a short time, and as I was leaving, I turned and apologized to the mayor and assured him nothing happened. However, not until I had a very serious talk with Tony, did I feel convinced I spoke the truth about the mayor's daughter.

Returning to the ranch, as I walked through the main ranch house, I yelled: "I want Tony in my office immediately."

One of my cowboy counselors replied, "But Tony is doing so and so."

I stopped abruptly, "I don't care if he is wiping his backside. I want him in my office NOW." Tony entered my office hangdog, with head hung down and eyes staring at his boots. I plowed into him with a tongue lashing of the proverbial kind. I'm not quite sure, but I think I felt smoke spewing out of my ears. "Tony, you can't have just any girl in your room, like the neighbor's daughter or the little girl down the street, which, by the way, would be bad enough. Oh, no, you have the audacity to invite the mayor's daughter to your room."

I had talked to myself all the way back to the ranch: "Be calm, keep your voice calm; you can handle this one calmly." Perhaps the first few words were calm, but my voice of its own volition gradually increased louder and louder until I was shouting. "Do you have any idea of the ramifications your actions could bring to this ranch?"

Tony still looking down, "Yes Ma am,' but Mom, it wasn't my idea."

I stood up. I was losing it on this statement. "I suppose she found your EXACT window by herself! Your little afternoon rendezvous could threaten the whole program and the other boys who call this ranch their home!" I barely noticed Tony's nervous fingers as he moved his hat brim through his hands. I put Tony on restriction for fifteen days.

Romance of this kind could cost the facility our state license. For the next week I had nightmares about lawsuits and the licensing foreclosure of the ranch. As it turned out, the mayor wrote a nice letter and asked that I not mention the incident to anyone. I called and thanked him for the letter, reassuring him that I had told no one. I laughed at the whole thing because of the upcoming elections. He couldn't afford a small town scandal, especially concerning his daughter. Sometimes God just looks down on us and smiles that wonderful big smile and blesses us just before we go down for the third time.

A different kind of romance took place at the ranch. I interviewed a rather nice looking young cowboy in his late twenties. During the interview, I told him I did not want to hire him because of my female counselors. Most of my male counselors were older. If I hired a young one more the age of my female counselors and it resulted in romance, which was not allowed at the ranch between counselors, I could lose both counselors.

Decisions about hiring a counselor must be evaluated in terms of my personal investment, which required a sixty to ninety day training period and at least nine thousand dollars in my personal time and effort. If I lose that person after the training period, I have just cost the corporation and myself time and money.

After further discussion Bob convinced me he would meet all my requirements. I handed him a contract to sign stating there would be no dating other counselors who worked on the ranch. I even had him read it out loud, so there would be no misunderstanding in this serious matter.

At that time, I employed Shelly and Leanne, two female counselors, and both were pretty easy on the eyes. Leanne originally hired as the ranch secretary. After completing her degree, I promoted her to counselor. I did not want to lose either one, because they were very good counselors.

Upon hiring new employees, I introduced them to the other counselors at a special group session. When I introduced the new counselor, the others came up and one by one welcomed the counselor to the ranch. When it was Leanne's turn, the two just stood there staring at each other. I finally told Leanne to close her mouth as it dropped open upon the introduction. Leanne immediately volunteered to show Bob around the ranch. She too had a no dating clause in her contract.

The days started getting longer and the winds began to change from cool to a welcome warm breeze signaling time for the summer trips to the High Country. I hired an administrator the year before, and he was chomping at the bit and pulling on the reins to take control at the ranch. Larry was working out rather well. The ranch was running smoothly, so I gave in and stepped down allowing him full administrative control. Executive Director would be my only position. This gave me the opportunity to do the things I liked to do, without the normal burden of paperwork. I spent most of my time that summer in the mountains taking boys into the High Country.

The mountain trips offered the greatest of both worlds—teaching and watching boys grow in the mountains while experiencing the ever presence of God's greatest landscapes, the high Sierra country of Yosemite National Forest. Not all the boys went on the mountain excursions. Some stayed home and participated in other activities the ranch offered. One such activity was roller skating at the local skating rink.

Always when the boys went skating, two counselors accompanied them. Leanne was a good skater and assigned to this activity, which also meant she could influence the choice of who the second counselor would be.

When Leanne asked for a volunteer, Bob immediately volunteered for the job. Most of the counselors that went along on these skating trips knew how to skate. It was assumed if you volunteered for the skating activity, you knew how to skate. Well, I guess Bob was so busy volunteering looking into Leanne's blue eyes that he overlooked this fact.

After the first outing to the skating rink, the boys told me, "Mom, you should have seen how many times Bob fell at the skating rink." I can just imagine how he must have looked on skates: good-looking, sandy brown hair, and absolutely gorgeous eyes, cowboy hat, six three, big shoulders, and a thirty-four inch waist in Wranglers that stretched down his lean frame to those funny looking scuffed skates. All this on roller skates!

The months went by, and fall came with damp cold rains, and howling winds. Winter had arrived.

Bob continued to accompany Leanne to the skating rink and Leanne finally accomplished the impossible, teaching Bob how to skate.

I started noticing things about Leanne that could only mean one thing. She was spending a lot of time running to the bathroom, throwing up, and looking very pale. Although they had been dating, they kept it away from the ranch. I did not have a clue.

One day following our regular counselors' meeting, I asked Leanne to stay because I wanted to visit with her on an important matter. As she sat down in the chair in front of my desk, I spoke softly, "Leanne, you're doing such a great job with the boys here at the ranch."

She replied, "It's the most rewarding job I have ever experienced." She began to look down at the floor.

I continued, "Sometimes we as directors are so busy we forget to tell the people working the ranch how much they are appreciated." I asked the question lingering between us. "Are you pregnant?"

She started to cry. She looked at me as if to say, how did you know? She was scared and worried. "Yes," she said, followed by more tears.

"Does he love you?" She did not answer, just more tears. I read this to mean that he did not love her, or she did not know. "Is this worthless excuse of a boyfriend going to marry you, or am I just going to have to hang him from the nearest tree?" After a long pause, I continued, "What do you want me to do? How can I help you?" My counselors also became my family. Not overnight, but it did happen.

Leanne was from a divorced family; her dad left home when she was young. Her mother left Leanne with her grandmother at a very early age.

Leanne looked so surprised. She said, "I do not want to lose my job."

"Who in the world told you that you were going to lose your job if you got pregnant?" I asked.

She looked at me bewildered. "You did."

Sometimes I made so many rules trying to cover everything I forgot about the pregnancy clause. This was not the clause she was thinking about!

"Well, Sis," I said, "If I made the darn rule, I can sure break it."

So back to who's the father? Does he live in town? Did he work on one of the nearby ranches, and was he going to marry her? My volley of questions triggered tears, tears, and more tears. I assumed these tears meant that he wasn't going to marry her.

I slowly walked around from behind my desk putting my hand on her shoulder, "I will find this worthless crow bait and he WILL marry you!" My solution to resolve this matter only spurred her to heavier sobbing. I tried to figure out why she was still crying. Was I talking too loud? Did she think I was mad at her? Her sobs increased my sympathy. I truly cared for this twenty-three-year old girl and wanted with all my heart to make everything right for her. I continued, "Just tell me who this yellow belly lowlife is, and I will see that he does the right thing."

She looked at me with those big blue eyes and said, "If I tell you, he will get fired from his job."

"Is that what you're worried about? Is that what all these unhappy tears are about?" I asked. "Well, you stop crying," I continued. "I'll talk to his boss and tell him not to fire this young man because he is going to be a husband and a father which will make a better employee because he will be more settled. Now, what is this boy's name, and who is his boss?"

Leanne said, "The boys name is Bob." With a little hesitation in her voice, she added, "and the boss is you, ma'am!"

Well, we had the wedding. And it was a real wedding. About three months after the marriage Bob came to the office very long faced. He and Leanne were having some problems. He could not figure it out. He sent her flowers two and three times a week and continued buying her things as if they were dating, anything she wanted and then some. He wanted my advice. The cost was too great to keep doing these things, and she seemed unhappy. "Bob" I said, "Your situation reminds me of that ol' saying, "It's kind of like a cog that turns the wagon-wheel. You need to keep it greased to keep the wheel running smoothly; however, I've seen wealthy men over-grease the cog that turns the wheel until it begins to slip out of control. Leanne will appreciate you more if you point out to her the flowers purchased and other things that are costly are going to stop because there are other more important things coming your way, such as the baby. Leanne will appreciate your conservative attitude. And don't forget the, "I love you," statement everyday—it does not hurt nor cost you anything, but will be appreciated by your wife."

A few days later Bob poked his head in the door of my office, thanked me and said, "I have quit greasing the cog, except on special occasions."

The boys got quite an education out of this romance. None of my little ones knew about the baby until Leanne's stomach started to grow. Then the questions started to come, especially from my little ones. The little ones were full of questions about how the baby was made and how it was growing.

The growth of the baby increasingly enlarged Leanne's stomach. She was so good with my younger inquisitive boys, allowing them to feel the baby kick. They entered my office one day and asked, "Mom, did you know Leanne is going to have one of us?"

For just a fleeting moment, I thought, "OH NO!"

David continued. "And, how is this going to be Bob's baby too when it's in Leanne's stomach?"

"Well, David, he helped make it." With this one statement, I spent the next hour trying to satisfy my young one's inquisitiveness. In some cases speaking the truth can create a continuation of the subject matter, especially with nine-year-olds.

The baby shower was one of a kind, especially when the cowboys at the ranch found out it was going to be a boy. At the shower, the baby, who had not yet arrived, received presents including a very small bull-riding rope which was hand plaited by one of my cowboys. Of course, the little guy wouldn't be able to use it until he was four. That's the age when young ones start riding sheep at the rodeo, in a special event known as mutton busting. The association even gives a belt buckle to the winner.

Some of the other gifts were a pair of spurs, a stuffed rocking horse, and naturally a small custom-made cowboy hat. Tom had ordered the darn baby hat from Forth Worth, Texas. It probably would not fit until he was around three. One of the cowboys made a baby pair of chaps, the smallest I had ever seen. Two of the teenage boys helped the younger ones make a variety of little things, including a hand-painted big cowbell to hang on the end of the crib that said BABY on the sides.

After I finished telling everyone how they made fools of themselves and should have realized the baby was going to need diapers and sensible things, they asked what I had bought for the "baby boy that had not yet arrived."

"Yeah, Mom, what did you buy for a present?"

"Well, it's in that big box sitting in the corner," I answered with a big smile.

When Leanne unwrapped the box with Bob sitting by her side and saw what was in the box, they both hugged me. I had done the more "sensible" thing. I had a saddle maker in Fort Worth; make a very special little saddle the baby probably could not use until he was at least three-years old.

The night Leanne had the baby, nearly everyone at the ranch went to the hospital; it was something to see. I looked down the hallway to see eighteen boys, cowboys, and Tom. The doctor asked who the father was, and all the cowboys raised their hands, jokingly, of course; then pointing to Bob, they pushed him in the delivery room. After fainting shortly thereafter, Bob was carried out on a stretcher with the cowboy hat lying on his chest.

We nicknamed the baby Scooter, for his delivery was a short one. This very special family stayed at the ranch for more than three years before they moved onto other things in their lives. I shall never forget the excitement this family brought to the ranch, and the pleasure received from that very tiny human being.

~ Chapter 32 ~

THE MOUNTAIN HIKE-IN

Every summer, we planned a hike into the High Country for the younger boys. At this time of year, the older boys were using all our horses for roping and rodeo practice and the younger ones felt left out. A five-mile hike into Kibby Lake, with its wide shady trails that were not too steep, was exactly what they needed. One of the older boys named this trip "the shoelace hike-in," because all my little ones wore tennis shoes for this trip. The backpacks the boys carried containing lunch and snacks for the day trip of hiking up to Kibby were being checked. Excitement was in the air for the upcoming trip. The conversation drifted back and forth from the rainbow trout that populated the lake to the enticing swimming hole with its clear blue water.

Unfortunately, the ranch hand that I scheduled to accompany the boys and me came down with some kind of stomach virus, so I decided to take the boys by myself to avoid leaving the ranch shorthanded. I had traveled alone with groups of boys before, and everything went according to plan. After all Tom would be only a few hours behind us with the pack horses carrying our supplies, which included our dinner, and all our overnight camping supplies.

The boys loaded their backpacks into the camper shell of my pickup; we hooked up the horse trailer, loaded my horse G.B., and headed out. Eight very excited young boys scrambled into my truck. Four rode up front in the four-door truck, and four rode in the back with a covered camper. The ones in the back could open the sliding windows, plus there was no counselor in the back to be condescending on their behalf.

As we were getting ready to leave the ranch, I noticed Tom had not gathered the packhorses out of the pasture. Tom assured me not to worry: "We will arrive with the supplies in time for the evening meal." We both knew the boys moved slower walking than the horses. Tom didn't want to catch up with us because of all the dust the horses would create passing us on the trail. Tom selected a cowboy who was new to the ranch to help with the packhorses so the new hand could get some experience in the high country.

The drive to the High Country was always exciting for the boys and entertaining for me. The air in the valley was hot. Driving farther into the Sierras, we could feel the air getting cooler. With each stop we made, the boys sensed the changes and became more eager about our trip.

I still remember one conversation I had with nine-year old David during the trip. We were stopped at a traffic light in Sonora, when he saw a restaurant sign that read, "Buffet lunch five-ninety-five." It caught David's attention.

"Mom," he said, "what does b-u-f-f-e-t mean? I've never heard of buff-it."

"David, it is not buff-it. The (t) at the end of the word is silent. A buffet is a lunch that is served on trays, and you help yourself to whatever you want."

David thought for just a moment about what I'd told him, and then he said, "Mom, I really don't think I said that word wrong, 'cause if it didn't need a (t) on it, then why did they put one there?" I knew if I continued with the conversation in this direction, it would probably last for the rest of the trip. Later the buffet restaurants became the boy's favorite places to eat during special outings from the ranch.

We arrived at the main trailhead around ten o'clock in the morning; the boys were chomping at the bit, eager to get started on the hike. Before I could saddle G.B., they were ready and waiting. Their backpacks were loaded with snacks and trail goodies, insect repellant, fishing gear, and their lunches. I considered the trip a pretty normal one with the usual arguments and two or three of my whiners protesting anything and everything to do with the trip. Of course there were the normal stops to go to water the trees. And not all would participate at the same time. So taking this part of the trip wearing a smile on my face I considered very important for my sanity.

Willie, who was my stout little four-by-four boy, told me how tired he was before we started up the trailhead. He was fairly new to the ranch program and whining was one of his favorite pastimes. That, along with his temper tantrums, caused every foster home and Social Services a continuing replacement. Walking was not one of Willie's favorite things—he preferred eating. I noticed his pace became slower and slower. Finally, I announced, "We will eat as soon as we arrive at the lower springs." Willie instantly found a new burst of energy.

After lunch, we traveled a mere half mile when Willie and David lagged behind. They decided they were not going any farther and sat down. New boys often tested me with a little rebellion. On nearly every trip, one or two boys struggled against the bit. I rode back and informed the two of them, "The Mountains can be such a beautiful place, with all its natural beauty—the mountains can be your best friend or your worst enemy."

David quickly picked up on the enemy part. "What enemy, Mom?"

I said, "There are many reasons why you boys should be keeping up with the rest of us. You see bears and mountain lions roam freely in this area. If I were a bear or mountain lion looking for an easy meal, I would think a small boy would be easy pickin's." I turned my horse around on the trail, and as I rode off, I said, "Suit yourselves. I would think really hard about that hungry old bear or mountain lion."

I heard David tell Willie, "You can sit here if you want, but I am going to catch up with the other boys." Willie jumped to his feet as fast as David. They both passed me on my horse, and by the time we took our next little break, they were as talkative and compliant as the rest of the boys.

The conversation during this break was mostly about who was going to be first off the rocky granite bolder into the swimming hole or where the best spot was for fishing. The boys, visualizing Kibby Lake, began to plan where they would drop their hooks in the water. I knew immediately when the conversation shifted to a setup for the new boys—the old swimming-hole trick. Year after year, I watched the same feat. The seasoned boys jumped off a big high boulder hanging out over the lake into the icy water and began to swim around and tease the newer ones, "Come on in, sissies.

The water is warm." Before long, they pulled me into the prank. "Show them Mom, just how warm the water is."

I would jump in and as I was coming out of the water say, "Not bad, not bad at all." I joined in their joke so many times that I had lost count. Finally, they encouraged the new boys to jump together. A loud gasp always followed as they shot up out of the chilly water. We always encouraged a good laugh because laughter cures a troubled heart. I listened with amazement and joy when a boy began to laugh with the others, especially when all our in-house counseling sessions failed.

After the short break, we continued up the trail. We took breaks every so often and walked the next two miles with normal conversation. I loved stopping along the way to point out something I thought the boys should see, like the pretty mountain-snow flowers that only bloom in the High Country. This was definitely God's flower because for years people had been trying to grow this plant in hothouses without success. Each plant has only one flower. I heard it was impossible to transplant. I think this was God's way of showing us this beautiful white flower, His flower, should stay in the mountains. On one of these breaks near a wooded hillside, a doe and her fawn grazed on the rich new grass in the shade of the Ponderosa pine trees. They were undisturbed by our presence, as the boys sat down to eat their snack. I pointed to the deer and told the children to be very quiet (an impossible task). We sat there watching as the mother raised her head every now and then to check our presence with her watchful eyes. She really did not seem to be afraid of us.

With another mile to go to the stream crossing, I hoped the water would not be too high. The storms in the Sierras that year had deposited an unusual amount of snow. This meant the stream crossing going into Kibby Lake could be higher than usual.

We didn't have far to go when Willie decided he was lost and started throwing a temper tantrum. We had gone through some brush about three feet high on both sides of the trail; the trail itself was clear and wide. I looked back and saw Willie's head above the brush; I encouraged him to keep up with the other boys, who by this time were also tired of his whining. He informed me, "The bears can have me."

The other boys told him, "Stop being a wimp and keep up." Willie began to cry and scream at me, calling me those all-too-familiar, not-so-nice names. Finally, I rode back and informed him he was not lost, but we were going to continue up the trail without him. I looked down at his face, red from crying, and about that time, something moved in the brush behind him. He said, "I'm really *scared* and tired Mom." So I told him that just this once, I would let him ride on the back of G.B. with me. There was a time to be firm, and there was a time for compassion.

This horse was so good with my boys, and the boys loved him. Sometimes I looked out into the corral from my office and saw three or four of my little ones in G.B.'s corral sitting on the old horse's back, while G.B. gave them a walk around the corral. When he wearied of their foolishness, he went to a corner of the corral and stood there. Were they supposed to be riding horses without a bridle or saddle in the corrals? Of course not, but sometimes I just looked the other way and let boys be boys.

I took Willie back to where the other boys were waiting, and we continued on up the trail. We approached the stream crossing; I cautioned them about the water and told the boys not to attempt to cross until I had checked on the depth of the stream.

Danny was another new boy on this trip who was twelve-years old and not that familiar with listening to an adult. Danny fit the mold of those know-it-all types who constantly informed the others on, "how much they *think* they knew."

As I begin to study the stream, it looked too swift and deep to cross. I reinforced my discussion earlier about NOT crossing and informed them the swift water could be dangerous. They were told to go water a tree and wait for me to return. I mounted the old horse and asked if anyone in the group had a hearing problem. They said, "No." I assumed everyone knew I meant for them not to go near the water until I returned.

The stream normally ran a foot or two deep at this time of year, but as G.B. got closer to the middle, the water leveled off at his stomach; it was twenty five feet across. I looked back to see most of my boys watching me from the top of a huge rock. Danny was nowhere in sight.

I turned G.B. around slowly and headed back. The rocky bottom of the stream made it difficult for the horse to keep his footing because some of the rocks were covered in slippery green moss. With every step G.B. took, he carefully found his footing. Returning to the other side, I informed the boys the water was too high to wade across. They all started to talk at once. "Are we going home, Mom?" "Can we camp here?"

Meanwhile, Danny was still nowhere in sight. Just as I was about to ask where he was, I heard him say, "Up here, Mom. We can cross up here." He was up above the main crossing where the water in the stream dropped rapidly.

"No, Danny, don't!" Those were the only words I managed to get out before he slipped on a rock and fell into the swift water. He bobbed up and down, shouting for help at the top of his lungs. I jumped off my horse jerking off my boots as fast as I could. I needed to get to the middle of the stream before he passed the crossing area. Beyond the crossing a short waterfall spilled into a dangerously deep pool of water.

I knew Danny wasn't in danger of drowning on the way down. The biggest danger was he could hit his head on one of the big protruding rocks, and that, indeed, could be a very big problem in the middle of nowhere.

Danny was shouting so loud we probably wouldn't see another animal in these parts for the rest of the week.

I stood in the middle of the stream, about waist high, in frigid cold water. The first thing I caught was Danny's backpack, then his jacket—all soaking wet; then came Danny. I caught him and helped him to shore. He was shaken up a bit, but otherwise, he was okay. He was pretty embarrassed about the whole thing, especially when I told him in front of the other boys all he had to do was stop shouting and stand up.

It was getting late in the day, and the wind had a chill to it. We took an inventory of the clothes in the backpacks and found enough for Danny to change into dry clothes. I took out a pair of Wranglers and a sweat shirt from my saddlebag and went behind a rock. Then I turned my attention to the other boys. They were in full discussion as to how they were all going to get to the other side, that is, without getting wet.

"Here's what we are going to do," I said. "G.B. and I are going to carry you, one by one, to the other side. When it is your turn, you will stand on the large rock, climb aboard the horse behind me, and put your arms around my waist and hold on tightly."

We all said the rider's prayer out loud, "Please, Lord, make this a safe one." G.B. walked so very carefully back and forth across the stream, as if he knew each boy was a very special cargo he was carrying. When the boys were all on the other side, we continued over the granite-rocky ledge up the path and over to Kibby Lake.

In all my years of going into the wilderness area, there had never been a time when I didn't go through my checklist and check everything in my saddlebags, except this trip.

As experienced as we think we are, human error still exists, and this time it was my mistake. As the boys started gathering the wood, I unsaddled my horse and took him to the meadow. I searched for the matches in my saddlebag and finally spotted the little metal box that held the matches. When I opened the box, it was empty. NO Matches.

This meant no fire and a very cold time ahead of us unless Tom arrived with the supplies soon. The sun had noticeably begun to set. No fire also meant NO protection from bears and mountain lions. Most will not come near a campfire; however, I didn't let the boys know my fears. I fought going into an unnerving female panic mode.

I got a hold of my feelings and began to prepare for the cold. I told the boys I needed to take an inventory of what we brought. As each boy unloaded his backpack, I was proud to see each had packed according to the checklist. I was the only one who hadn't.

We moved a couple of logs up against a stand of young thick pine trees to help keep the wind off of us. One of the most important things the boys had packed was their own metal cup and silverware. These later proved to be lifesaving tools.

As night descended, I brought G.B. out of the meadow below for our guard in camp. Horses sense a bear's presence before a human can see or hear one. It became clear the night temperatures were getting colder so I gathered the boys up and covered them with G.B.'s two wonderfully warm but very smelly doubled folded saddle blankets. We sat as close together as possible, letting the warmth from our bodies keep each other warm. I told each boy to keep his metal cup and spoon nearby.

Three hours of darkness with eight scared little boys was not part of the plan. I kept them talking and telling stories so they would not panic. The conversation worked well until the wind came up and the wolves started to howl. Then I felt the little ones moving closer and closer to me.

The boys kept asking when Tom was going to arrive. I made excuses, trying not to show my concern. Only an experienced mountain guide would ride in the dark, and there was NO full moon tonight. Tom had never ridden in the mountains in the dark, and he didn't know the trail that well. By midnight, I knew Tom would not be there until morning, but the boys needed to believe he was going to ride down the path and into camp any minute.

Their little conversations by this time went something like this: "Mom, do bears eat at night?"

"No, boys, I've never heard of bears eating at night." Truthfully I did not know the answer; I just knew the importance of reassuring the boys.

When the wolves started their howling again, Willie asked if wolves like eating at night.

"No, they are just talking; the wolves are calling their young in for the night and visiting with the other wolves," I reassured him, "Besides, these cups you have are a true weapon. When you hear a noise, just take your spoon and bang it around inside the cup. It will hurt their ears, and they will go away."

"Now," I said, "would be a good time to confess to God and ask for forgiveness of our sins and to thank him for something special he has done in our lives. When we have done this, we can ask for his protection through the night."

Children, eight through twelve, have the most entertaining minds. As we started around the group, each boy stood up in the dark and thanked God for something that was special in his life. Then the fun part began with each boy taking his turn asking for forgiveness.

There, in the dark of night, I found out more about what went on at my ranch than I ever had before. We had a truce of sorts when they were confessing to God in my presence, knowing there would be no ramifications.

David said he needed forgiveness for the underwear he had stuffed down the toilet the week before and for putting a large box of starch into the washing machine while the sheets were being washed. The house mother, unaware, had put the sheets in the dryer and was "way past mad" when she held those very stiff sheets up in my office. Personally I thought the young creative mind that did the deed was something I might have done as a child, but then I did not have to re-wash the sheets. Conway said he would return all of John's comic books he had hidden. Then he said if God would just not let the bears eat him, he would be good for at least one day. I reminded him this session was about asking forgiveness, not bargaining with God. We all joined in and asked God for protection, especially for David.

Next was Danny's confession. He began telling God about his week at the ranch and about all the sins he had committed, beginning with Tony's bike disappearing. Danny had sworn to me in my office he was innocent and accused Tony of selling the bike. He had actually worked very hard in the middle of the night and buried the bike in the manure pile. Then Danny asked forgiveness for telling the younger ones they couldn't join his special club unless they ate worms. He blindfolded them and fed them spaghetti sprinkled with dirt.

One by one, each of the boys stood up and confessed. I thought the boys would be tired after all this confessing and praying, and suggested we go to sleep for a while. I was exhausted by this time. But my little ones were wide awake. A deer or something moved through the brush about this time, and the boys started to panic. They reached for their tin cups and began banging with the spoons. Whatever it was ran out of the area, and things quieted down.

I had always encouraged singing, and one of the boys asked me to sing, and they all joined me in a somewhat humorous harmony. David said we should sing loud, so God would be sure to know where we were.

For the next hour or so, we sang religious songs. Pretty soon, most of them were fast asleep. I thanked the good Lord for providing protection for all of us on one of the longest nights I've ever spent in the mountains. Now I was not only tired but hoarse as well from singing in the cold night air.

When Tom and the new hand rode into camp the next morning with their heads hung down, it was nine o'clock, and my young ones, especially Willie, had been asking for the past two hours if we were ever going to eat again. Willie kept it up until one of the other boys threatened him with bodily harm.

Sonora is a cowboy-mountain town and is on the route to Yosemite National Forest; it has more bars than town. There had been a weekend roping during the day. One thing led to another, and Tom was invited to go downtown with some of his roping friends. Tom had always been so responsible when it came to the boys. What happened? It was a combination of things, including the fact that he was showing off a little to the new ranch hand.

Before they knew it, it was dark, and they still had two hours of driving to get to the trailhead. They said they had tried to ride the path at night and almost got lost. Tom told me they slept on the trail and waited until daylight. I later found out they did not make it to the trailhead until daylight early the next morning. They spent the night out at the ol' rodeo arena in Sonora.

I have never been as close to losing control as I was that morning. I got so very quiet it scared me. I finally found my voice and told Tom, "If you ever put my boys in danger again, I will shoot you."

As I turned to walk away, I heard the new ranch hand ask Tom if I was serious about shooting him. "Son, she meant every word."

~ Chapter 33 ~

THE REVIVAL

Confusion should be the title that covers all religions, for at the boy's ranch, the boys chose their own religious beliefs. This practice is required by law in most state-licensed children's facilities.

I attended various churches with some of the boys going to one church one Sunday and another church the following Sunday. This practical experience gave me an unexpected education on the way each religion interpreted the Bible.

As a metaphysician, I am open to most religious views. Metaphysicians are positive in our attitude about God and believe God is the inner strength that guides us to our highest good. Metaphysics consists of three components, mind, body, and spirit. Mind, representing the study of science of the mind, has no connection with scientology. Body is the study of health and well-being, and of course, spirit is the meaning of the soul and the God power which exists in us all. You will never be in a more positive atmosphere than at an international convention of metaphysicians. Hugs and blessings are shared by all.

Someday I believe the public will look for doctors who will not write prescriptions but will direct his or her patients toward better diets, vigorous exercise, and other forms of preventive medicine. Some doctors are open minded to alternative medicine today and are living in a more open and productive space.

Exposure to religion of any kind is better than none. I tried very hard to see the boys were exposed to different views of the Bible. On one occasion, they were really overexposed, and we all learned a very important lesson.

It was August and my boys were out of school. Their leisure time was great for them, but not always good for me. I had never closed my office to the boys and so in the summer, they dropped in to talk and talk some more. The little ones, who I thoroughly enjoyed, were in and out of my office all day long. Their visits were not bad when I had ten boys, but when we grew to sixteen, and then eighteen, I couldn't get anything done for all the interruptions. I really needed to concentrate on doing the monthly reports or I would fall behind; the latter situation could create a nightmare.

One day I called Tom into the office and asked him to come up with some solution to this problem. He said, "I will give it some thought and try to have something within the week that would handle the situation."

Sometimes I was too close to the problem to see the simple solution. Tom's down-to-earth solutions amazed me with their simplicity and practicality. One evening over dinner, we came up with several options; most we dismissed because of the little ones. I did not want them to get the idea that I was inaccessible or that I was rejecting them. They had quite enough of that already in their lives. I just needed to get some work done.

Tom suggested we use a light bulb over my office door, green for "Yes, it is all right to enter," and red for "Stop, it is not all right to enter." I thought this was a good plan, for even the little ones could understand this system.

We called a group session the following evening and discussed this procedure. For once, everyone seemed to understand what the meeting was about. I talked about why the red and green lights were on the door of my office and what they meant.

Tom installed the lights, and for the first few days after they were installed, things went rather well. About the fourth day, the phone rang, and when I answered it, a little voice on the other end asked, "Is this Mom?"

I said, "Yes, David, what are you doing calling me, and how did you get this number?"

He replied, "You gave me the number when I came to the ranch and told me to call you if it was important. I put it on my cork board, and now I am calling you cause it's really important."

All the boys were given a card with my private office telephone number during orientation, the first day of their arrival at the ranch, so he was calling to tell me he and Willie along with Conway needed to see me right away because it was important.

"David, did you not see the red light on my door was on?" I asked.

David answered with a sigh, "I did and that's why Willie and Conway and me are calling 'cause we cannot come down and talk without getting in trouble, 'cause the red light is on."

Again they had me. The logic of a nine-year-old was amazing to me, so I told them to come on over to the office and we would discuss what was troubling them. In less than five minutes, all three of the boys came running into the office and began talking at once.

Their excitement was over a conversation they had with one of the boys at Bible school. There was a revival coming to town, and their friend was going with "his mom," and the boys wanted to know if they could go and if I would take them. Willie spoke up and said, "Mom they are having homemade cookies and everything."

David said, "Everyone," meaning mothers "are bringing homemade desserts. You need to bring something too. Mom, you can bring chocolate-chip cookies, 'cause I don't think the other mom's are bringing any."

I asked the boys, "Do you boys know what a revival is?"

David said, "No." After a short pause he continued, "But if you will take us, then we will know." Through all of this conversation Conway said nothing. He remained silent. He was my quiet one until someone irritated him; then he lost it. I called these three my little musketeers.

In truth what happened, the boys told their little friends that "their mom" was going to take them to the revival, too. They probably volunteered "their mom" to bring something. I thought for a minute and asked myself, "What could it hurt?"

It might actually be enlightening for them. Any spiritual guidance willingly requested was always a step in the right direction

"Okay," I said, "You can go, and yes, I will take you and bake the cookies." David said, "Gee, mom thanks!" They scurried off before my eyes, leaving with the same exuberance and energy, slamming my office door behind them.

Three days later, David, Willie, and Conway loaded into my pickup with Willie's watchful eye guarding the cookies. It reminded me of leaving the wolf to guard the henhouse. Off to the revival we went looking ever so fine, the boys in their Sunday best and I naturally in my dress and pillbox hat. The revival was being held on the outskirts of town. Upon our arrival there in the distance stood a big tent, typical of a traveling revival. Conway asked if they were camping out in their big tent. I assured him they were not.

As we drove into the parking area, I could see our arrival was early, and so we had our choice of where to sit. The old benches were just that, very old with two or three put together making a row. They had no backs on them and no arm rest at the end. As with most churches, the rows consisted of the left side, the middle and the right side. I thought it a good idea at the time to sit on the front row, middle aisle with my boys, the boys sitting inside while I sat on the aisle, the outside.

I had been so busy before the revival I had not checked out the preacher and what his sermon was about. I would soon find out about his sermon, and so would the boys.

If you go to church and you sit on the very front row, there are advantages and disadvantages. The advantages are you can hear better and, for that matter, see well. At my age, this was becoming more and more important. The disadvantages are you don't dare get up to go to the bathroom, because everybody knows where you're going and what you are going to do. Besides it is terrible etiquette to leave while the minister or preacher is giving the sermon.

So I had my boys all take that trip before the preacher started his sermon and explained to them the importance of sitting through the whole sermon. The benches, worn slick from age, required a certain kind of balance. These short benches held four to six people.

The preacher was a big man, maybe six three or four weighing around three hundred and twenty pounds most of which was in front of his body. My motley crew was settled in on the front row looking up at the stage more than able to hear every syllable.

The revival started with some good old-fashioned singing, and my boys and I sang along. You know the kind of music: "The Old Rugged Cross" and "Just a Closer Walk with Thee." These were the old gospel hymns I sang as a child with my family. The boys looked at their song books and did their best to keep up. They were really trying to impress everyone they knew what they were doing. After only a few songs, Willie asked if it was time for intermission. "No, Willie," I replied, and we sang another old church song.

Just as I was beginning to think this was a pretty good idea, the singing stopped, and this goliath of a gentleman stepped to the pulpit and began to preach, or rather shout. "HALLELUJAH." He was right in front of us, standing on the stage; he began to walk back and forth. "All ye'all have sinned and come short of the glory of God." His loud rough voice compounded with his huge stature standing on a stage right in front of us made this man appear to be a giant. The boys' eyes popped out of their heads with the mere sound of the preacher's booming voice.

His sermon was on the sacrificing of animals, and he continually shouted about damnation, going to hell, the blood of the animals saving you from hell, and more blood, and more killing of the animals, and more sacrificing to go to heaven. He continued with the penalty of sin—"Death!" But he was not talking about any ordinary kind of death. He explained from Revelation, "In one hour your doom is come.

You will be gathered with Satan and thrown into the lake of burning sulfur with the beast. You will be tormented day and night forever and ever." David's voice shaking with fear asked, "Are we gonna die, Mom?"

I whispered back, "Of course not, son."

The preacher continued, moving from Revelation to Leviticus. "Your only salvation is to be covered by the Blood of the Lamb. Hallelujah!"

The crowd shouted back "Amen!"

I glanced at the boys a couple of times, and their little eyes were twice the size of normal. David kept scooting closer to me on the old bench. I was on the very end of the bench and losing ground inch by inch. The preacher raised his fist high and brought it down like a knife, stabbing the pulpit to demonstrate Aaron's stabbing of the goat. Conway gasped and shoved Willie over closer to David. Just as the preacher flicked his fingers wet with water up in the air to demonstrate the sprinkling of blood on our front-row seats, it happened in front of God and everyone: David and I went sprawling onto the dirt floor, me in my motherly looking shirtdress with David landing on top of me while my pillbox hat flew into the air; the bench teeter-tottered for just a moment before flipping upward and dumped Conway and Willie on top of us. There we sat in the dust on the dirt floor. I scrambled to find my hat and gain some kind of composure. Needless to say, we did not stay for the intermission or the chocolate-chip cookies.

Do these adults actually think, when they are preaching and shouting, that the children understand what they are saying? Every time he shouted about killing little lambs or blood flowing, he shouted "Hallelujah," and the adults in the crowd shouted "Amen." My little ones were scared out of their minds.

The next day I planned to call the three boys to my office in an effort to explain what happened at the revival. However, before that could happen, the boys called me and asked if they could come down and naturally "it was real important." According to David, the problem could not wait for the red light on my door to turn green. I could tell David had been crying. I gave them permission, and it was a good thing I did for good old Charlie the cat's sake.

We had a dearly beloved old cat at the ranch. He was a grossly overweight yellow tabby and could easily pass for Garfield's double. Perhaps reincarnation does exist, for Charlie had all of Garfield's habits, lazy personality, a love for food, and the ability to sleep in a variety of positions.

The little ones dressed him in all kinds of doll clothes, which were mostly girl clothes, and carried him around like a sack of potatoes. He really did not seem to mind the dresses they put on him. Charlie had been retired as stud long ago, which probably had something to do with his good disposition; he was always so trusting and good-natured with my boys.

In walked David carrying Charlie, and all three were crying big crocodile tears. They began to talk at once, telling me they did not want to go to hell or be burned up in that lake. They had thought about everything the preacher said, and they had decided to "sacrifice" Charlie. Meanwhile, good ol' Charlie was relaxed and content laying upside down in David's arms, not knowing, of course, what the boys were talking about, which was his demise.

I said, "Give me Charlie." David handed Charlie to me with tears in his eyes, like someone had opened the floodgates.

I begin to explain, you do not have to kill something to go to heaven. God just wants you to be good; some adults, such as the preacher, do not always explain things very well to children. Besides, there may have been a reason to sacrifice animals a long time ago, but God does not expect us to do that anymore.

David asked, "How long ago—before I was born?"

"Yes," I said, "and even before, *I* was born!"

David's eyes looked bigger than usual. "Golly, Mom that was really a long time ago!" emphasizing the word *really*.

I told them I know all children have a place in heaven, and they do not have to kill anything to go there. They just have to be good little boys, and God knows whether they are good or bad. David spoke up and said, "You mean that we have someone else watching us besides Santa Claus?"

"Yes, David you do," I put Charlie the cat on my desk and told them it was surely time for "hugs." I hugged each of my boys and dried their tears.

In my desk, I had a surprise drawer where I kept hard candy. Although I limited their sweet intake, certain special times called for the surprise drawer, which really came in handy. This was one of those times, and so after they each chose a very special piece of candy, Willie and Conway left. David walked out shortly afterward, carrying Charlie and telling that darned ol' cat how sorry he was and that he would never let anything happen to him ever. Needless to say, I never took my boys to another revival, and that's not all. They never asked to go again.

~ Chapter 34 ~

CHRISTMAS AT THE RANCH

Christmas at the ranch—oh, what a very special time!

A few weeks before Christmas, I walked over to the main house for my usual visit with Bertha, our cook, by now a very close friend. We discussed the holiday-dinner menu and the amount of fudge we planned to make for gifts. Every year before Christmas, we made fudge for all the merchants in town to thank them for doing business with us throughout the year. The ranch required all the boys to participate in making the fudge; the principle learning lesson was giving before they could receive. With the fudge making the kitchen became the local spot for the boys, and, of course, every batch of chocolate fudge had to pass the taste test by the boys. Sometimes one or the other would suggest, "I don't think this batch has enough walnuts," and, of course, that meant another taste test. Often, the little ones wore enough fudge on the outside of their faces to feed a hungry cowboy, which filled my heart with such joy. Everyone became caught up in the excitement of preparing the many boxes of fudge, from wrapping the boxes to delivering them to the merchants.

Bertha said her favorite thing at Christmas was watching the boys unwrap their presents, which were always plentiful. She remarked to me, "You probably didn't have much of a Christmas as a child, did you?" And as usual, she was right.

A trip to town at Christmas offered many learning and teaching experiences for the boys. Christmas presented the perfect time of year to make sure my boys remembered others who, like the boys backgrounds before the ranch, had no Christmas. The appreciation my mother had taught me as a child, I was now teaching the boys in a real, but visual way. On one particular trip to town, the boys started arguing in the back seat about their jackets being the wrong colors. They insisted they "needed" new ones for Christmas.

Interrupting their conversation, I said, "Boys, this is such trivia." For a moment, the vehicle was silent.

Willie asked, "Mom, what's trivia?" "Trivia is something that is uncalled for, such as arguing over the color of your jackets." As I was driving, I made a sharp turn to the right and headed for old Sacramento area. Some of old Sacramento was under new development, but some remained the shady side of life most cities do not want to admit exits. It was right after dark and a misty rain created a shivering, cold atmosphere. I locked all four doors to the vehicle and slowed down. The dark, dreary spooky night offered a teaching visual that spoke volumes. On the first corner standing there in the cold night air was a boy with no coat and tennis shoes so worn through that his toes stuck out. I stopped at the stop sign and pointed the boy out and said, "Do you think he would care what color a jacket was or would he appreciate the warmth? Trivia can also show lack of appreciation for what you have." I drove down to the next block and then turned down an alleyway, finding people sleeping under cardboard boxes and children, young children, cold and wet from the night air. "Do you think they would argue over a warm place to stay or the color of a warm blanket? I think not. Trivia, trivia, trivia."

All the way home we discussed the word "trivia" and the word "appreciation." I suggested, "Think how blessed you are and how perhaps to help the boy on the street or the two young ones sleeping in the alley."

Joe spoke up, "Mom, I know what it's like to be on the street at Christmas time hoping to catch a rat to eat."

My David picked up on the new word trivia, and for the next few days, he drove everyone up the wall. He was like a kink in a rope at the national finals. If someone decided to argue with David, he would simply hold a hand up and say, "Trivia, trivia."

The next week I held a group session on the subject matter. I had each of the boys stand up and tell the others what we had seen. Then I asked, "What do you intend to do about helping the boys on the street?"

Jake stood up, "What can we do to help these kids; we are just kids ourselves?"

I countered, "Well, let me see; most of you have been at the ranch long enough and have saving accounts and checking accounts."

Danny interrupted me, "We have clothes we have outgrown,"

"Yes" I said, "Great idea."

Jimmy stood up and asked, "Is there a Goodwill store around, 'cause I know from personal experience, if we give the kids on the streets new clothes they will be forced to sell them by the 'toughs' that run the streets."

This group session began to buzz with excitement; I decided to help the situation and offered to match what the boys spent.

The very next day we went to town with each boy at the ranch waving their check books around in the Goodwill store. The boys, quite the traders, loved bargaining for the items with the clerks. The manager came out and saw what my boys were doing and announced they could buy the children clothes for half the price. Trevor had been in the back in bedding and said to the manager, "What about the new blankets in the back? You know you could throw them in free; after all, it is Christmas." His voice projected so loudly that everyone in the store was looking at the manager. The manager replied, "Well, okay, but you have to load them." I glanced over giving Trevor a smile of approval and reserved a huge hug for later.

I watched the boys pick out certain items for the street children such as coats, tennis shoes, jeans and lots of socks and gloves. We loaded the back end of both trucks and drove to old town. The boys climbed in the back and began to hand out clothes to the boys on the streets. It was so amazing to see boys who had been on the street taking time to help others still there. By the next year the boys had saved some of their clothing ready for old town. I did notice little David's bag being rather large. After Christmas David's clothes closet was nearly bare. Only then did we discover that David had given most of his clothes away at old town. And yes, he received a shopping trip to the city to refurbish his clothing, including his underwear.

The old town trip became a practice every year thereafter, and in many ways it brought home the best teaching tool ever, giving to others, as Christmas is meant to be.

One of my favorite things at the ranch was watching my boys get excited about Christmas. And watching Joe! What was so special about Joe? He reminded me of myself when I was growing up. His curiosity overwhelmed him. One Christmas Eve when everyone was asleep, he quietly went from house to house, very carefully un-wrapping all the packages to see what everyone was getting.

The next year, I anticipated his plot. I followed him into the first house at midnight and helped him unwrap and rewrap packages; we limited it to five in each house. Joe was unaware the counselors knew what we were doing, for it surely would have spoiled his whole adventure. We both swore an oath of silence. Sometimes the little girl in me just came out, so I steered clear of punishing Joe for the same kind of transgressions that I committed as a child.

We prepared great dinners with all the trimmings at the ranch. I always knew where I was going to be on Thanksgiving and Christmas, and that was in the kitchen with Bertha fixing a great feast. The menu included ham, turkey, and dressing, Jell-O molds salads, yams, and all the different desserts.

Most of my boys did not know the joy of the holiday traditions, so Tom and I showed them the holidays could be fun and enjoyable. I hoped our "family" feast, Christmas cards, shopping and decorating the Christmas tree at the ranch would create lasting memories to pass on to their children.

The tree at the main house, a big part of Christmas at the ranch, was decorated with all sorts of homemade Christmas ornaments, and at night the normal stringing of popcorn to adorn every limb. The smell of popcorn in the main house brought all in to help. The popcorn, most of which was digested before using it for the purpose intended, required our keeping the Pepto-Bismol handy for the tummy aches that popped up during this joyful time. I caught Bertha one day looking at the Christmas tree. "What's wrong?" I asked.

She replied, "I can't figure out how such a small string of popcorn ended up on this big tree when I popped more popcorn than last year." I had to admit this looked a little straggly as though someone had helped themselves along the way.

The Christmas holidays were so hard on these children at school; their classmates talked about parties with their parents and extended families coming to visit for the holidays. So I tried to spend time with the children, keeping them busy doing normal Christmas things. Each house threw a Christmas party for the foster grandparents program, which served two purposes. One, the children could brag about having their "family" over and having a real Christmas party. Two, This created a need for both side of the fence; the young and the elderly.

Christmas lists along with letters were handed to me right after Thanksgiving, and some things on those letters to Santa were heart breaking—things like "Dear Santa Claus, I wish for Christmas to know who my daddy really is," or "I want to know why my mother didn't love me enough to keep me."

Tom and I were excluded from the Christmas list. They could make us something but not buy it from a store. One Christmas little Neal made me an ornament with his photo glued inside a cardboard frame with a hook to hang on the tree. When he gave it to me, he said, "Mom, every Christmas you can remember me." I told him I would keep it always. I still have this ornament today.

One year, we had the prettiest snowstorm just in time for Christmas, and the boys made a snowman, with everyone on the ranch getting involved. The snowman was dressed a little differently than most snowmen. It wore an old cowboy hat, a western belt, a pair of old chaps, and somebody's old boots. Two of my young ones came running to the house wanting Tom and me to come outside. We did—only to find the whole ranch waiting with snowballs in hand. After the snowball fight, I had no problem getting the boys to bring firewood to build a big fire in the old fireplace. By the way, Tom and I lost that battle. We were wet from head to toe and enjoyed every minute of it.

After dinner, we made hot chocolate and I watched with joy as my young ones roasted marshmallows 'round the stone fireplace. The conversation I guided towards our goals for the next year and gave thanks to God for our many blessings. The children had no idea with the fun we had that day; I was taking full advantage of the situation for their future. Goal setting at the ranch was nothing new; they would someday need this very important tool to better survive the real world.

No matter how hard we tried to make every Christmas a great time, there was always state licensing finding some way to screw it up, or they tried.

One Christmas, Willie's drug-addict parents wanted him for a Christmas visit, and naturally, Willie did not want to go. They had lost their welfare check on Willie, and now they wanted the income back; and the only way they could sell the idea to Social Services was to make an effort to take Willie for a visit over the holidays.

After the telephone conversation with Social Services, I called Willie into the office and told him his parents would like their son home for Christmas. Willie looked at me as if I had betrayed him. "Do I have to go on this visit, AT CHRISTMAS? Have I done something wrong; have I been bad Mom? I thought this was my home now."

"No, Willie, you have done nothing wrong, and you are welcome to stay at the ranch. This is your home too. However, you must tell your social worker it is your decision to stay with us for Christmas, so that she knows from you what you want to do."

Three days later, the social worker, Willie, and I met in my office. She asked him questions I felt went over the line. "Don't you still love your parents? After all, they have been going to counseling once a week for their drug problems."

I nearly threw up on this statement. These so-called parents had abused Willie and his sister so much. One of the many things they did included locking their children in an outdoor dog pen and not feeding them for three days. In this book I devoted a chapter to this very overweight but precious child. The average family has no idea of the real world that my boys came from.

Willie insisted he wanted to spend Christmas at the ranch. When Willie left the office, the social worker accused me of influencing the child "against" his parents. She was probably right. I informed her that the child had made his choice and that she must honor the boy and his decision to stay at the ranch and added, "The law according to state codes and regulations allow the child the final say as to the decision of where he prefers to spend his holidays." She and the parents filed a grievance against me and the ranch for interfering with their reunification program. It went nowhere, of course, and Willie got the Christmas gift he wanted most, and so did I.

It was a cold, wintry December day. The boys were busy with Bertha in the kitchen and running from the kitchen to my office, bringing different desserts for me to taste. I recognized their sneaky ploy as they tried to see who was going on the special Christmas trips; one was to Disneyland and the other to the Christmas play for children at the community center downtown. The latter was a very special event sponsored by the local Chamber of Commerce. The event included a big community dinner, a Christmas play, and a personal talk with Santa Claus, who also gave the children a very special gift.

The boys, Santa, and Mom

By this time, my boys had western Resistol dress hats, western dress jackets, Wranglers, and Justin boots. Any event that came up where they could show off their "family," was something worth working for, and then there was Santa Claus!

It usually took me three or four days to figure each boys positive points for these trips. I must have gained five pounds from all the sweets they brought to my office. The boys reported their spying observations back to Bertha, and she reported back to me. It was quite an exhausting week, but nevertheless entertaining.

All of the boys were on their best behavior. Bertha put in a good word for her favorites. "Ms. René, you must cut little Neal some slack. You know he has no momma, and you are his only momma." This, of course, did not make my job any easier.

When I finally chose the boys for the Christmas community dinner, it was followed by an awards dinner at the ranch in which we all participated.

We kept the little ones busy this time of the year, from helping Bertha in the kitchen to making different decorations for the Christmas trees in all three houses. In fact, everyone at the ranch was busy during the Christmas season. It was the happiest time of the year.

We watched Christmas movies and read stories. There was also an English mastiff dog, by the name of Major, who thought the ranch and the boys all belonged to him.

During December when school was out, the boys could stay up later than their usual bedtime. Major joined the boys to watch movies and hear Christmas stories read aloud. This wonderful dog was as much a part of the family as anyone on the ranch.

One particular busy day, I asked Tom if he would mind handling the evening Christmas movie. This turned out

NOT to be a good decision on my part. It was the first original old movie, *How The Grinch Stole Christmas.* Two of the older boys picked out two more Christmas horror movies, and by the time I returned home from shopping, my little ones wanted to sleep in the living room in their sleeping bags with Major to protect them.

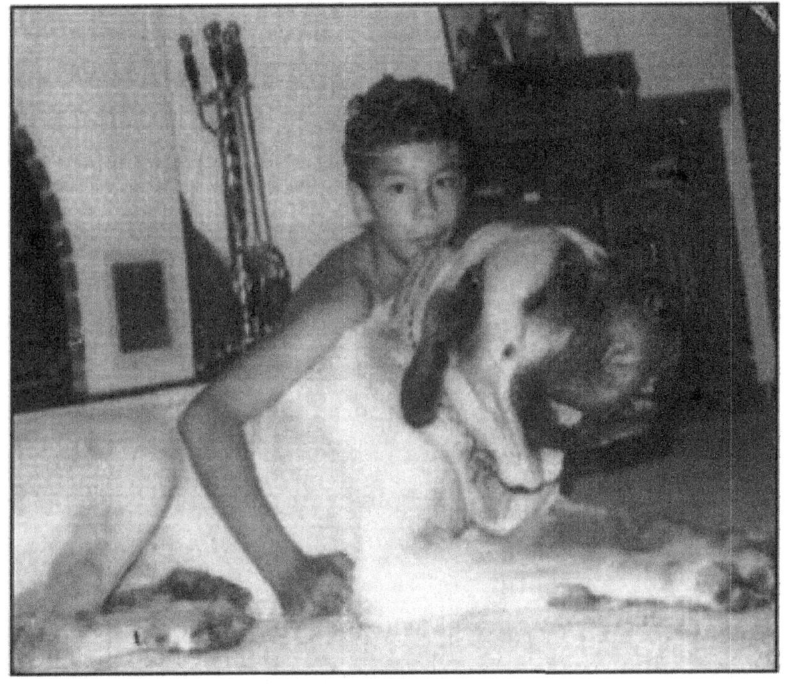

Major and Robert.

For the next few days, Major was a happy dog with all the boys giving him their undivided attention. Needless to say I picked out the next movies. The boys watched Peanuts Christmas videos and laughter flowed freely out of my living room.

There was a very special time for one of my older boys when Christmas arrived earlier than usual. When I found a boy had no parents (they all had parents somewhere) according to the Social Services history records, I searched hoping to find the parents to see if they wanted their child back. Sometimes I got lucky.

Three weeks before Christmas, one of my research people called to say he found John's mother. She, a Native American, had lost custody of John four years before. She was in rehab for her alcohol problems years earlier and was now sober and had re-married.

I set up a meeting and drove some distance to see their home. I was so protective of my boys. It would be a disaster of the worst kind to tell the boy we found his mother without first checking her out. I wanted to find out if she had a decent home, if she was able to support her son, and if she wanted him back before telling the boy.

As I drove down the dirt road to the address she gave me, I passed several older homes. I was trying to stay focused on the tasks at hand. Was she going to love John? Did she have a warm and loving home environment? And, did she really want him back? Most of the homes in this area were on five-acre parcels. This was great because John could take his horse and dog with him.

I rang the doorbell, and a very nice-looking lady answered the door. As I walked into her house, warm inviting smells of homemade apple pie surrounded my being. We visited for a while, and she introduced me to her husband of three years. They were thrilled to find John was doing so well, and her eyes filled with tears when I asked if she loved her son and wanted him back.

By the time the meeting was over, I was fighting with all kinds of emotions myself. On one hand, I had found John's mother, and she truly loved him. She was settled in a good home with her husband, and she wanted John back by Christmas, including his horse and dog.

On the other hand, John had been at the ranch for a few years, since he was fourteen, and was part of the ranch family. It was a long drive home that night as I wrestled with the decision I knew I would have to make.

The next day, I called Social Services who informed me John would not be going home before Christmas. She informed me that this matter had to go before the judge, which would take at least three months. The same social worker also told me she was going on vacation and would not be available until after New Years.

I thanked her for her time, hung up the phone, and proceeded to call a judge in the area. Yes, he was a friend of mine. I told him the situation, and within a week, the so-called paperwork was completed. Did I go over her head? You bet your sweet backside I did.

John was not informed of this until a week before Christmas. I told him Tom and I needed to take him shopping; we had a very special gift for him that required his presence.

When we drove up in front of his mother's house, I allowed him to walk in front of me and ring the door bell. His mother opened the door, and there stood her son. He hesitated just for a minute; then, they fell into each other's arms. The floodgates were open. In the three years I had John at the ranch, I never saw him cry. Now he was crying, but with tears of happiness.

This was a scene of joy both for the mother and her son. What a Christmas it was! John and his parents returned to the ranch for Christmas dinner and John's going-away-party.

John handed me a poem and stood there while I read it in silence; he had a talent for writing. Then he reached out and took the poem from me and tore it up. I understood it was for my eyes only. It spoke of his love for me as his Mother and the appreciation for giving him my love and understanding.

He was a quiet boy. As he was leaving the party with his family, John turned to give me that last hug, and spoke softly, "I can never repay you for what you have done for me."

I smiled and said, "You just did."

Our Christmas feast

~ Chapter 35 ~

BEAR-FIGHTING SLINGS

In the summer of 1988, while preparing for another mountain trip, I called Tom to the office and asked if he could spend some time with the younger boys at the ranch. I stressed the need for his participation in teaching them a skill or something, for lately, they were feeling left out. The younger ones asked me what they could do to make Tom like them, "like he liked the older boys."

Tom and the counselors were not really "into" the little ones. They weren't old enough to handle a rope, big enough for steer wrestling, or for that matter, strong enough for any of the events that the older boys accelerated in competing. The older boys, counselors, and Tom avoided the little ones whenever possible.

The younger boys adored Tom and thought he was just the greatest. Tom was not too excited about my suggestion, so I reminded him of his position by saying, "You are the vocational instructor for all the boys. He had little choice.

After much discussion, me talking and Tom listening, he promised me before the next mountain trip they would know a skill of some kind.

For the next few days, Tom worked in the shop with the younger boys. From my office, I could hear shop tools running and hammering every once in a while. I assumed Tom's ingenuity was at work. Then I heard a new sound, one I had not heard before. It sounded like rocks hitting the side of the shop building. I tried not to go out to the vocational shop, for that was Tom's territory and my way of showing Tom I trusted him and respected his space.

The next two evenings, not one of the little ones said a word about what they were making; the mountain trip was the coming weekend. Finally, I couldn't stand the suspense any longer.

"Boys, what have you been making in the shop?" I asked.

Little nine-year-old Tim spoke up and said, "Mom, Tom made us promise not to tell anyone especially you." And then continued, "I really would like to tell you, 'cause I like telling you things; but Tom made us all promise, so I guess I can't."

Later that night, I held a prayer time and Bible reading with the little ones, and Tim was there. We had a question and answer session after the readings, and Tim asked, "Does God know everybody's secrets?"

I answered, "Yes, he probably knows lots of secrets."

He asked, "Can I tell God a secret?

I told him, "Sure. You can tell God anything. God is the very best at keeping secrets." Then it was time for each of the little ones to say a short prayer out loud.

When it came time for Tim to pray, he said, "God, Tom gave me a secret to keep about the bear-fighting slings we are making in shop, and I am going to give the secret to you 'cause, I don't want it anymore. Amen."

They went off to bed with me trying hard to keep a straight face until they were out of sight. When the last one turned to go to bed, only then did I allow myself to laugh. Afterward I tried to figure out what in the world a bear-fighting sling could possibly be. Oh well, it was probably something Tom dreamed up to keep the little boys out of his hair. I really never thought much more about it. We packed everything for the High Country and left the next day.

We arrived at the lake and set up camp. The metal pan and spoon were sitting within easy reach of the campfire just in case we had unexpected visitors, the big four legged furry kind.

The next morning, I lined a pound of thick bacon strips in my iron skillet over a roaring fire. The boys loved their mountain bacon, cut thicker for the mountain trips by the local butcher. Unfortunately, bears can smell bacon from as far as three miles away. While cooking, I continuously kept a sharp eye for any uninvited guest. Just as I turned the bacon, I spotted a big black bear coming straight down the rocky landscape and into our camp. I knew he was big, but when he rose up on his hind legs to wiggle his nose in the air, I realized that he was huge. This area was the dumping area for bears that tourist had spoiled. Being afraid of humans he was NOT! He came back down on all fours and moved closer to the camp. The bacon smell was more tempting than the fear of humans, so he kept coming for our camp, throwing his nose in the air to smell the aroma. I reached for the big pan with the spoon inside, while calling out to Tom in a low voice, so as not to distract the bear. Tom picked up two hands full of rocks and said, "Boys, get your bear-fighting sling ready." I focused my entire concentration on the bear, not paying attention to the statement Tom had just made.

I took the spoon and began banging it around inside the big metal pan, and sure enough, the bear started to turn and head back up the rocky hill, shaking his head from side to side as the sound of the pan began to hurt his ears. As he turned, Tom started throwing rocks, and the second one hit him up under the tail; with this encouraging blow to his lower anatomy, he hit another speed and was up and over the mountain trail and out of sight.

Meanwhile rocks flew over my head and all around me, two of which hit me in the back. The boys were swinging their bear-fighting slings around their heads with rocks positioned in the leather pouches. Tom shouted encouraging words to them as they swung the ropes of their old-fashioned leather slings. He hollered, "Fire, boys, fire again!" These little boys slung their slingshots in every direction and let the rocks fly even though the intruder topped the hill and was long out of reach. The boys charged after the poor old bear; their big pursuit ended approximately twenty feet from us.

The rest of the day, Tom told those little ones what a great job they did, chasing that darn old bear away. Three of the older boys had been fishing, and when they came in for breakfast, the little ones told how they chased that big bear away from camp with their bear-fighting slings.

David stood up during breakfast with the older boys laughing and said, "Tell them, Mom, tell them we're not lying!"

Smiling I agreed, "Yep, they chased him right up and over the mountain."

I thought this story harmed no one, but boy, was I wrong! Two weeks later, an "old-maid social worker" dropped by the ranch. She was one-hundred percent city. In the two years coming to the ranch, she asked the most ridiculous prying questions designed solely to make her feel important. I never once saw her smile. She asked the boys, as she prepared to record their answers in her report, "What have you young boys been doing?"

Tim blurted out, "We have been on a really fun mountain trip."

She asked, "What did you do on this mountain trip?"

David had to get in on the conversation "We kids protected the camp from a big old bear." They told her Tom had made them bear-fighting slings, and one morning when the bear came into camp, they chased him up the mountain with their bear fighting slings and ran that darn old bear clean out of camp. The children's eyes were sparkling with excitement and of pride as they told this story.

Now I was in a bad position. If I told her Tom and I ran the bear out of camp with the noise from the pan and Tom's accurate rock throwing, my young ones would be devastated. If I did not speak up right now and straighten this matter out, I knew she would write a negative report in regard to this situation.

The social worker was having a field day with the story the little ones had just told. She peered at me over her glasses and asked, "Is this true?"

My boys were looking at me saying, "Tell her, Mom. Tell her we're not lying."

So I told her, "They are not lying."

She looked hard at me and asked, "You mean to tell me you let these little innocent nine-and ten-year-olds chase a bear up the mountain and put their lives at risk?"

I said to her, "I have never put my boys at risk, but you think what you want."

She took out her pen and started writing furiously. She wrote me up for section something another and wanted me to sign it. Legally, we were allowed to protest any and all reports written up during evaluation. Anything negative about me or the ranch, I protested by not signing, which meant I had the right to a hearing on the violation.

When I refused to sign her report, she was outraged. This woman never had anyone challenge her or refuse to sign her report. She left in a huff and sure enough, I received notice to appear for a hearing about the matter.

I have always felt if the state is going to cause me inconvenience, then it is only fair for me to cause them inconvenience. The state director was somewhat of a friend, and I knew he was scheduled for his vacation. I called my attorney and told him the date the state had set was impossible. I could not appear at that time; the only date I had open was the day the director was to leave on his vacation.

My attorney thought this a great idea and saw where I was going with it. My attorney told the state this was the only day he had available as well.

When they ordered a hearing and set a date on the matter, I had the right to object if it interfered with the operation of my facility. A hearing of this type had a deadline of thirty days.

With the director going on vacation, naturally, he would not be back in time to meet this requirement. They wrote me and confirmed the date I wanted.

I met with my attorney in front of the building. I found out from the director's secretary what exact time the director was scheduled to fly out. Our hearing was set for three o'clock in the afternoon, and the director's flight was scheduled for an hour and a half later, four-thirty.

I rather hated to mess up his vacation, but this hearing was causing me an awful lot of inconvenience. I asked Jim, my attorney, if he could stretch this meeting out until about five o'clock. He just grinned and said, "René, it's your money, and you know what I charge per hour."

After much discussion and after the director, who knew my reputation in the High Country, heard the whole story, the whole thing was thrown out. The director did miss his plane. And my attorney's bill was outrageous, but worth it.

Shortly after, this same social worker was transferred to the northern part of the state, where she could drive all winter in the snow and not see a soul. I sent her a congratulations card on her promotion.

~ Chapter 36 ~

WILLIE GOES HOME

The ranch in the 1980s

When Willie came to the ranch, he was horribly overweight. Every button on his shirt gapped; his stomach hung well over his faded jeans that surely required a coat hanger to zip. I feared the visual consequences if he tried to bend over. Nothing he was wearing fit. His sandy-colored hair needed a trim and a good washing. Willie's shoes were new, but they were purchased by Social Services—they were girl's white tennis shoes—not what little boys would wear. Knowing about the state funding, I recognized that they were probably the cheapest thing in the store. This poor child stood before me trying desperately to hide his feet.

The social worker said, "Willie has a younger sister, and they had no problem placing the little seven-year-old girl. But with Willie, foster parents are simply not qualified to handle Willie because of his temper tantrums and total defiance of authority."

Months earlier, I read in the Stockton newspaper about two children, ages seven and nine, found during a drug raid. They were locked in a dog pen in the backyard. They were Eating dog feces for food. The parents had drug parties that lasted three-to-four days. To keep the children from telling, they would take them to the store for candy and cupcakes after the party was over. They were the worst of the worst of so-called parents.

Willie was that boy, and here he stood in front of me with the saddest brown eyes. He had just had a birthday and already experienced more misery than most adults.

I looked at Willie and said, "Welcome to the ranch." He let me know he already had built up enough defiance to protect his feelings.

He glared at me and said, "I don't like it here; I don't like you, and you can't make me stay here."

I could see this was not going to be an easy walk in the park.

"Well, I am glad to meet you too! We will discuss why you are so lucky to be at my ranch a bit later."

Most of my orientations started off with; "GOD HAS BLESSED YOU in giving you the opportunity to be at my ranch." But with Willie being so defiant I used a different opening.

Willie and the social worker sat across from my desk. Willie slumped in the chair as the social worker poured out all of his life's mistakes to a perfect stranger. I finally stopped her rattling in front of the child long enough to say, "These things you're telling me about his past are just that, in the past, and need to stay there. Let's look to Willie's future. Everything you are discussing with me is in the file you handed me." I said this as I led her to the door.

I returned to my desk, and Willie and I became acquainted the very first day. He said, "I can throw a fit and I am stronger than any adult." Before I could bat my baby blues, he started shouting, kicking the chairs, and shoving my papers, files, ornaments and lamp off my desk. When I took hold of him, he shouted I could not stop him. I informed him, "At my discretion, I can restrain you to keep you from hurting yourself, and you are out of control." He looked shocked when I held him to the floor and he could not budge. I won a measure of respect that first day with Willie. I never let him know I wasn't sure how long I could have held him because he was a very strong nine-year-old boy and very much overweight.

During orientation we actually became "friends." I introduced him to David, his roommate, and they hit it off from the start. David was small for his age, and Willie was the muscle, such as it was. David thought it was neat having a big roommate.

Like most of my boys, Willie had many problems. One minute, he would touch your heart, and the next he was the child from h——.

I taught my older boys to defend themselves and each other in regard to the brotherhood of the ranch; of course, they needed to be sure they were right. An incident occurred one day at school. My phone rang and it was the principal of the school. He informed me, "Your boys are unruly and started a fight." I listened as he continued to put the blame on my boys, stating they left the school grounds without "his permission." He wanted to know what I was going to do about this matter because he was expelling them—all of them.

I responded to the principal trying to keep my voice in control, "I will see you in your office tomorrow morning after I have talked to my boys." It was not long until the door opened to my office, and in walked the boys. Their account of what happened that day was far from the principal's version.

Willie was getting teased at school because of his weight. The three boys teasing Willie, being older, came from families who were upper-middle class. Willie tried to take up for himself, but the three older boys were too much for him. At first, it was just pushing and shoving, with Willie being pushed to the ground. Two of my older boys saw what was happening and told the three mischievous boys to leave their "brother" alone. When the three boys laughed and proceeded to push Willie, my older boys jumped in, and the fight was on. With my boys street fighting experience, it was a short fight.

The other boys swung first. My boys took up for Willie. According to the principal, my boys had picked a fight "for no reason" and refused to get on the bus. They told the principal they were taking their brother Willie home and took off walking toward the ranch, which was about four miles.

After listening to my boys' side of the story, it made more sense how everything "really" happened. The reason the boys decided against riding the bus was simple—the three boys that picked on Willie threatened to start another fight on the bus, as they were on the same bus route as my boys.

The next morning, I entered the principal's office, ready for a straight-forward talk. The principal greeted me, "Dr. Monroe, how good to see you."

I responded, "This meeting is necessary so that I can tell you what really happened. You need to hear the truth, not some made-up baloney from your pampered spoiled upper class boys." After I told my boys side of the story, I said, "I think my boys are telling the truth, and if you have any information to prove otherwise, I want you to show me the proof. If you're not ready to settle this matter right now in this office, I am quite prepared to take it to the school board."

He suggested we discuss it some more. I suggested, "You put my boys back in school, end of the discussion." The last principal to challenge me in front of the school board was fired in a very public way.

The principal just shook his head and said, "Your boys are NOT suspended from school."

After that incident, Willie was a different boy because the bigger boys taking up for him made him feel he really did belong at the ranch.

One afternoon, Willie, Shawn, and David came into my office, all three talking at once. The boys had seen Tom practicing with the "dogging steers" (steers that are young and lightweight are ideal for this particular sport) and wanted my permission to dog the old steer, known for his gentle nature. I gave my permission mainly because I figured they could not catch this smart old steer, plus it would entertain them for the rest of the day. We kept this old steer just for situations like this. Off they went back to the arena.

There is a feeling of sorts that comes over you when things are too quiet, especially at a boys ranch. Call it a premonition or just years of experience that tell you something is wrong. I turned and peered out my office window to check on the boys. The steer was nowhere to be found.

After spending a couple of hours trying to corral the steer without success, they came up with their second best solution. They made Willie their steer. By the time I got out there, Willie was loaded in the chute. When the gate opened, he shot out with the little would be cowboys riding their small pint size horses in fast pursuit. Fast pursuit at this young age was a slow trout. They jumped Willie's back, and down to the ground they collapsed. I could not believe my eyes.

By the time I discovered their game, Willie was exhausted and relieved that I halted the whole thing. Always, when I gave permission for the boys to do something, I needed to be specific with the details.

I shouted, "What in the world are you boys doing? You could have hurt Willie."

David, getting up off the ground and dusting himself off, explained, "Mom, Willie is really strong and makes a great steer."

Willie stayed at the ranch for two-and-a-half years when good ole "Social Services" came by one day to inform me Willie's parents had completed their therapy counseling and met the requirements to regain custody of their son. Translated, this meant the drug-hippie parents attended one hour a week in counseling for six months and now had the right, by the court's decision, to take Willie home with them. Did the parents wake up one day and decide to love their children? NO.

It was my experience they were doing this for one reason and one reason only—the money! You see, welfare in California (and perhaps other states) is a mess. The drug-hippie parents get paid so much a month for each child. If they lose the child, they also lose the welfare check, which means they have less money to buy drugs.

Running a boys ranch includes a difficult, gut-wrenching side. Try loving a child for a two-and-a-half year period and then having to tell that happy and settled child that his drug-addict parents earned their legal right to take him from the ranch. When I told Willie that his parents were coming to take him home, I knew that home meant an eight by forty foot trailer house that was cold in the winter and hot in the summer. I knew the trailer lot offered no yard. And, yes, I saw the dog pen that Willie and his sister knew so well, was still there.

The day Willie left was a downright "tearjerker." I could not cry in front of the boy. He had to feel the one person whom he trusted for over two years was being strong for him. It's called a "smooth-transition process for the child's sake."

WHAT A BIG FRIGGIN' LIE THIS IS.

I dream one day of having a boy's ranch where the boys do not have to leave. This, of course, would mean the funding is NOT controlled by the STATE.

We gave Willie a going-away party with presents and cake. The boys were crying, and Willie was crying; and I was crying inside for such a brave child.

I had no idea how painful it would be, but I always told myself I could handle it. The problem in "handling it" is that I became very aware of the dreadful truth. The reality is I knew what was really happening—this child is not the parents' main interest! Yet, here we were giving him a party to go home, where I knew he would just be abused again. This is our "great" children's system that costs a considerable amount of taxpayers' money. This reunification in the majority of cases does not work. This program continues to fill our prison systems by creating more insecure children who then become insecure adults, not because of the directors or administrators that run these programs, but due to the constant moving of children right back into abusive situations because of state mandated-misguided regulations.

The doorbell chimed; there at the ranch door stood two drug addicts, ready to take this child, collect their welfare checks, and abuse the child again. They would just be smarter about it. Willie started crying, begging me for the umpteenth time not to make him go with them.

I soothed him, "It will be okay" and whispered, "You have my number; you can call me." My God, the lies we tell these children as it falls on our shoulders to make sure a transition from the ranch setting back to reunification with their parents is a positive one. This is the reunification program that was written by someone sitting behind a desk in a government office that knew nothing of these children's needs. We are not supposed to have any contact with the children when they leave our facility. Do these people working for the state and making these regulations think love just shuts off like a faucet? Is this not crazy, or what?

With Willie, the judge and I petitioned for and got a terms-of-condition clause included in the release papers, making it mandatory for the parents to bring Willie back to the ranch for monthly visits. I was given permission to visit Willie at his home one weekend per month for a period of six months, plus allowing Willie phone privileges to visit with the ranch. At least it was something to let Willie know he was still loved and the ranch was still available should he need us, which was another lie.

The ranch could not take a child back until he qualified again for the program. In other words, if the child wanted to come back to the ranch, he would have to go to several foster homes, become destructive all over again, and then maybe find a social worker that has a heart and place him back with the ranch.

The monthly visits to the ranch were great except Willie always left crying, knowing he had to go back home. Invariably just before the visit to the ranch the parents would call with some lame excuse, such as their car wasn't running or they were sick et cetera, so I would go pick Willie up and he would spend the weekend. Sixty miles there and sixty miles back.

To this day, I have fond memories of Willie riding his horse around the arena with the other happy kids, laughing and teasing each other. I affectionately dwell on Willie catching that first fish in the High Country or jumping off the high rock for the first time and into the cold mountain water shouting at the top of his lungs, "I did it; I did it like the rest of the boys. Did you see it? Did you see how I just jumped right in there?"

Whether I saw it or not, I always told them, "I didn't see it, could you please do it again." Why did I encourage them to jump off this high rock and into the mountain lake? It was such a big thing for the boys to go to Kibby Lake. Jumping off the big rock into the swimming hole helped them build more character than ten counseling sessions.

One day I went to visit Willie only to find that the trailer had been sold and the family left no forwarding address. I pray for Willie and hope he still remembers the ranch and that I did everything within my power to protect him.

~ Chapter 37 ~

THE DRIVING LESSONS

Driving in traffic never used to bother me, but I have lost the recklessness of my youth (well, almost). Over the years, I have been stopped for speeding so often that the local highway patrolman and I exchanged conversations on a first-name basis. He informed me, "Rene` I know exactly what your problem is; you have lead in your right foot," He humorously referred to it as an "excessive mineral overload; lead." I am sure back then I held some kind of record for talking my way out of speeding tickets. Now, at my age, I seem to be slowing down, and/or, everyone else seems to be speeding up. Come to think of it, I have not had a "warning" ticket for speeding in over ten years.

My fifteen-year-old boys were no different than any other red-blooded American boys. When my boys turned fifteen, they all came down with the "driving disease." I called it a disease because it consumes every brain cell and every thought pattern of a teenage boy, second only to girls. I'll give you a few examples: put pay jobs on the bulletin board, and the fifteen year old will opt to mow the lawn for free, because he can, "drive something." Should you want the leaves raked, get rid of the rake and buy an attachment that fits the riding lawn mower, and what do you know? Every fifteen-year old will volunteer to "rake" those darn leaves.

My big problem was finding someone at the ranch crazy enough to give driving lessons. The counselors vigorously shook their heads "No." They did not want any of my persuasive conversation, stating, "It's not my job description, or, do you think we're crazy." The bottom line is that I just didn't have anyone willing to risk his or her life just so another teenager could drive.

I decided the good Lord probably wanted me to do the teaching, so I quit asking the counselors and took on another specialized job description.

We leased a large pasture with a few roads going through the middle. This pasture provided the safest place to teach the boys to drive. I looked for a special type of pickup to use during the driving lessons. I finally bought a dark blue Dodge. You know the kind, early '60s, that looked like a square box. The old Dodge truck resembled the likeness of a tank. I just knew I had found the perfect vehicle. Trevor was the first to test my physiological theory and logic.

My mother taught me how to drive before I could see over the steering wheel. I remember a comment I made to her, "But Mom, my feet won't touch the pedals," she looked at me and said, "No excuses, you are going to drive this hay truck, and that is the end of this discussion!" She put a rather big heavy pillow underneath me, and I had to slide down to shift gears and to push the clutch and then slide back up again. I navigated the hay truck up and down the alfalfa rows while my family loaded the hay bales. All the while, my mother screaming at me, "Stop jerking the clutch. Let it out slowly! Stop gunning it! Slow down! You're going to kill the engine!" I think I was twelve. I don't remember much about it, except my mother's constant shouting at me.

My great uncle would shout back at her, "Leave her alone. She's just a kid."

Needless to say, it wasn't a pleasant memory. I was determined to teach my boys with "patience and understanding." I wanted them to look back with fondness on their driving lessons and focus on that godly calmness I portrayed.

The morning of Trevor's first driving lesson, he stood at my office door, chomping at the bit like a young racehorse.

I said, responding to his excitement, setting in my swivel chair, "Trevor, we need to wait an hour or so until the sun dries the dew on the pasture grass. The dew makes the grass too slick."

He replied, "That's okay, Mom. I'll wait here in your office and watch you work."

Trevor could not sit still, nor keep quiet; he tapped his foot and then twirled his hat in his hands and began pacing the floor.

I looked up from my desk and said, "Trevor sit down!" Then the finger tapping started on my desk. I finally gave in to his persistent nonsense.

We climbed into the old Dodge and he drove out through the gate, past the barn and horse corrals to the big pasture. Just this short distance created an emotional storm.

Trevor jabbered to me about how much he knew, "I know quite a bit about driving already because I have been watching you and Tom. I know about clutches and accelerators. Which one is the brake?"

When he stopped to take a breath, I begin telling him how much he did not know.

"Easy on the brake, Trev, easy; I said EASY!"

All the while, Trevor continued to talk, "Mom, you just need to 'chill out.' I had a chill all right, a chill that scuttled up my spine, not from the cold, but from the realization that a gangly fifteen-year-old boy held my life in his hands and feet. We stopped for a few more braking lessons, sliding a bit on the grassy pasture. His "know-it-all" idea of braking was to put his foot on the brake and slam it to the floorboard. After several braking lessons, my finger imprints were clearly visible on the dash.

The key to good teaching is the adult educated mind must take over and become understanding and patient. I chanted this to myself a few times before I decided Trevor needed to relax and settle his mind by talking about school, his friends, or girls. Perhaps he would surprise me and I could live to teach another day. As I opened our discussion about girls, he began to drive through the wet pasture with a little more ease, but still entirely too fast.

I gave him permission to drive anywhere he wished to drive, as long as he stayed in the two-hundred acre pasture.

During late spring it was still cold and damp in the morning, but sunny in the afternoon. Irrigation on the ranch pasture had begun by flood irrigation. This meant that across the middle and at each end was a rather large ditch. This ditch was about six feet in width and about four feet deep and full of water.

As we drove along, I tried to tell Trevor, whenever I could get a word in, that he needed to slow down; my warning had the reverse effect. I could see the irrigation ditch in the distance and mentioned this fact in between his conversation about how great he was doing. Meanwhile, we were traveling at a rather high speed, closer and closer to the irrigation ditch, Trevor still driving at the same fast speed, talking a mile a minute.

"Ah, Trev, there IS a ditch up ahead of us." I was still talking softly so as not to upset him. The passenger is at the mercy of the driver, so I felt the need to keep the driver as calm as possible, that is, if I wanted to continue with the process of living.

I tightened my seat belt and proceeded to listen to this teenager talk, thinking he was going to react at the last minute and throw on the brake. I prepared myself for the sudden stop.

Well, sure enough, when he finally saw the ditch, it was too late to stop. When he put his foot on the brake, instead of stopping, he locked the brakes up, and we slid on the damp pasture grass. The front end of the old Dodge pickup dropped into the ditch. Both front wheels ended up in the water with the front end planted in the opposite bank.

We sat there for a minute just looking straight ahead. He still gripped the steering wheel with his tight fists, while his lips trembled in his ashen face. I could tell he was scared to death.

All the questions he must have going through his mind. Was Mom hurt? Am I grounded for life?

Finally, I broke the silence. "Trev, that was the absolute best example of how NOT to drive in the pasture or on the road; therefore, we surely do not need to experience this again."

"No, ma'am, we surely don't," he said.

I gave him a little grin to let him know it was okay and said, "We'll try again tomorrow." I made a mental note to myself, "Tomorrow's lesson we will concentrate on going slower and more carefully."

It was Saturday and everyone wanted to see Trevor's first driving lesson. We both looked back to see the boys and counselors running toward the truck. They had been watching the entire episode. Tom was first to arrive and helped me out of the truck. In between the chatter I heard someone ask if I was all right. I replied, "Oh yes, Mom's just fine." Underneath my breath I mumbled, if you think being scared out of my wits is all right!

Trevor and the boys moved the truck out of the ditch, and the lesson continued the next day.

By the third afternoon, I was relaxed and laughing and telling Trevor what great entertainment he had provided for me. We were both laughing when he swerved to miss a cow and wiped out four fence posts and a section of fence.

That poor Dodge truck went through various crashes that summer, but it was a great old truck for boys learning how to drive. We experienced several different little accidents, but my boys and I survived the ordeal without a scratch. Praying for our safety became a morning ritual. I accumulated a few more gray hairs that summer, which I would have had anyway, just maybe not as soon, and increased my purchasing investment with Miss Clairol.

When the boys received their driver's license, we introduced vocational training in how to drive a cattle truck, pull a horse trailer, and become helpful to the ranch. These skills could help take them into their adult years. For this driving lesson, we needed an area where we could set up the orange cones for backing the trailers. There was a graveled area not far from the horse barn that looked like the perfect spot. I've had a class one driver's license, or 'A' as some call it, for many years and was proud that I was qualified to drive anything on the road. I still keep it current today.

Tom had been a truck driver, so he was elected to teach without really running for the position—he was simply the best man for the job. Needless to say, he was not thrilled about being assigned this task. It looked like an easy walk in the park when we added this course to our vocational training program. Wrong! I neglected to take Trevor into consideration.

Tom taught the fundamentals of driving a cattle truck in class. He was a great teacher because the boys totally respected him. I tested them on the fundamentals after they attended these classes. One such fundamental task concerned backing up. After passing the fundamentals of truck driving on the ranch, Tom took them on the road.

The air was crisp this particular morning, and things were going along smoothly, that is, for the ranch. Each boy took his turn in backing the truck and trailer. Then there was Trevor. When Trevor's turn came, he told me, "Don't worry, I haven't had time to attend Tom's class or practice, but I think I can do this, 'cause I watched the other boys."

Trevor climbed into the truck and ground the gears to find reverse. Finally, he and reverse found each other, and back he came. I stood at the very back of the cattle trailer helping the boys with hand signals. Trevor missed that class, which also included looking in the rear-view mirror and watching for my signals. Behind me was a great big horse manure pile where the boys dumped their wheelbarrows after cleaning the stalls. Trevor never saw me, and so he just kept coming. By this time, Tom yelled at Trevor, "Stop, stop the truck!" But it was too late. Trevor did stop, but not before I fell backward into the manure compost pile.

When Trevor crawled out of the truck, he had successfully knocked over every orange cone—not one was left standing. I congratulated him on his genius accomplishment and suggested, "Why don't you take another approach to learning other than watching the other boys, for instance, ATTENDING CLASS!"

As I was getting out of the horse manure pile, Trevor asked, "Mom, what are you doing in the manure pile?"

I replied, "Getting away from a runaway truck and its driver."

How to pull trailers with horses and cattle behind a pickup was taught by demonstration and inductive reasoning. I had a sure fire way of teaching that made a lot of sense to me. Our rodeo horses were expensive animals, and the livestock investment needed protection. A driver could seriously injure an animal if he drove recklessly. The boys taking the lessons were assigned the trailer we would use a day before the actual lesson. The trailer was usually the eighteen foot gooseneck cattle trailer, which hauled either horses or cattle.

Before the lessons, I loaded cattle from the wheat pasture and let them stand in the trailer for a few hours. Allow me to paint the proper picture for you. These cattle have very runny bowel movements from being on wheat pasture.

The counselors could not tell the boys what to do with the trailer, such as wash it. If they figured it out by themselves, well, that meant the next day would not be as entertaining. For you see, I believed before they learned to pull livestock, they had to experience first-hand how the horse or cow felt going down the road.

I told them to draw straws to see who got to drive, then the remaining boys could load up and ride in the cattle trailer.

Usually you had two to three boys in the trailer, and the boy driving was told to go on the back roads through the countryside, which were pretty rough. By allowing one of the boys to drive, I avoided their blaming me for the rough ride. Normally the boy drove too fast over the rough road. I rode on the passenger side of the pickup. If the boys thought to wash the inside of the trailer the day before, then it wasn't too bad of a ride. But if they neglected washing the cattle trailer, then by the time we arrived back at the ranch, well, they were pretty messy. On more than one occasion, the boys would get out of the trailer, and proceed to roll the designated driver around in the floor of the trailer.

This method taught them two very important things: (1) to keep the horse and cattle trailers clean and (2) to drive with the utmost care. The boys who had experienced this type of teaching were the best I could ask for to haul horses or cattle.

Teenagers learn more through experience than someone verbally teaching them. Some of the boys actually became good truck drivers and made it their profession in their adult lives.

~ Chapter 38 ~

ROUGH-STOCK RIDING

I banned bull riding at the ranch. This sport prodded my overprotective spirit almost as much as drug-addict, abusive parents. I could not help myself. I saw some of the damages that a raging two-thousand-pound bull commits as he bucks, and stomps, and tosses bodies into the air. I had no intentions of letting my boys get hurt, run over, or stepped on by such an unpredictable beast. Bulls in the pasture to breed cows I could fully appreciate, but bulls for my boys to ride, absolutely NOT! In junior rodeo circuits, steer riding represented a form of bull riding; however, the steers weighed six to seven hundred pounds, usually had no horns, and bucked easier than the bulls. This I allowed; the steers were not as heavy or as aggressive. I didn't believe my young boys needed to experience bull riding. In actuality, I was being overly protective, but I could not help myself.

At the end of every month, the mail arrived with entry forms for the junior rodeos scheduled for the following month. Trevor, now sixteen and like most sixteen-year olds, if I told him he couldn't do something, he was going to do his best to change my mind. He started watching the mail for the entry forms to arrive. Trevor decided bull riding was what he wanted to do and informed me, "Mom, I am sixteen and it is an older boys sport."

He was right, bull riding was the older boys' event, and even though Trevor could not walk without stumbling over his feet, he could sit a horse and had a natural riding ability. I had given him permission to ride rough stock (bareback horses—another rodeo event), and surprisingly, he was doing rather well. Trevor had qualified for the finals in this event in junior rodeo the year before.

We did have one incident that is still as vivid in my mind as if it happened today. It was a hometown junior rodeo in Oakdale, California. Joe had ridden his steer and won the round, which qualified him for the district finals. Trevor and Joe did the high five thing and then it was Trevor's turn. Trevor was up in the bareback riding, and I was sitting in the third row waiting for the chute to open.

The announcer introduced Trevor; the chute opened, and out came the rankest horse with Trevor spurring and doing a balancing act to stay on for the legal eight seconds. The horse was wild-eyed and turning and twisting, while bucking left, then right, trying to throw Trevor off. Eight seconds does not seem very long unless you are riding an animal that is trying with all his might to throw you off, or a mom sitting in the stands praying God is truly watching.

Suddenly, the bucking horse turned back and fish-tailed, rolling his back in the air throwing Trevor into a section of the rodeo fence that appeared to be a concrete wall. He lay very still on the ground.

To this day, I don't know how I managed to make it over the spectator's fence. A friend sitting beside me said, "Rene' you flew from the stands, over the fence, and was the first person to arrive at Trevor's side." He was out cold; my heart sank. The paramedics arrived and began putting on the neck brace, when he started coming around with eyes fluttering; Trevor going in and out of consciousness opened his eyes and asked, "Mom, did I make it to the eight-second whistle."

"Yes, Son you made a great ride and are probably going to the finals."

I rode to the hospital with Trevor, and fortunately, he suffered only minor abrasions. He made the whistle and qualified for district finals. I postponed my nervous breakdown for another day. That night, I was thankful to relax with meditation and my usual conversation about God's chosen Journey for me. I suggested he try in my next lifetime to choose something not quite so stressful.

A week later, I went over to the rodeo arena and tried to figure out how I managed to clear the seven foot high spectator's fence. I could not even get to the six foot marker.

Instant motherhood to some eighteen boys with behavioral problems was not boring by any stretch of the imagination. God, through his plan, has a way of helping us survive it all.

Meanwhile, Trevor continued pursuing his need to ride bulls. Every first of the month when the entry forms arrived, he delivered the mail to my office, asking the same question: "Can I enter the bull riding?"

I simply said, "No."

"But, but Mom," said Trevor.

I interrupted him by saying, "End of discussion!"

We repeated the same conversation every month until one day I called Tom to the office and asked him how I could get past this ongoing conversation with Trevor. Tom's suggestion was not exactly what I was looking for, but it did seem to make some sense. Tom suggested we let him enter the next rodeo, and if he got bucked off, then that would be the end of it and I would have my sanity back.

When Trevor entered my office at the first of the month with the same song and dance, I kept it simple; "The answer is yes," and then explained the conditions.

He hugged me, taking me by surprise, and said, "Thanks, Mom," and ran out of the office shouting to everyone. "I'm entered; I am entered in the bull riding."

Two weeks later we traveled to Orland, California. The boys were abuzz about Trevor entering the bull-riding event. Even though I agreed to let him ride, I was ill at the thought of one of my boys riding one of these powerful, aggressive bulls. On that day, I told myself it was going to be okay and prayed as I did for all my boys' safety.

Trevor had never ridden an actual bull before, steers yes, bulls no. Tom assured me Trevor would get bucked off, and that would be the end of it.

The chute opened, and I could not bear to watch. The eight-second whistle blew, and I opened my eyes to see Trevor finish his ride and step off without as much as a hair out of place. He not only rode his bull the first day, but also placed second in the first go-around. On the second day of this three-day rodeo, he won the round.

He rode the third bull and successfully rode his bareback horse too, qualifying him for all around. That third day, he was simply unbearable to be around. "Mom, did you see that ride I made? Did you see it? Did you?"

Trevor at the district rodeo finals

"Yes, Trevor, I saw it." Actually, I had my eyes closed on each of his rides.

I said if he rode his first bull, I would consider letting him ride bulls the rest of the year, thinking he would get bucked off. For the next week, Tom stayed busy with the cattle and the horses until I had time to cool off a little. Tom's sensible plan to get Trevor off the bulls failed miserably.

Trevor made it to district and placed in the finals, coming in third in the all-around. Joe won the steer riding that year. Both the boys grew in self-esteem. As for me, I gained twice as many gray hairs; you guessed it, causing me to double up on Miss Clairol.

To practice rough stock riding it was necessary to buy two-and-three-year old colts and steers at the local sale. So horse and cattle sales were as much a part of the ranch duties as riding and sometimes very educational. While attending one of the many horse sales, the boys learned an important lesson about horse traders; that is, to pay very close attention to how and what the horse trader says.

Two of my boys came running up to me, telling me they had found me the perfect hunting horse. They both began to talk at once, "Mom, he is real big, just like you like'em."

Joe chimed in, "Mom, the guy said, you can shoot off of him and everything."

I stood there a minute and figured it would not hurt to visit with this gentleman. Besides it could be very educational for the boys. We walked toward the horse trader and sure enough, the horse had the size and appeared fairly calm. I asked the gentleman the question, "Can you shoot off this horse?"

The gentleman said, "Oh, yes ma'am, *you* can shoot off of him."

I smiled and asked the determining factor, "But is he *trained* to shoot off of?"

"Ahhh, I didn't say he was trained to be shot off of; I just said that YOU can shoot off him if you are a mind to."

"Would you, sir, shoot off of him?" I continued the conversation. By this time, the horse trader had his hat off in his hand fiddling with it and wishing this lady in front of him would go away and stop talking so loudly.

"Well, no, I don't rightly think I would do such a thing." He knew he was caught and smiled with a hangdog look on his face, both of us retreating in opposite directions.

Horse traders become professionals with word usage, tricks of their trade. Having a conversation with a gentleman horse trader one afternoon became a play on words. I spotted a big stout paint horse gelding at a local sale and asked the horse trader, "Have you owned this horse long?"

"Oh, yes, ma'am."

He did not say how long, so I continued my questioning.

"How long have you owned him?"

"Well, a long time," was his answer.

"And just what do you call a long time? Months? Years?

"Well, you got me; a few months" was his answer.

Still being cautious I asked, "Is he registered with the paint horse association?"

"Oh, yes ma'am." Again he told me no more than he had to.

"Let's go to the sales office and have a look see at the horse's papers."

We both strolled into the office to look at the papers, which are required by horse sales if an owner claims the horse is registered. Meanwhile this horse trader showed all the signs of not being truthful, nervously glancing from side to side. He had stated the paint gelding was seven years old. When I examined the papers on the horse, what do you know? His age turned out to be eleven years old. "A little older than you stated to me," I remarked.

"Well, ma'am, I must have mixed this horse up with another one I have." He still failed to admit his fabrication.

When I looked further there was no date on transfer of ownership, which meant he probably traded for this one last week. We walked back out to give the horse one last look and I asked, "Is he healthy? Can he see? Is there anything you can tell me about his health?"

Then came the typical answer: "Yes, ma'am. This horse here looks real good."

With this answer I looked closer at the horse's eyes, and sure enough his eyes were unhealthy looking.

My next question came as a surprise to this old horse trader, "Ah yes, I know he looks good but can he see?"

With this question he did not answer but walked away

The boys were all ears and Trevor spoke up, "But Mom, he said, the horse looked real good."

I turned to respond to Trevor's remark, "Yes son, the horse does look good, but that does not mean he can see good."

As it turned out, he could not see well and the auctioneer pointed out his poor eyesight condition when the horse came through the sale ring. The boys learned to be sure and question horse traders, for they are the best at telling only half of the story.

~ Chapter 39 ~

PLAYFUL TIMES

When Allen, Tom's son from a previous marriage, hired on at the ranch, I consulted with Allen during orientation in regard to special treatment, there would be none. Simplifying it considerably I said, "Do your job and do it well; you will be respected "accordingly." As it turned out, Allen made a super counselor, maybe because he inherited his dad's easy-going nature or maybe his desire to be close to his dad inspired him to make an extra effort. Whatever his reason, I was glad to have him at the ranch. Being six foot and five inches tall and weighing two hundred and fifty pounds was an advantage at the ranch. He was twenty-two years old when I hired him.

Sometimes Allen took four or five of the little ones out on the front lawn for a down-on-the-ground wrestling match. They scuffled as if they intended to defeat this big galoot of a man. The boys pounced on his back and clung to his shirt as he bucked them off, rolling with them on the grass, sometimes allowing the boys to hogtie him. Of course, with their tying ability he easily slipped out of their ropes. On occasion he let them think they won; they genuinely loved Allen. In his Wranglers and western clothes, he looked like a cowboy and was trying very hard to learn how to be one.

Within a year at the ranch and combined with his determination to please his dad, Allen competed in the steer wrestling at the rodeos alongside his dad, while I chased the buckets (barrel raced). If I went along, the rodeo had to be close to the area of the ranch. We never lacked for a cheering section when the boys accompanied us.

In February, a storm came through and blew leaves and other small debris into the in-ground swimming pool. I asked Allen to clean the pool as I was leaving for the bank with the checks for the monthly deposit.

At the beginning of the month, going to the bank became one of my monthly rituals. I needed enough cash to pay the boys for their pay jobs completed the previous month. I always paid the boys in cash, they understood cash; checks looked more like notes from their teachers.

Every month, I held our group session with money lying on my desk in plain view for all to see. Those new to the program, which refused to work, found themselves watching as I handed out a lot of cash to the other boys. Psychologically, this system worked. Watching other boys payday turned into a grand incentive for wanting to participate legitimately in pay jobs at the ranch.

I never bothered to carry a purse when wearing Wranglers; I carried my cash in my back pocket. So this particular morning after the deposit of my monthly checks, I received the cash from the bank and automatically put it in my back pocket.

Arriving back at the ranch I headed for the backyard where Allen continued cleaning the pool with a straining bag attached to a long pole, I walked north toward the end of the pool area, through the gate and into the pantry to inventory the food in the pantry. Finishing my task, clipboard in hand, I started back around the pool headed for my office. I noticed two of the older boys, Joe and Harry, standing at the south end of the pool with silly grins on their faces. I knew their intentions immediately. They planned to toss good ol' Mom into the cold, icy waters.

About this time they confirmed my suspicions when Joe stated; "Mom how'd you like to take a swim."

I issued an open invitation, "Just come on, but remember, I fully intend to take one or both of you with me." I hoped the chilly February day topped off with my open invitation would give them something to think about.

Harry gazed down at the ice floating around the edges of the pool and darted back into the house; Joe, unable to resist the playful invitation, strolled forward, acting like he planned to head to the barn. I pretended I did not see him make the turn around the pool and come up behind me. We both figured that the element of surprise was on our side. I waited until he closed in and quickly tossed my clipboard toward my office; for I did not want to do the food inventory over. I was about four feet from Allen when I turned and grabbed Joe, jumping into the deepest part of the pool. I held on tight as we plunged to the bottom in the icy waters of the pool. When we came up sputtering and laughing, we shivered so badly from the icy waters and the cold air it stole our breath away. We both climbed out quickly and headed for dry clothes and a warm fire.

Meanwhile, Allen, still working at the pool, stood there with his mouth gaping open. He could hardly believe that his boss and Joe just took a dip in the pool in February and that we were laughing and playing. As I rushed past him, I said, "Close your mouth Allen, before you catch your death."

I had only thirty minutes to change before the monthly group session started. The cash, oh my gosh! I had completely forgotten about the cash in my back pocket. Sure enough, it was very wet, all sixteen hundred dollars.

I changed clothes and made it in time for the group session where I paid the boys with soggy wet bills. Joe and I were still shivering. Every now and then, I looked over at Joe, and we grinned at each other. By this time, everyone at the meeting had heard about the winter dip in the outside pool. Harry, of course, sat there all warm and dry.

The boys took their money to their rooms to dry with hair dryers before going to the bank. I personally escorted the boys back to the bank to make deposits into their private checking accounts. Before they left the ranch at the end of their stay, they understood the significance of earning and managing money.

The boys continued teasing Joe about his polar bear winter swim. I truly believe I had more fun and experienced more satisfaction in what I was doing with the boys than anyone. It was just such a great and rewarding time in my life. It allowed me to experience the childhood robbed from me.

Early in the ranch program, we didn't have enough horses to go around. One of the favorite things to do was take the boys skating; this was a fifteen-mile trip to Modesto. During this trip the boys, true to their nature, determined that the best traveling game involved a flatulence contest, yes, that age old contest of farting. Naturally in the dead of winter I couldn't find a safe place to pull over and give them a piece of my mind, so I continued driving to the stench of different volumes coming from different directions. And of course, no one stepped forward to confess who was doing this distasteful smelly deed. It was time to call the professional in and discuss this matter to find a solution.

The next morning when I told Tom of my predicament, he smiled and said, "This problem is fixable. Leave it to me. I'll take care of it." The next time, we planned a skating expedition, Tom true to his word, volunteered to drive the boys. The day of the trip, I caught Tom in the kitchen cooking and eating a mess of beans, cabbage, and jalapeno peppers.

That night Tom drove my car because I had those new fangled locks on the driver's side that controlled the locks and windows. None of the doors or windows opened until the driver released the lock button. In the boy's ranch business, this safety feature turned out to be a necessity.

Tom traveled about five miles down the road, when the game started one of the boys in the back released a gas bomb. "Want to play games, do we? This is one game I know how to play." Tom blasted away his special odorous bomb of beans, cabbage, and jalapenos.

One of the boys started screaming, "Open the windows! I need air." Tom drove around the countryside with locked windows and doors for more than an hour and completely avoided the skating rink. When the joyride ended, the boys climbed out of the truck quietly. I don't know if Tom said anything more to the boys, but they refused to go skating again unless someone other than Tom drove. They also promised me no more odoriferous games. Tom, the faithful crime stopper, solved another problem. Of course, I couldn't drive the car until we fumigated it.

At the beginning of spring, I taught horsemanship to make sure the boys were capable of surviving the trips to the high country. In my teachings I reminded them by saying, "Each one of you will remember the mountain trips as one of your best childhood memories, provided you are listening and learning enough to survive the trip. I cannot stress enough the importance of these adventures."

Boys find solitude and often recover a lost freedom in the mountains. If they are lucky enough, they may find the important thing in their young lives that will carry them through the rest of life's Journey—the inner most spiritual soul. I saw this happen with my own eyes as the mountains turned young ruffians into young gentleman growing toward manhood.

One afternoon the boys were not in a listening mode; they had spring fever. I lowered my diction a little and remarked, "The horses must have the best of care, for you are responsible for taking care of your horse while in the high country. If the horse is left standing and tied to a tree or fence, loosen the cinches to the saddle so the horse may rest." I continued, "It is so important for the rider to check the cinches before mounting your horse. The reason for this procedure is so the saddle will not slip, causing a wreck, your wreck. If your horse bolts and Gets away in the mountains, you will simply be afoot."

Soon it was time for a break, and the boys tied their horses to the fence and made a mad dash for the kitchen. This is just one of several times on the ranch I felt boys sometimes actually needed to experience what I was teaching. So I began to loosen the saddle cinches on the horses. They returned from the break. Immediately I saw who was listening and who was not. It was entertainment of the best kind. Three of my boys, when I said, "Mount up" did check their cinches; as for the rest we had ourselves a wild horse ride. When the boys put their weight in the stirrup the saddle pulled over to one side by the total weight of the boy. This caused the tamest of horses to buck, and if six were bucking, those six boys were busted!

Some of the counselors came out to see this chain of events take place. It was the entertainment of the day, with the horses bucking and the boys scatting in all directions. Amazingly, fun and games taught the boys they needed to pay more attention to Mom's teachings. This technique became such a learning experience that everyone, including me, remained cautious and always checked their cinches before mounting our horses. Well, almost always.

What's good for the goose—you know that saying—the boys loosened our cinches in hopes Tom and I would forget, and we did. We were both caught on this matter. On one occasion I left the arena to go to the restroom and returned to find my cinch was loose. When my weight hit the stirrup, the saddle slid to one side, I landed on my backside looking up. Thank goodness, the horse was gentle. The old roan just turned his head toward me, as if to say, "Get your s—— together."

No one lasted at this ranch unless he or she had a great sense of humor!

~ Chapter 40 ~

DAVID LEARNS TO MEDITATE

At no time in this book do I claim to be the only force running this boys ranch. Everyone contributed to the success of the boy's ranch. God's strength and guidance were the true reason for my success.

I started to study religion and found the subject matter of spiritual metaphysics an interesting subject. It answered a lot of questions and helped me become more successful with my career and the boys at the ranch. Religion is a point in one's mind as to how individuals perceive God as our strength, each determining one's own definition according to his or her translation.

Meditation, as a form of religious practice, is gratifying and based in theological theory to be the most believable; guided by an inner strength on a Journey that is more powerful than just our own ideas. Wherever I am, whatever I may do, in reality, it is God who is there and God who is controlling the path and Journey within.

I still lose my temper on occasion and let fly with cuss words, especially when playing golf. I do try very hard to clean it up a bit, saying, "Oh holy ca-ca," instead of that other word. These deeply imbedded words, (habits from having too many behavioral problem children's programs, and yes, lousy shots in golf.) did not miraculously disappear when I became ordained as a minister. In my childhood my mother would wash our mouths out with soap. It was next to death for us to use such language.

Unfortunately, I have discovered that it is an impossibility to live perfectly. I believe God knows this bit of information; consequently, I imagine that our heavenly Father never rests and certainly does not complain of boredom when I come calling each evening. If in fact we were perfect, God would be bored to death.

At the ranch, hands down, I was the biggest contributor to the "Cuss for cash jar."

The cuss jar helped pay for the boys many privilege trips, and everyone at the ranch was required to participate. The counselors, the house parents, cowboys, and the boys all contributed to the cuss jar; I, however, had to contribute five dollars while everyone else fed a dollar in the jar.

One evening at the ranch, I was deep in meditation when there was a brief knock at the door, and I do mean brief—in walked David. There I sat with lighted candle, eyes focused, mentally talking to God, asking his forgiveness for my mistakes of the day, and thanking him for all the gifts we had received. I was in the process of thanking God for another boy accepted at the ranch. Meditation and prayer are similar in structure; however, meditation is a deeper fulfillment of oneness.

The boys were not allowed in my bedroom at any time, unless, of course, they had a question that could not wait until morning. This was my personal and private time. With a boy's ranch, rarely did I have total privacy, especially with David in the house. He could always find a question or two that simply could not wait until the next morning.

It surprised David to see me kneeling on the floor, with, of all things, a candle burning in the room. David, being David never shied away from questions: "What are you doing, Mom; are you saving on the elect-electpricity?"

Bless his heart. "You mean electricity, David." I always said the word he was meaning to confirm the correctness to the boy. "No, David, I am meditating with God." Why I did not just say "yes" and let it go at that, I don't know. With this reply, I opened a whole list of questions David thought of immediately.

"What's med-a-fu-cation?" David asked. David's speech problem arose from a hearing impairment from untreated ear infections when he was a toddler, which caused him to say the words wrong.

"Well, son, it's when I reach into my mind and talk to God. A candle in a dark room helps me relax and think, so I can have a better visit with God. The thought power of our minds control basically what we do and how we react to our surroundings." With this last statement I buried myself, and for the next twenty minutes of my somewhat-limited private time, I talked to David about meditation. We talked about things he did not understand.

"You have heard people comment about how positive thinking I am; even in a crisis, there is always something positive, if we just look hard enough. Well, David, that positive flow of energy comes from the God power within me, as it is in you."

I looked at his face for signs he understood what I was saying. "There are also prayers that I say each night.

These prayers give me strength and carry us all safely through the night. There is a purpose and a principle to each thought pattern we have, and when combined with metaphysical techniques, like meditation, they have a strong influence in our lives. Jesus said, "For it is not what goes into the mouth of man that defies the man, but what issues forth."

David was so confused, and knowing David, this conversation could go well into the night. I asked David if he would like to pray with me. So we both could get some sleep, I kept it short: "Dear Divine Presence of God within me, upon all those near and dear to me, bestow your love and blessings, peace of mind, health of mind and body, and your presence. God within me ..."

David interrupted, "God is within me too."

"Yes, David. To you almighty God I dedicate the efforts of this day, my soul, and my existence, and I thank you for having lived in your presence one more day. And so it is."

"Do we say 'amen' now, Mom?" David asked.

"Yes, son, we can say amen. Oh, by the way, David, what did you come in here for?" By this time, it was past bedtime for the boys.

He said, "Sorry, Mom, it's too late to ask." At that time of night, it was always the same question: "Can we stay up just a few more minutes?"

As he left, I heard another boy say, "David, thanks a lot; now we 'really' have to go to bed!"

David was unaware I had used meditation on him when he first arrived at the ranch, but since we were not allowed to use that terminology, I simply used semantics and called it a relaxation session. Meditation today is proven most effective on children of all ages with social behavioral problems, especially teenagers.

David's relaxation session went something like this;

Speaking to David in a soft voice I said, "Please lay down on the coach, put you head on top of the pillow and close your eyes...now take deep breaths and relax.

David asked opening his eyes, "Am I gonna take a nap Mom."

"No David, close your eyes and keep them closed. This is about relaxing and visualization to relax."

"What's bisuali...whatever you said Mom," opening his eyes again?

"David, close your eyes and let's get started, and David do not open your eyes again," I remarked.

David's eyes closed and I began the process. "David, pretend to see a blue sky with white fluffy clouds. Can you see the blue sky?" Again, talking in a rather soft voice; Nine year old little boys have a habit of literally throwing your education out the window in a mere simple statement.

David being a nine year old, said in a whispered voice, "Mom, can I open my eyes."

"No David," I replied with a sigh.

I continued, "David do you feel relaxed and can you see the blue sky with white clouds?"

David by this time had his arms crossed in total disgust with me and sat up, eyes still closed and replied, "Mom, I can't see anything 'cause you won't let me open my eyes!"

The rest of the afternoon I spent with little David trying to make him understand what meditation and visualization through the mind's eye could accomplish for him.

The next day and through the next week, everyone was busy going about their chores, and I thought the subject of meditation had been answered to David's satisfaction. Wrong. Never, underestimate the powerful mind of a nine-year-old.

The boys were not allowed to have matches or candles for all the obvious reasons. If I caught them with either, the boy received a mandatory thirty day restriction and could be suspended from the ranch program. They were thoroughly aware of this rule. However, with a little boy and his great imagination, rules sometimes become secondary.

David told Willie, "I know how Mom talks to God, and we can do the same thing. All we need are some matches and a candle."

Toward the end of the week, I noticed David's presence lacking, running in and out of my office with the normal visits. So I began to ask around and found out he and Willie were trying to save the world through "med-a-fu-cation." David told the boys and counselors he was going to pray for them in such a way he would be talking directly to God. It is odd to me none of us picked up on David's dangerous mission—we just thought it was entertaining and worthwhile for a nine-year-old to be that interested in praying for everyone.

Friday night a trip was planned to the shopping mall for the boys. I decided to go along with the two counselors. Most of the time I supervised the little ones and the counselors took the older boys with them. On this particular shopping trip, somehow David and Willie, knowing the counselors' supervision would not be supervised as closely as mine, ended up with one of the other counselors. Their conniving overzealous little minds planned it that way. Willie probably distracted the counselor, while David snuck around to purchase a scented candle and some matches. I am not sure the matches weren't snatched by David.

Earlier in the week, a ranching family invited the two of us to dinner, and Tom looked forward to a night out. With my busy schedule, the neighbors were aware that any plans with me were subject to change, with a "no-hard-feelings agreement."

As I was getting ready for the evening, Tom kept saying, "We are going, right?"

I answered for the third time, "Of course, dear, we're going." As I took one final look into the mirror and turned to tell Tom I was ready; I glanced out the back patio and down toward the barn and the houses below the main house. I checked to see if everything was still standing. A flicker of light caught my eye. The light glowed off in the distance. FIRE WAS COMING FROM THE HORSE BARN. After one panicked moment, it dawned on me what was happening. As I ran toward the hallway, I began yelling, "FIRE! FIRE IN THE BARN!" I kicked off my high-heel shoes and ran; I managed to put on a pair of slip-on tennis shoes as I dashed through the house.

Fire in a barn could easily wipe out most of our horses. Never mind the loss of hay, equipment, or saddles—it could be a nightmare of the worst kind. Tom had already called the fire department. He ran into the yard to ring the big church bell to alert the other two houses and the cowboys to the emergency. I installed the big bell the year before, and we used it for practice fire drills.

I purchased the old church bell at a local antique shop. It could be heard for miles, according to our neighbors.

As I made my way down the road to the barn, I could see lights and commotion all over the ranch. I continued running down the gradual slope to the barn about two hundred yards from the house. By the time I reached the barn area, the cowboys were out and about, and the house parents were getting everyone out of the other houses. We immediately did a head count of the boys; Willie and David were missing! Due to our dinner engagement, my little ones were at the main ranch house next to the barn.

The flicker of light grew bigger as flames leapt into the air from the very back of the barn where the hay was stored. Things could not be worse. The hands had already let the horses out of their stalls, and horses were running everywhere. With the horses in front of the barn, most had run down the shed row, but some were being led out blindfolded because of the smoke that had consumed the shed row. Some horses are just like people—they panic and will not leave their stalls. With blindfolds the cowboys led them to safety.

One of the hands was leading two horses out of the barn; the back of his jacket was on fire. Two of the other hands hit the horses on the butt and immediately threw the cowboy to the ground putting the fire out

I heard David and Willie screaming, their little voices coming from the back of the barn. It is amazing how my motherly instincts kicked in; even though they were not my birth children—they were still mine, and they were in deep trouble. By this time, Tom was in the barn.

I grabbed a big horse blanket, dipped it in a watering trough, pulled it over my head, and followed sounds of terror coming from my boys. Firemen and fire trucks arrived on the scene.

Their sirens stifled out David and Willie's screams—with the noise from the fire and everyone yelling, I could not hear them.

At one time, the barn had been a very long chicken barn. We built twenty stalls in front and had the other half filled with hay. It was a very long barn. The previous year I had extra water outlets placed along the entire barn. Everyone complained about the extra work, but now they were being put to use. By the time I was halfway down the barn, I could see David and Willie. Tom and one of the hands grabbed me and carried me out of the burning barn. I kicked and screamed for them to let me go! Two ranch hands went into the burning barn, found the boys, and came running toward me with both of them safely wrapped in wet blankets. Needless to say, by this time, I had completely lost it and was out of control until the boys were at my side.

We rushed David and Willie to the hospital to make sure they were okay. Both of their little faces were so black with smoke, we did not know whether they were hurt or not. I rode to the hospital in the ambulance, praying harder than I had prayed in a while that both of my boys would be all right. I insisted the hospital keep the boys overnight. I slept in their room that night in case they needed something or woke up. My dress was a mess. One of the female nurses offered me a set of scrubs from the hospital and showed me to the shower room; I appreciated both the shower and the clean clothes.

As it turned out, David and Willie snuck out of the house with a candle and matches, intending to talk to God. While meditating, Willie accidentally knocked over the candle.

Thanks to the fire drills we practiced on a regular basis, we avoided a big disaster. No one was really hurt, and all the animals escaped without burns. The fire hoses installed saved the barn and probably the boys lives. We did lose most of our hay. I knew how dangerous it was to store hay in the same barn as the horses, especially a wooden barn. The next year, we built a steel-constructed barn just for hay.

Were David and Willie grounded for life? Well, no, because this incident had been my fault. Mimicking adult habits is a natural thing for children to do. I prayed with a candle and they wanted to talk with God just as Mom did. The boys did get a rather strong talking to, but I was so glad they were all right that I just wanted to hold them and never let them go.

I held a group session on the matter of meditation and talking to God. The point of the conversation was about where, when, and how to talk to God. I explained that candles help you relax, but are not necessary to visit with God. God, as I told my boys, is a great listener and listens if you sit underneath a tree or even while you are fishing. "Until you are older and understand more about life, I suggest you talk to God without using candles."

Tom bought David a prayer light with an angel face and wings on the front for his bedroom. Tom told him it was not to be used as a night light, but rather it was to be used only when he prayed. We hoped the angel light would deter any further prayer candles.

In the following group session, I said, "David, would you like to come up in front and tell your brothers what you learned from this experience?" The boys often shared their learning experiences.

David walked to the front and replied in a rather loud voice, "It was the loudest conversation with God I have ever had, and the scariest one. From now on, you guys can just pray for yourselves!"

His declaration was not exactly what I had hoped David would say, but then again, it was David.

During the counselors' sixty-day training period, I stressed they be very careful of what they say to the boys, especially the young ones. Children's minds are so very fresh, and assume adults know everything.

What happened with David was really my fault; if I had been more understanding and explained meditation on his level, I would have realized he was not ready for such lessons.

After everyone left group session, I had a talk with David regarding his feelings on the matter. Understand that when asking David a question of this kind, well, you just never knew what he was going to say.

David was mad at God. He told me, "If there was a God, the fire in the barn would not have happened, and I would not have gotten in trouble trying to talk to God."

I wanted to tread lightly and hoped whatever I said would clear the air a little. "David, don't you know God was there in the barn all the time with you and Willie? It was God who saved you. He saved the horses, and absolutely no one was hurt. Even though the cowboys carried you out of the burning barn, God was most definitely showing them the way in the smoke-filled barn. God does not promise he will prevent bad things from happening, but he does promise he will be there by our side when they do."

In our western culture that helped make this great country of ours strong, prayer is a center piece for family.

In November of this last year we attended a national finals ranch rodeo. The cowboys riding in the arena mounted on their horses to exercise them before the rodeo started. About thirty minutes went by when the announcer asked them to clear the arena. Instead of clearing the arena; they circled their horses, and as every cowboy dismounted their horses, hats came off. There in the middle of mother earth arena knelt down on one knee was some of the toughest looking ranch hands with humble heads bowed listening to a cowboy minister say a prayer before the rodeo started. The lights were dimmed and a brilliant white spotlight appeared on the minister as he prayed for the cowboys safety in their events. I have never in my life been so proud of my western heritage. It brought the audience to a silence of total respect and a unity that filled the auditorium with Christ's awesome presence.

We must carry this tradition forward into the modern world we live in today, as this is our heritage established centuries ago by our forefathers before us. The old fashion morals and standards most lived by today. Remember, its God, Country, and Family.

~ Chapter 41 ~

JOE'S PLANE RIDE

Joe was twelve when he gave me his "special wish letter," or perhaps I should say "note." This note was folded numerous times, handed to me by Joe, and by the time I unfolded the darn peace of paper, Joe had left my office. This special wish letter concerned something special that the boys wanted to do. This had nothing to do with the Christmas list or for that matter birthdays; although I sometimes granted a special wish on birthdays.

I often noticed Joe gazing into the sky and watching the jet streams or smaller aircraft buzzing the ranch. He watched with more intensity than most boys at his age. When he heard the engine sounds, he stopped whatever he was doing to look up and watch the plane soar until it faded completely out of sight. If we attended the state fair and rodeo, Joe gravitated to the displays of airplanes from the past. He poured over every detail, sometimes irritating the other boys, who chimed, "Come on, Joe, we don't want to miss the rodeo." It came as no surprise to me when I opened the note simply put, "I would like to go flying," and it was signed "Joe."

For a few days, I said nothing, and Joe said nothing. Finally, he asked, "Mom, did you read my letter that I gave you?"

I replied, "I have, and I will consider your request."

Nothing else was said until his thirteenth birthday, a month later. Birthdays at the ranch were always special, with cake and lots of presents. Joe received his birthday gifts as usual.

With eighteen boys running around, we sometimes had as many as three birthday parties in one month. In retrospect, I know that I celebrated my own missed childhood birthdays vicariously through the boys. A part of me wanted to make sure that if they remembered nothing else about the ranch, they would remember fondly their special birthdays.

I jumped through hoops and over hay bales to make every birthday party unique. Most seemed surprised when we held Joe's thirteenth birthday party in the morning instead of the afternoon. My present consisted of a white envelope, simply stating, "One flying lesson." After the party, I loaded Joe and two of his friends (for moral support), Jake and Harry, in the crew cab pickup. As far as the boys were concerned, our destination was unknown. I headed to an airstrip for glider flying just outside of Fairfield, California. The airstrip was approximately three hours from the ranch. I knew the route like I knew the German braids on the side of my head, because I too had taken glider lessons at one time to get away from the phones and to seek a different perspective on life. I had some of my best conversations with God while soaring in a glider over the Delta area in northern California.

I insisted that Joe not eat anything for lunch because I wanted him to enjoy his day fully. However, the boys became hungry, and finally I gave in and stopped for lunch. We played the usual guessing games about his birthday present through lunch. What kind of flying lesson? What kind of plane? These questions consumed the rest of the trip. When I finally pulled into the little airstrip, the excitement mounted.

I knew the instructor and felt he would give us a safe ride and make it enjoyable for Joe. When Joe finally put it together, he was excited until he saw the plane I chartered; it had NO engine! I wanted him to enjoy flying and to be able to feel the plane. Joe had mixed emotions about going, as would all young boys; however, his two buddies wished him a great flight with all kinds of reassuring support. I informed Joe of its safety features, "And Joe," I said, "I will be going flying with you."

It was about this time that Joe remarked, "Mom, I really want to go flying, but it has NO engine!"

I answered, "Joe your letter did not specify whether you wanted an engine or not, so perhaps next time you will make the effort to write a little bit more and clarify specifics." I paused for just a moment, then said, "Well, do you want to go or not?"

"Oh yes ma'am," Joe replied.

The instructor put us together in the front seat while he took the back seat. The seating gave us an eagle's view of the landscape. We were strapped in, as the "pilot plane" pulled us up, higher and higher. When a pilot plane hits a certain altitude, the glider is set free of the towing rope. If the passenger is not familiar with this procedure, it will definitely get your attention. My intention for Joe was that he needed to enjoy this special experience, not be scared to death. I explained that this procedure creates an awesome loud noise and to be prepared for the noise.

By this time, Joe was totally taken by the flight and started asking all sorts of questions: "Do we have parachutes, and if we don't have an engine, how are we going to land?"

"To answer both of your questions, son, NO we don't have parachutes, and as for the landing, we hope it will be a good one the first time around." I neglected to mention that we wouldn't have a second shot at landing, especially if the glider dropped below a thousand feet. If you are in a glider and you are below one thousand feet, you are going to land one way or another.

It takes skill and professional knowledge to fly a glider. Our pilot's safety record, plus his twenty years as an instructor gave me the assurance we were in good hands. Most importantly, I had spoken to God about the whole thing and felt protected by His presence. The feeling of reassurance comes in different forms, but for me, it was simply a warm and fuzzy feeling of total confidence.

Finally, when Joe started to relax, he began to enjoy the wind going by the wings and the quietness of the glider. I pointed out things to Joe from the air, and he was in awe of the magnificence of flight. Soon he had forgotten we had no engine in the plane. Joe's reaction to the release of the tow rope from the pilot plane suggested he had also forgotten my warning about this little matter earlier. All of a sudden the rope was released and sure enough the loud sound that followed included an elbow in my side.

Joe asked a question that strongly embedded in my spiritual mind. "Mom, is this what God sees?"

"I suppose so, son, except he has a much bigger picture."

About this time, the instructor asked if Joe wanted to take the stick. The stick is the basic driving mechanism that guides the glider. I knew the instructor would not let us get into trouble. So for just a few minutes this thirteen-year old was living out a dream of flying, plane and all. The instructor retrieved the controls in preparation of our landing. We hit an air pocket, and Joe's face became pale. We landed and took about ten steps when Joe's lunch came up. I washed Joe's face with a cold washcloth handed to me by the kind instructor, and said, "See, son, this is why I didn't want you to eat."

He said, "That's okay, Mom; it was worth it."

"Oh, by the way Joe, thanks ever so much for holding your lunch until we landed. That was extremely considerate of you."

That evening when we arrived at the ranch, and for the next week, all of us heard repeatedly about the glider ride, the flight, and his ability to fly the glider, all of five minutes. Of course, he neglected to tell everyone the amount of time he was flying.

The following week his probation office showed up. In his excitement, Joe told his probation officer about the glider flight.

His account brought down a barrage of questions on me: "Was this approved by state licensing?"

"NO, it wasn't." In fact, I didn't ask, for I knew they would refuse because glider flying, I was quiet sure, was egregiously omitted from the manual. Soon afterwards, I received a letter of do's and don'ts from the state followed by a visit by Social Services. I wrote a letter and apologized for my behavior, after the fact, of course.

Joe heard of the incident and worriedly asked, "Mom, did I cause you to get into trouble?"

I comforted him, "No, son. I never regret anything I do for any of my boys, especially if it gives them fond memories. That includes you, Joe."

Like little Shawn and his symphony, I bought books on aviation and other things, such as model airplanes, that made Joe's heart smile from the inside out. Joe's room was full of rodeo pictures, but also included numerous pictures of airplanes.

I don't know what happened to most of my boys after they left the ranch; for this was another one of the state's silly rules—no contact after they left. But I have no doubt that Joe is probably flying somewhere, maybe in the Air Force, or perhaps flying commercial. Sometimes, when I am flying commercial across country, I wonder if Joe perhaps is piloting the plane.

Wherever Joe and the other boys are today, I pray that their memories keep coming back to special times at the ranch. And yes, perhaps "Joe, that special day, put out his hand and touched the face of God."

~ Chapter 42 ~

DAVID'S BANK LOAN

One of the main teaching goals in my program encompassed handling money and financial responsibility. Adults fall short in teaching children at a young age simple things that can be so important before they become eighteen, For instance; how to balance a checking account or how to qualify for a loan and pay it off. These things, when taught at an early age, may make the difference between success and failure in their adult lives.

Experts claim that training in financial responsibility needs to begin almost as soon as a child learns to count. Trust me, some age groups in children learn more quickly than others. I discovered learning occurred readily in my boys between the ages of eight through twelve. My little ones' fresh minds eagerly embraced the learning, especially when it included money. To arouse the older ones' interest, I had to sneak in the two equations that controlled their entire minds: girls and wheels. I constantly reminded the older ones,' "Remember, to date the girl of your dreams you must have money, your own checking account makes you look very stable to a young girl." Then adding, "The purchase of your own vehicle, shows responsibility to the parents of the girl you wish to date." Through these two wonderful components of a teenage boy, learning about financing became an easy stretch of the legs in the park!

At the ranch, we granted permission to a child to open his own checking account when he reached Level Two. It was the child's responsibility to keep up with his money, or at least that is what we allowed him to think. All checking accounts at the ranch required two signatures with both his name and mine on the check. This great solution kept everything in balance. The boy reported to his counselor every week and requested permission to spend his money.

The first of many financial responsibilities for the boys began with the offering at church. During the week, they would write a check for spending money and included one dollar for the offering at church. Sometimes the checks were only five dollars. Most banks were not understanding in this matter and resisted cashing so many small checks. I met with the officers of the local bank about our program. They agreed to cooperate with our checking account program in handling the boys pay job money and cash their checks. If both signatures were not signed, the bank would not cash the check. The tellers where I had the corporate accounts were friendly and made the boys feel important. The bank made a little wooden box, furnishing my little ones something to stand on at the teller's window.

My David received his Level Two and opened his checking account the day after his ninth birthday. The mind of a nine-year-old is at that wonderful stage—the brain is actually starting to kick in, and the beautiful part is, they are so honest in their thinking. It did not take David long to figure out if he wrote a check out for the church offering, then that money was gone.

My older boys were so good with the younger ones. The big-brother program I developed was working very well, but with one little kink. David figured it was much easier to "borrow" from the older boys and the counselors when he needed money for church or skating. If he borrowed the money, only one or two dollars at a time, he would not necessarily have to pay it back, and *his* money was safe in the bank. Most of the time, the ranch had so many things going on at once everyone simply forgot about the money David had "borrowed." He even borrowed from me, and I forgot about it. So began a habit that became all too easy.

The older boys would not ask to be paid back, and the counselors did not want to ask David for a dollar or two. After all, he was just "nine." So basically, David made out like a very young thief in the night.

One evening during a monthly group session (meaning everyone usually attended), John, one of my older boys, asked about the policy for borrowing money at the ranch. I replied, "We do not allow borrowing unless the borrower writes a note made directly through the ranch." I continued to talk about the subject at hand, which was planning trips for that particular month.

Pretty soon, Trevor asked about borrowing between the boys. I stopped and asked, "Is there something I am not hearing or seeing about borrowing money? Will someone please tell me what is going on?" Everyone started talking at once. I finally managed to quiet the room, including house parents and counselors.

When I asked who had borrowed money from whom, it was amazing the fingers that simultaneously pointed to my David. Somehow the older boys gossip session turned toward David and they discovered that he had been mooching from all of them. Since the little professional manipulator had managed to fool them all, their embarrassment quickly changed to anger. David shrunk down in his chair; he knew he was in trouble, not big trouble, but trouble nevertheless.

"Who has David borrowed from?" I asked.

All of the older boys and counselors raised their hands. It was unanimous. I asked David to come to the front of the room and defend himself.

"David, do you know what the word 'borrow' means?"

He looked straight at me and said, "Yes, ma'am, I don't have to write a check if I borrow, and if I don't have to write a check, I get to keep my own money."

Was that an honest answer or what? David's honesty revealed his total misunderstanding of financial integrity. I needed to solve his money management problems, his ethics, and his indebtedness right away. First, I needed to figure out how much he owed. Not one single individual offered any physical evidence of a loan—no one, including the counselors had anything in writing, in regard to David's borrowing. The borrowing transpired for so long that nobody had a clue how much he owed. In fact, no one even discussed with David any terms for paying back the loans. We all just handed the boy with the soft, big brown pitiful looking eyes the couple of dollars he requested and made erroneous assumptions about his payments. As eloquently as Judge Judy, I declared, "Since no one has written any notes about the transactions, David cannot be required to repay the loans." David's sigh of relief was covered by the mass of groans coming from the rest of the group. I knew I literally saved David from being tossed and rolled in the manure pile.

So we made another ranch rule: I announced, "No one, including me, will lend any money to anyone, no matter how small the amount, unless it is sanctioned by the head office; and I am the head office."

I confronted David in front of the group to make sure he and everyone else fully understood. He said, "Yes, ma'am." I assumed mission accomplished. This would put an end to David's borrowing, and I, being the authoritative figure, had handled this situation.

Never underestimate a nine-year-old, especially if his name is David. Remember once upon a time there was a "David" who won a big fight with a rather large giant called Goliath.

Two months later, David came into my office, thinking I just might have forgotten everything about borrowing. There was a rodeo coming up, and the ranch paid for the tickets for the boys who went just to watch. The other boys paid their entry fees to participate through the ranch account. It was up to the boys themselves to have their own spending money at the rodeo.

David and I had a conversation that went something like this: "Mom, if I ask you something and it is something you might say yes to, I can't get in trouble if you say yes, or no, right? You always told us if we had something on our minds, to be sure and ask, because you just might say yes."

On this particular Friday morning, I was rather busy with the end-of-the-week reports. So basically I answered David without too much thought or attention to what the question might be.

"So, Mom, if you say no, then I'm not in trouble for asking; and if you say yes, I'm not in trouble?"

"Yes, David, I guess that's what I told you."

David immediately asked me for a loan. I was astonished.

"ABSOLUTELY NOT! Are you broke, David?" I asked. "Did you forget about the no-borrowing rule? You know the trouble you may be in if you borrow money from anyone at the ranch."

"Well, Mom," he said, "if this means no, you are not lending me any money, then I guess I am not getting in trouble." David undoubtedly thought his strategy out before entering my office. He was my little thinker, and in many ways, I so enjoyed his absolutely honest approach to everything.

I asked, "Do you have any money in your checking account?" Before he could answer, I reminded him: "David, you were paid just three days ago."

David said, "Yes, I have money in my checking account, but it is in the bank and the rodeo is tonight."

With firmness in my voice, "It is your responsibility to see that you have your own spending money for the rodeo and the church offering on Sunday. You know I expect you to take care of your financial responsibilities. You know the drill. Get Shelly or one of the counselors to take you to the bank. David, do we fully understand each other on this matter?"

David said, "Yes, ma'am," and left the office.

Willie was ten, and Conway was eleven. Conway at birth came with slow learning disabilities. They were waiting outside to offer moral support. I stood in the office doorway and watched the three of them leave. Willie told David, "I knew this would not work. But, David, you are the bravest person I've ever known."

Conway commented, "Boy, you could have gotten grounded for life."

I took a moment to look up and thank the good Lord for the morning's entertainment and went back to work. I waited for a while, and then called Shelly to see if David had asked her about going to the bank. Shelly told me she would bring the three little musketeers up to the main house to get my signature on their checks after lunch. The last thing I said to Shelly was "Do not take your eyes off these boys."

That afternoon, after taking David, Conway and Willie to the bank, Shelly came in the office. She was laughing and trying to talk at the same time. According to Shelly, David asked the bank receptionist to see the banker, "the one that has all the money." The receptionist asked, "Do you have an appointment."

David said, "I don't need one of those things 'cause me and Willie are one of the bank's 'custom people' (meaning customers), and we have lots of money in this bank." David's balance was fifty-eight dollars at the time.

To a nine-year old, fifty-eight dollars is a lot of money. David accompanied me on several occasions when I handled my banking business. David was "all ears" as I discussed business with Jim, the president of the bank, regarding different money matters.

Shelly made a big mistake with the boys. She was laughing as she said, "I know now what you were talking about when you said, "Never let the boys out of my sight for one minute." She had sent the boys into the bank by themselves. By the time she figured out they were taking too much time just to cash their checks, it was too late.

David was in front of Jim, the president of the bank, asking for a bank loan of ten dollars. Jim knew about my boys and told Shelly he was amazed at David's confidence. Shelly and I sat there laughing, and then I called Jim. He too being entertained remarked, "David was the youngest customer to ever ask me for a loan."

Jim told David he would have to check and see if his bank had that much money. David immediately told Jim he did, "cause he had made a deposit of fifteen dollars three days ago bringing his account up to fifty-eight dollars." The banker and I, when we were finally able to control our laughter, decided to work together to teach David a lesson on borrowing. After I discussed my plans with Jim, he agreed to cooperate fully. Of course, none of this loan business would actually be through the bank.

I called a group session and told the boys David was going to borrow money from the bank; the purpose of this transaction would show the rest of the group both the advantages and the disadvantages of borrowing money.

I accompanied David to the bank the next day and sat down in front of Jim's desk, and again, David asked for a loan. Jim asked, "What collateral do you have?

And David asked, "What's that word Mom, do I have it?" Before I could answer, Jim answered David's question.

Jim said, "Well, David, it's something you own that you can give to the bank to hold until the loan is paid in full. And of course, there is something called interest, which means if you borrow ten dollars, you have to pay back that amount plus one dollar and fifty cents interest."

David looked at me and asked, "Can Jim do whatever that word means and make me pay a whole dollar and fifty cents."

I assured him, "Yes, that's how it works. You know, David, you must make payments, and if you miss a payment, the bank gets to keep whatever you put up for collateral." David had a little toy-car collection he dearly loved. I suggested the bank could hold the collection for collateral.

Jim asked if he had a job, and David said he did and that he made big money. "How much do you make at this job?" Jim asked.

"I make about eighty dollars a month—sometimes more," was David's answer.

Jim asked, "Are you in debt?"

David looked at me and asked, "Am I whatever that banker said?"

I said, "Yes, David, you are in debt to the ranch. Remember, you have a note with a payment of ten dollars a month on your battery-operated race car." The ranch carried the note. Jim and I were trying very hard not to laugh because David was so very serious about his loan request.

Jim told David he would probably qualify for the loan, but first, he would have to fill out some papers. Jim handed him more paperwork than even I would have bothered to fill out. Jim explained how to fill out each document and what each document meant. "Why don't you take them home; then you can bring them back to me when they're completed."

Jim handed David a folder to carry his bank papers home. Jim also told David to be sure to call and make an appointment before David came back to the bank. Jim put out his hand shaking David's hand with Jim commenting, "It's truly been a pleasure doing business with you, young man."

In my mind's eye I still see David walking through the bank with a serious expression, with his head held high, folder in hand. One of the window tellers said, "Hello David, how are you today?"

As he walked past her, he looked back and remarked, "I'm just fine. I'm here at the bank on personal business." We left the bank with David opening the door for me. I guess you just had to be there to feel that very special moment.

David was determined! He asked the counselors to help him fill out the papers, and everyone got into the act. By the beginning of the next week, David had all his papers ready, with each and every line filled out, including multiple N/A's in the spaces.

A few days later David sat down in my office and asked to make his phone call to Jim. I dialed the number and then handed David the phone. When the receptionist answered, David asked, "May I speak with Jim, my banker?"

Naturally, they put him through to Jim's secretary. The secretary told him the usual, as though she was talking to an adult. David said, "Yes, ma'am, but, ma'am, if he's in a meeting, then go tell him I am on the phone and that it's important. He will talk to me, 'cause he told me to call him personally."

I just sat there listening as David told this secretary exactly what he needed without accepting any of her so-called excuses. She must have asked him if Jim was his dad, for David sighed and said, "No, I'm not his son, but I have lots of money in this bank and need to talk to him about my loan." The next thing I knew, David was talking to Jim about his "big bank loan" and his appointment.

The next day, David went to the office to see his banker. David had in tow his toy sports-car collection. Shelly helped pick out his attire. He was dressed for the occasion in a white western shirt, ironed and creased Wrangler jeans, his boots shined, and his Resistol hat set just right on his head, with one of the cowboys making an adjustment or too. Shelly fixed him up with a small briefcase to carry his papers to the bank. David had also helped himself to Tom's after shave cologne, filling the air with an over abundance of fragrance.

I remarked, "David, you look so handsome."

He simply looked up at me and said, "Mom, I know all that stuff. Let's hook 'em."

When we entered the bank, one of the tellers said, "Hi, David, I can help you over here."

David thanked her and said, "I'm here to do business with my personal banker. I'll see you next time." He kept walking down the hallway to Jim's office.

Jim the banker was ready to see us and began by explaining to David how serious it is not to pay a loan back. He looked over David's papers and asked David a few simple questions. Jim then asked for David's collateral.

David looked first at me and then back at Jim, asking Jim; "Do you have my money?" David wanted the money before he would let go of his toy-car collection.

Jim gave David a cashier's check for ten dollars and a note for eleven dollars and fifty cents. He looked at the piece of small paper Jim had just handed him and immediately asked me if it was any good. I assured him indeed it was good. David gave Jim his cars and made Jim assure him he would take very good care of his collateral.

I spoke to David, "Go to the teller's window and they will cash you cashier's check, then wait in the lobby, because I need to speak to Jim about something." When Jim and I finished our business, I thanked Jim for taking David's call.

He had a silly grin on his face and said, "No problem. It was just the monthly board meeting." When he hung up the phone after talking to David, Jim told the board of directors it was a customer who had "quite a bit of money in the bank." I apologized for my David, and we both had a pretty good laugh.

Willie and Conway were waiting when we arrived home to greet David. As they were walking away, I heard Willie tell David, "You are really in debt now and probably will go to jail if you don't pay the money back." Undoubtedly the cowboys had joined our conspiracy to educate David about borrowing money.

All at the ranch conspired in this lesson to break David from borrowing money. So that night, and throughout the next week, the cowboys told all sorts of stories. The older boys jumped in and started telling David how the bank would probably keep his car collection. This was one very worried nine-year old.

Another week went by. David came into my office one afternoon and asked if he could speak with his banker. It was real important.

I called Jim and told him one of his customers wished to speak with him. David asked Jim if he could go to jail if he did not pay the loan back. Jim said, "Well, that's possible, if you don't pay the note to the bank, then the bank could file charges on you. Yes, you may go to jail. However, if you pay the note off, you will have good credit."

David paid the money back the next day, including the extra one dollar and fifty cents. He also picked up his collateral. Jim thanked David for his business and told David, "You are now in good standing at the bank."

David looked straight at Jim and put his hand out. As they shook hands, David thanked him for the loan.

When we got back to the pickup, David looked at me and asked, "Why did Mr. Jim say I am standing good? I thought I was standing pretty good before I paid the money back to the bank."

I think this adventure taught David a good lesson, for after this experience with the bank, he didn't borrow any more money—that I know of. The real lesson David taught us all was never to underestimate a nine-year-old. I've always told my counselors, "With every lesson we teach, we can also count on learning one of our own."

~ Chapter 43 ~

OATS

Oakdale, California 2006

My face felt the warmth of the sun peering through the leaves of the old walnut tree. At my age, taking a nap on the ground aroused my aches and pains, speaking to me in plain English, reminding me how many birthdays I had accomplished.

"Ma'am, are you all right? You've been here all afternoon. It's not that I mind you being here; looks like the nap rested you a bit." I looked up at this kind gentleman; his leathered face revealed the years of riding horseback in the sun and of much hard work with faded wranglers and a faded shirt to match. Perhaps the grandfather of the boys I had seen earlier in the week. He sensed my attachment to this ranch, and I more than welcomed his western manner.

He spoke softly as he introduced himself, "My name is Jack, and yours?" We did the introductions and as I rose to my knees, Jack put out a hand and helped me to my feet.

I eased into a familiar conversation with the old western gentleman as if I had known him my whole life. As we walked toward the alleyway between the house and barn, I spoke of great memories here on this ranch. I thanked him and asked that he pass my gratitude along to his family for allowing me the pleasant reverie of visiting my former home. (Without words, his eyes revealed he understood the heart's attachment to places and events means everything in the twist and turns of our Journey.) As we walked past the barn area, I looked down the shed row and swore I saw old Oats sitting in his chair, leaning back against the wall, telling his stories to my boys. Oats looked like he leapt off a film clip from a Zane Gray western, like Gabby Hayes or a Welfred Brimley character. I felt honored to know this old seasoned cowboy. *My afternoon of reminiscing at the ranch along with the old cowboys polite manners invoked a new awareness and sense of purpose in me.*

Tom brought Oats to the ranch and introduced him as someone I "really needed to hire." Tom, who ordinarily meditated on every word, spit out his words with such speed that all I could do was listen. He said, "We really need a supervisor in the barn at all times during the day because of the safety factor. You know how the boys act before they think, and they surely don't understand caution. Oats, here, is our man."

Here before me stood the most bowlegged, elderly man I had ever seen. His white mustache matched his salt-and-pepper hair that he covered with a cowboy hat. The hat, darkened around the band and pleasantly bent in places, looked as though the barn cats had used it for a nap rag. There was a perfect hoof print on the back of the ol' felt hat brim. I am sure visiting with this gentleman about his well-seasoned hat could take the rest of the afternoon.

After a short introduction of, "how do you dos", I asked him, "Where did you get your name?"

He replied, "Well, Ma'am, my parents tell me I was one of those babies that loved to eat horse oats better than most horses." He answered with a genuine twinkle in his eye that even Santa Claus would envy. I noted a dip of Copenhagen in the mouth of this ancient man who wore suspenders to hold up his Wranglers, which hung low leaving room for his rather extended stomach.

I asked, "Are you a hand with horses and cattle?"

His reply was that of an old cowboy, "Ma, am, you asked me two questions, and I will do my best to answer them in the order that you asked them." He pulled a ragged, red handkerchief from his back pocket and politely wiped the tobacco from his mouth, dabbing at the corners of his mouth before continuing. "They say I could break a horse to ride better than anyone in this county; however, I'm not of a mind to break horses anymore. Next question; about them ol' cows. Yes, ma'am, I did a lot of just plain ol' cowboy'n in my day. However, I am not of a mind to do that anymore either."

I looked at Tom, then back at Oats, and said, after a moment, "Well, I guess you're just what we are looking for because we do need someone to watch after the boys when they're in the barn working with the horses. You know an extra set of eyes around the barn area. Just hang out around the barn and see the boys don't tear the darn barn down." Tom stood conveniently behind this old gentleman shaking his head up and down encouraging me to continue. "The job pays six hundred dollars a month, room and board." I'd already figured he wanted some extra income but had to be careful how he got paid.

He looked at me and then at Tom. "Can I take it under the fence?" he asked.

I said, "Yes," and we shook hands the old fashion way. I was trying to figure out how Tom coerced me into hiring a charity case to take care of the barn with such a smooth tongue, matching any horse traders' hood winkled play of words, treating me like I was some kind of greenhorn.

When Tom finished showing him the ranch, he went to the bunkhouse to show Oats his quarters. Tom came back to the office to thank me. I was not in a thanking mood. I had just hired an elderly man that probably would not be able to do anything. I simply did not see what Tom saw in this broken-down old cowboy.

Tom told me, "Oats was quite a hand in his day; now he has no family left. He lives by himself in that dilapidated old hotel downtown, above the bar and, well, I think he needs a shot at a better ending."

I asked very few questions about his private life. It was just the respectable western way to do things. One day, I went out to the barn, pulled up a chair, and sat down beside Oats. He said nothing at first; we both just sat there taking in the great smells of the old barn. The shed row recently sprinkled down with water for the evening gave the true smells of the dirt floor.

Finally, he looked at me and said, "You know, I was married once."

I sat there a few minutes before I spoke. "How long were you married?"

Taking his time to think about his answer, he said, "Oh, long enough, about five years."

Neither one of us was in a talkative mood. I waited a while then asked, "Did you ever re-marry?"

"Oh, I came close a couple a times, but thought I made such a mess out of the first one, I really didn't want to do it again." Oats just sat there and continued his whittling; neither of us said a thing. After a little while, I got up and walked back to the office.

This old gentleman became one of my best employees. He was also a great storyteller. If the counselors missed a boy and started looking for him, especially the little ones, more than likely, they would be with Oats. The boys were not the only ones that became attached to this old gentleman. After supper was over and everyone else busied themselves with getting ready for bed, I found myself looking forward to the barn trips and sitting there talking to this wise old gentleman, finding comfort in each visit.

Oats greeted me with a nod and sometimes a silly grin through the long horned mustache. He often offered simple down-to-earth solutions for the problems that my mind tied into complicated knots. As if he had eyes into my soul, he knew I let my emotions strangle my brain, especially when one of the boys troubled me. He could lead the boys out of their doldrums easier than tethering a wild goat. He introduced them to cloud watching. One afternoon, I walked down by the barn, and there sitting on a long bench outside the barn were three little boys and Oats gazing up at the white puffy clouds. I sat down beside them and pretended I knew what they were doing. I was simply witnessing a miracle in front of my eyes for ten minutes elapsed before the three moved. Soon, one of the boys exclaimed, "There, there's one. Can you see it, Mom? Well, can you?"

I replied, "Well, no. Can you point it out to me?" I looked up into the clouded sky and then over toward the boy. His eyes were filled with excitement.

Oats spoke up about that time and said, "Well, boy, you won. Sure enough, you are the winner, 'cause I can see her wings and all."

He reached into his pocket and pulled out a little wooden horse. Oats was a great wood-carver and could carve anything, but creating horses in different shapes and sizes was his greatest love. He would create a game and then reward them with some little wood carving. After the boys left, I asked what game he and the boys were playing.

"It's very simple. You just look up into the sky, and the first one to see a cloud that looks like an angel is the winner." Of course this game had to be played on a white cloudy day.

One of his favorite stories was also one of mine. When a new boy came to the ranch, the younger ones proceeded taking him to meet Oats and insisted on the story about the ducks and the lake.

Oats would grin and take the boys over to the white rail fence and point to a low area in the pasture. "You see that low area there; well, it used to be a lake." Oats paused to give the child a chance to visualize the lake. "Well, one winter, the ducks landed on it. It froze with those darn ducks sittin' right on the lake."

"Tell 'em, Oats, what happened to our lake," the little ones chimed.

"Well, when them darn ducks the next mornin' went to flap-pin' their wings with their legs frozen in the lake, those darn old ducks flew off with our lake."

Oats meant more to me than any vocabulary could ever put into words. He never held back saying what was on his mind. Sometimes he gave his opinion, when I really didn't want to hear it. Then at the end of the day when I did my best thinking, there would be Oats and his wisdom ringing in my ears. I began to listen to his "opinions" because he sometimes could see things I somehow overlooked.

Just before I sold the boys ranch, Oats died. I knew he was sick but the old man was "set in his ways" and would not go to the doctor. So we just went about our business at the ranch and did our best to keep him happy.

He asked me one morning, "What's for dinner tonight?" He said, "I really would like one of Bertha's roast dinners, with maybe a cobbler. Blackberry is my favorite." This was unlike Oats to ask for something special. He looked bad, and so Bertha and I fixed the special dinner he requested without questioning the reasoning of the special request.

That night, I took his meal down to the bunkhouse, and he asked me to sit so we could visit a while. By this time Tom had added a bedroom on to the old bunk house for Oats. I felt the need to stay longer than usual, and we visited about a lot of things. By this time we had purchased an old cow horse for Oats, to brush, feed and sometimes ride. I don't know how he knew, but that night, he asked me to give his horse to a friend of his in town if something should happen to him. I kidded him a little, telling him he was too ornery and stubborn to die, and that he would probably out live us all.

Early the next morning one of the hands came up to my house and told me Oats had passed away in the middle of the night. His heart had just stopped beating. This was the way he would have wanted to die. Oats was so afraid of being a burden to us no matter how many times Tom and I told him he was family, our family, and we would take care of him to the end, he still worried.

Oats left me a note, it read,

Dear Ms. René,

"If 'in ida had a daughter, I would have wanted her to be just like you."

He signed it, "Oats." I considered this one of the nicest and most sincere compliments an old cow gal could receive.

For months after his death, I walked by the barn and paused looking down the shed row expecting him to say something to me, only to realize that I had lost a very beloved and trusted friend.

I'd catch myself looking up in the sky watching for white clouds going over, looking for a special bowlegged angel with spurs on his boots and wings so deserved. I still do this little habit today.

Walking by my side, the old western gentleman, who reminded me so much of Oats, asked, "You have a very serious look on your face, are you thinking about the future?"

"Yes," I said, "My Journey I know now is unfinished. There is much more I need to accomplish in my life. I fully intend to do something more about the injustices of our street children. I think I shall write a book and tell the real stories about the lonely and abandoned children, the street children—many who are ignored while others are abused or exploited. I want government officials to understand the failed government system that affects these children.

With God to guide me, and if I remember doctors I go to for an opinion, not necessarily a cure, perhaps I can stay healthy enough to finish my Journey as God intended. What do I want?"

"I want to run a privately funded ranch program, provided a trust could be set up for the children, removing the insecurities created by our government programs. The abundant street children should be afforded the opportunity

to become productive adults. I know I could set the standard for other providers to follow. This would be such a great way to end my Journey, leaving a legacy of the best kind."

"That sounds like a lot of sacrifice." he added.

"Gracious sakes, no," I said, "Quite the opposite! A Journey is not a true spiritual Journey unless you are God's true messenger, and a true messenger is one who gives of oneself for the betterment of others."

I shook his hand with a firm hand shake and climbed into my truck and drove down the old ranch road to the highway. I stopped just before entering the highway and looked up into the sky of puffy white clouds. I swore I saw a beautiful but funny looking, bowlegged, pot-bellied angel with wings. As the cloud dissipated, Oaks flapped his wings, tipped his hat, grinned down giving me his approval.

HISTORY

This short history provides you with a better understanding of how and what went wrong in the development and implementation of our government's youth programs.

The major approach to delinquency prior to the mid 1960s was traditional casework, based on prominent personality and sociological theory. Such a position fit well with the *individual* treatment and *parens patriae doctrines* on which the court was based.

This rather simple program included two major branches (1) the foster care and family setting and (2) the institutional setting.

However, the sociological turmoil of the 1960s did not leave the juvenile justice system unscathed. Three major lines of criticism can be identified.

First, the juvenile court was under considerable attack for the limitations placed on a youth's constitutional rights. In Kent v. United States (1966), the juvenile courts were warned against procedural arbitrariness.

Next, in the landmark case of Gault (1967), the Supreme Court recognized the juveniles constitutionally guaranteed rights to due process.

A second set of criticisms focused on the severe mistreatment frequently experienced by youth in juvenile correctional institutions. This was an area that was in need of correction. A series of documentaries and media exposés described the inhumane details of juvenile institutions in the country (James, 1960). Concern over the quality of treatment was combined with criticisms of the efficacy of treatment in very serious indictments of the practices of the juvenile justice system. It was obvious at this time there was a great need for change in our youth's programs—the government and the politicians were being pushed for change and the public was outraged.

The third set of criticisms grew out of the four-step evaluation (Klein et al., 1978) that determined the child's placement. The first step was the commission of an illegal act, apprehension, and the attachment of the formal label of "delinquent." The second was the spread of the delinquent label to other individuals in the youth's environment. Step three involves internalization of the label by the youth. The fourth step is continued contact with the juvenile justice system as a function of the first three. Specifically, the concern expressed by many (Gold & Williams, 1969) was that formal processing of the child through the juvenile system resulted in *more delinquency* than merely leaving the child alone.

Why was this last evaluation not recognized as a main point between the failure and the success of such an evaluation? The politicians could have seen it as a source of free media coverage for their personal use. The media was all over anything that had to do with negative children's programs, and any one that was running for office that favored an improvement to solve this problem would surely get the taxpayers' vote.

At this time I was questioning whether a child's right was being violated because of uncontrollable circumstance, such as both parents being killed in an auto or plane crash. There were children being placed into group homes and even held in the juvenile system, while they waited for placements to be found. The placement of a child, especially a naïve child, into the juvenile system, allowed him or her to learn the negative behaviors of others. I fought against this damaging procedure, but without much success because the state and federal governments would not recognize there was a problem. In my experience, this thoughtless misplacement was just one of the many cruelties that our society enacted upon our youth, which increased rather than healed their psychological wounds.

Were these problems not being solved because of the political and theoretical events happening at that time? Probably. In the context of these political and theoretical events, behavioral procedures saw an increased application to delinquent populations. Given these events, the history had disappointing results with traditional modes of treatment (Levitt, 1971; Lipton, Martinson, & Wilks, 1975) resulting in behaviorally oriented interventions with delinquent populations growing and becoming extremely prevalent over the last three decades.

The behavioral perspective had appeal on several grounds. One could, for example, attempt to change delinquent behavior through the use of behavior technologies regardless of one's ideological perspectives. Behavioral approaches frequently resulted in more easily measurable behaviors or outcomes. Behavioral interventions were implemented in juvenile justice settings, given the professional levels of staff availability. In addition, behavioral strategies were frequently used in attempts to modify theoretically post-related determinants of correlates of delinquent behavior.

For example, many argued that academic behaviors (achievement, attendance, on-task behavior), program-specific behaviors (in residential programs meaning promptness, following rules and pro-social behaviors) were causally related to delinquent behavior. In order to maximize and fully utilize the above for the practitioner, the studies examined were classified in the following manner:

- First, the setting was identified as institutional (psychiatric hospital settings), residential (psychological) group homes, and residential (foster homes and/or community) based homes.
- Second, the specific behavior targeted by intervention was categorized as academic achievement, program related, or delinquent.
- Third, the type of intervention implemented was identified as a token economy, behavioral economy, behavioral contracting, modeling or role-playing, and positive reinforcement / punishment.

The main problem with all of this evaluation is that most of the evaluators and educators had parents that cared about them. The researchers, without being fully aware, did not realize how bad the program really was. Research was done mainly on a child that HAD parents. And they had again missed the mark because they were putting adolescents in a percentage group rather than individually noting that each child is not just a child, but an individual with individual needs. These programs were called re-unification programs.

Another factor was the failure in their research to do percentage comparison as to how many children were on the street and *did not* have parents to be re-unified with. The researchers had left out the reality of the situation and/or its severity. Thus began one of the most tragic injustices ever perpetrated against our youth.

Because the researchers had to submit their evaluations and stated a time limit on each program, the time limit factor had everything to do about money and very little to do about a program that worked for the child. For instance, the government programs were written not for the child to improve, but the determining factor was how much money was available for the program.

The next mistake was limiting all programs to short-term: six weeks, three months, or six months.

After a child was moved from a foster parent, the foster parent was not allowed to contact the child. This strategy was devastating for the adolescent child.

Without parents to reunite with the child, who was distrusting because of the unsettledness of his or her life in the first place, he or she became more and more unsettled as the state moved him or her from placement to placement. By the time the child was eighteen, he had no faith with the people he had been with in the system. Our government-run children's programs had just created another criminal for America's already overcrowded prison systems.

I was convinced that when involved in long-term programs, the child would have a chance to become a productive adult. This premise is the basis of my boys ranch program.

I wrote and developed one of the first long-term programs for adolescents with behavioral problems. The government would only allow placements with me for a-year-and-a-half, and I fought hard to get it. The court was set to review each case file every six months. Evaluation as to the child's progress was submitted for review by the court system. If the evaluation of the child's behavior was good and he or she was doing well, the system moved him or her to a foster home that was less expensive.

This logic was so backward from the standpoint of helping the child! If one of my boys were to reach the year-and-a-half mark and was doing well in school, had regained his self confidence, made friends, had his own horse and dog, and was basically a settled child, this should have been viewed as a positive step, rather than a negative.

Finally, I was so tired of State Licensing taking a child and destroying what I had gained that I began to manipulate the system in the child's favor. Several judges saw the progress these children were making, and they began to back me and support my efforts, knowing full well the fate of the child now lay in their hands.

Example: John had been in my program for a year-and-a-half. My evaluation stated that John's behavior was showing signs of regress, and he dropped from Level Three to Level Two. I recommended against moving John, and the judge merely extended his stay. Did John actually regress in the program? According to my evaluation he did. By using this tactic, we managed to keep most of my boys for at least two or three years.

I conducted research to prove my point to Congress. The research, which took five years to complete, involved interviewing criminals concerning their backgrounds. Sixty-eight percent of the prisoners were from government-run programs. I have heard that other researchers found the number to be even higher. And the government wonders why our prisons are overcrowded!

This book actually tells it for the most part as it really happened and gives the public an inside look at the injustices that were created by these programs. Many of these stories will rip your heart out, but there is also a great deal of laughter and adventures in the wilderness backcountry of Yosemite. No matter how much my boys enjoyed being at the ranch, they feared the day they would have to leave due to state regulations.

Private entities must get involved to correct this serious problem. We cannot wait for the government to correct this situation. We, as Americans, need to step forward to correct it ourselves. I am <u>committed</u> to doing my part, but the question is: Will you do yours?

MORE INFORMATION AVAILABLE

If, after reading this book, you decide you are interested in helping the children in America, the unwanted, the forgotten, the throw-a ways, the street children, please feel free to contact me.

Perhaps you are an investor looking for an investment that will make a difference by helping others less fortunate move forward for a better tomorrow. Please contact me.

Perhaps you are a corporation looking to invest or just an individual looking for property investment that will provide homes for street children. Please contact us.

On our Web page you will see where there are donations needed for the Scholarship programs. These Scholarship programs are for the average income family and for the child that may not have a 4.0 but has the drive and the desire to continue his/ her education. Parents, single mothers and single fathers who are raising their children with good morals and standards may qualify. The majority of Scholarships provided by Constructive Youth of America will be in the rural areas and with the smaller colleges. These areas are for the most part over looked.

Orders are taken from our web and some discounts are available.

	Renemonroe.net
Web	drrenemonroe.com
E-mail	youthamerica@sbcglobal.net

Look for the following books in 2015 & 2016

- **The Epidemic** Written on behalf of our youth in this country who are being drugged, at an ever rapid increase, with prescription drugs. We have a major epidemic in our society; over seven million children are being prescribed drugs for Behavioral Problems. This book will bring to the public the facts of the damaging affect drugs have on our children. This book is written for parents who are concerned, to give you a better insight into alternatives and solutions. I have not only studied and researched this epidemic; I have personally experienced it with my Behavioral Psychological programs from the youth on my boys' ranch. There is a better healthier solution.
- **THE DIVORCE; IT COULD HAPPEN TO YOU;** This book is based on my own personal experiences, taking you through a real live divorce; The mental and physical abuse of a very educated woman but naïve`lady who did trust her partner in life only to find a person who betrayed her trust and used her for his financial gain. The lies and cruelties he puts her through, and the failure of the court system which is supposed to uphold the truth and the laws to protect her fails. I am writing this book to go public with what can happen to you; a TRUE STORY, THIS IS WHAT HAPPEN TO ME. I lost my retirement of $380,000 at the age of 69, It tells how the court that is supposed to protect you can simply look the other way. Texas is a community property state and yet that too failed do to the lies that were told in court, His lies, His attorneys lies. My story was never heard in the

court room. So I am going public with this in hopes it will save you the reader from it happening to you.

"WHEN YOU DO NOT HAVE IT IN WRITING", And, have the wrong attorneys.

Due out in 2017.

- **METAPHSICS, "What's That"** An educational book on the funny side of a very serious subject, regarding the mind, body, and spirit; and how to benefit from this knowledge.
- Other short booklets will also be available upon request
- Boys ranch program packages and training are also available through my web.

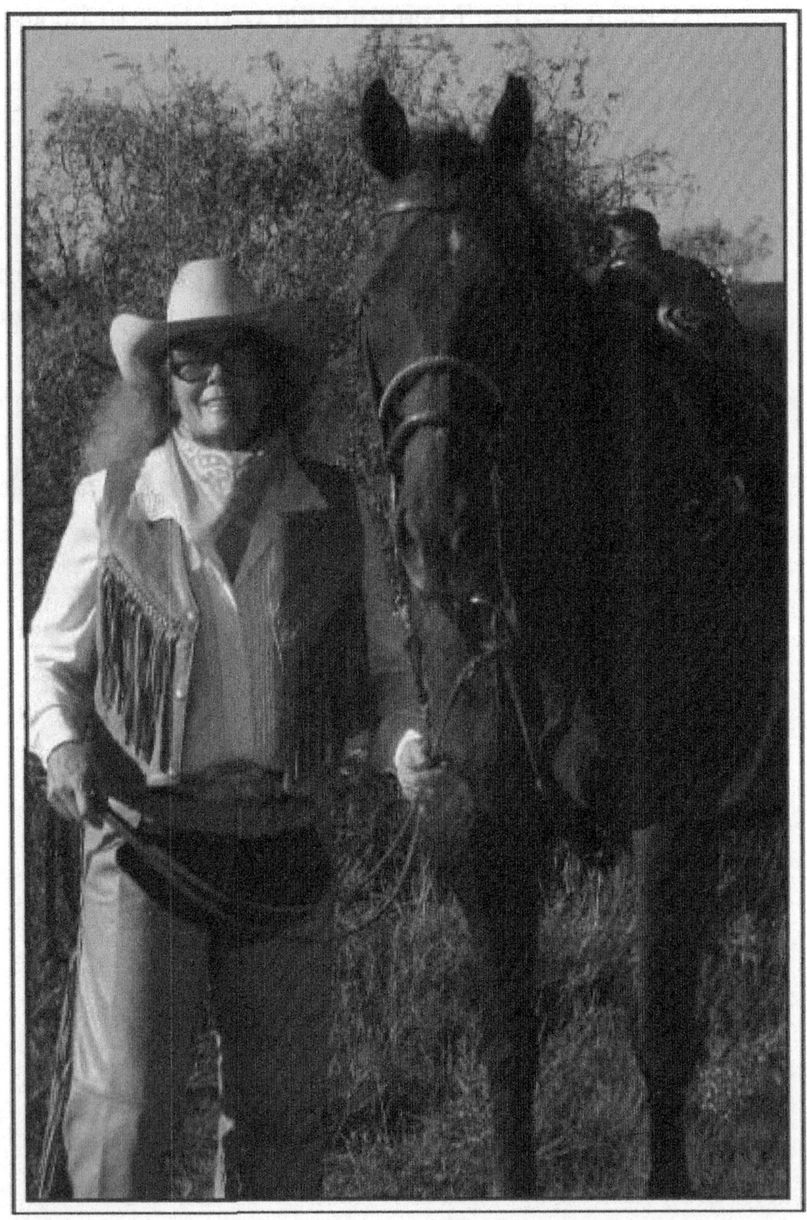

Come ride with me for a better tomorrow for our youth.

Made in the USA
Middletown, DE
19 October 2022